国际新闻听力教程

LISTEN TO THE INTERNATIONAL NEWS

李异平 编著

暨南大学出版社
JINAN UNIVERSITY PRESS
中国·广州

图书在版编目（CIP）数据

国际新闻听力教程/李异平编著．—广州：暨南大学出版社，2010.9（2011.6 重印）
ISBN 978－7－81135－626－7

Ⅰ.①国…　Ⅱ.①李…　Ⅲ.①新闻—英语—听说教学—教材　Ⅳ.①H319.9

中国版本图书馆 CIP 数据核字(2010)第 169557 号

出版发行：暨南大学出版社

地　　址：中国广州暨南大学
电　　话：总编室（8620）85221601
　　　　　营销部（8620）85225284　85228291　85228292（邮购）
传　　真：（8620）85221583（办公室）　85223774（营销部）
邮　　编：510630
网　　址：http：//www.jnupress.com　http：//press.jnu.edu.cn

排　　版：广州市天河星辰文化发展部照排中心
印　　刷：佛山市浩文彩色印刷有限公司

开　　本：787mm×1092mm　1/16
印　　张：15.625
字　　数：380 千
版　　次：2010 年 9 月第 1 版
印　　次：2011 年 6 月第 2 次
印　　数：1001—2000 册

定　　价：28.00 元

获得成功最容易、最迅速的方法之一就是有意识地扩大你的词汇知识。

——美国语言学家威尔福若德·芬克

导 言

传播国际化的趋势迫使我国新闻业迅速加入国际传播论坛，以提升我国政府及媒介在国际上的影响力。这股趋势加速了我国媒介对英语新闻人才的需求，新闻学院毕业生因而常常面临着使用英语采访、报道或编辑各类新闻的工作需要。然而，据业界反映，新闻专业的毕业生常因为语言问题而难以报道或翻译国际或国内新闻热点，而英语专业的毕业生却由于不懂新闻规律或因专业知识局限而难以理解经济、法律等专业性较强的英语新闻。

要解决这个问题，需要对英语新闻的教学进行全方位的改革，首先要通过更新教材来改变传统的英语新闻教学方式和教学内容，使英语新闻教学的内容与当今社会新闻业的发展进程紧密相连；其次是将学生从那种以“打钩”练习为主的学习方式中解放出来，培养他们听说英语新闻的能力。

目前高校的英语新闻教学存在一个普遍的问题，那就是将英语新闻课程当作英语专业课程来教，局限在对英语词句的理解和练习上。担任这门课的教师大都各自为政，教材散而乱，缺乏系统的英语新闻材料，造成新闻专业学生不熟悉英语新闻的结构、写作特征、词汇及发音特征，更谈不上用英语报道或编辑新闻了。新闻单位因此不得不先引进英语专业的学生，然后再进行新闻专业培训。结果是，新闻学院的国际新闻专业形同虚设。与此同时，我国高中的英语教学水平日益提高，考入高校的高中毕业生英语听说能力也随之“水涨船高”。如果英语新闻课程继续按照传统的教学内容和方式教学的话，既不能适应新闻业的发展，也无法满足新时代学生的求知欲望。

本教材以“美国之音”新闻综述节目中的各类国际新闻为切入点，将国际新闻按内容、类别编纂成层次分明的教学单元，不仅整合了当前国际社会在政治、法律、文化等方面普遍认同的新闻价值观，还将各类介绍经济常识的经济新闻纳入“听”和“说”的练习范畴。此外，本教材在编写上还进行了一大创新，即在每课前引用相关专业人士对各类新闻所涉及的事件进行的评论或综述，使学生在学习本教材的过程中，不仅可以系统地了解国际新闻的发展趋势，还能够消除对政治、经济及法律等英语新闻内容和语句的陌生感，在掌握新闻背景知识的基础上，提高对新闻价值的辨识能力和理解能力。换言之，本教材在教授英语新闻知识的基础上，再辅之以各专业（如经济、科技等）的新闻知识，既可培养学生在实践中从事英语新闻编辑和报道的专业能力，又可使之熟悉各类英语新闻的写作结构和表达方法，改变过去教授学生在纯粹机械的“打钩”中“学习”语言的传统方式。

学习国际新闻，之所以要从听力入手，一是因为当今社会通过广播电视获取和传播新闻更为便捷，且其受众面非常广；二是因为当前我国英语教学主要以阅读和理解为主，学生的英语“阅读词汇”比较丰富，而“听力词汇”相当匮乏。很典型的一个例子是，学生对英语经济新闻词汇和政治人物名字及组织名称充满了陌生感和恐惧感，这些词汇成了他们理解英语新闻的障碍，其原因就是他们没听过，更没有“说”过此类新闻。为此，教材中加入了复述所听新闻并直接进行口头翻译的练习。

在校新闻专业或英语专业的学生以及准备从事国际新闻报道的媒体从业人员均可使用本教材，以增强对国际新闻词汇和语句的理解，了解国际新闻事件报道的发展趋势，熟悉各类国际新闻的历史背景和价值判断。

编　者

目 录

第三部分　政治、法律、科学报道、文化等新闻

第一部分　经济新闻

Lesson 1　Stock Market Investors Count Their Losses after a Bad Week Felt Near and Far

By Brianna Blake

March 3, 2007

Part One　Background Information

金融危机来临的前兆

近年来，全球股市的震荡成为牵动媒体报道的一个“主旋律”，因为股市的“阴晴”关系到经济发展趋势的稳定与否。2007 年初，美国市场的信贷危机导致全球股市连续数周动荡。美国几家对冲基金因损失惨重而不得不抛售其资产的消息令市场愈加脆弱。美国房地产市场因此迅速降温，曾经一度红火的次级抵押贷款市场早在 2006 年就开始走软，到 2007 年第一季度，次级抵押贷款市场问题恶化，其中浮动利率贷款逾期还款的比例和借款人丧失抵押品赎回权的比例双双升至历史最高点。2007 年 3 月 13 日，全美第二大次级抵押贷款机构——新世纪金融公司濒临破产的消息使纽约股市首次因次级抵押贷款市场危机而遭受重创，道琼斯指数当天下跌了 240 多点。但是投资者当时并未意识到危机的严重性，股市很快重拾升势。6 月，纽约股市再次大跌，其诱因是美国第五大投资银行贝尔斯登公司旗下两只基金因涉足次级抵押贷款债券市场而出现亏损。之后随着企业和投资机构公布业绩，次级抵押贷款市场越来越多的问题被曝光，使股市接连遭受重创。业绩缩水最严重的是次级抵押贷款公司。

本课选自 2007 年 3 月初的新闻。当时，自 1929 年美国大萧条以来最严重的一次金融危机即将来临，美联储主席伯南克却仍然故作镇静，强调“美国经济运行正常”，唯有美联储前主席格林斯潘说了句真话：“一场经济大萧条可能来临。”时至今日，人们如梦初醒，过度的金融投机是此次经济危机的祸首。但直至“黄花菜都已经凉了”的时候，伯南克才在 2007 年 7 月 19 日参议院银行业委员会举行的年中经济评估听证会上如实报告说，次级抵押贷款市场造成的损失可能达到 1 000 亿美元，“次级抵押贷款造成的信贷损失已经显现，而且相当严重。对于次级抵押贷款给相关信贷产品造成的损失，估计在 500 亿美元到 1 000 亿美元之间”①。

---

① 任洪源. 美国次按风暴蔓延　中国能否独善其身. http://web.jrj.com.cn/news/2007-09-19/000002697986.html

Part Two　Exercises

Ⅰ. Listen to the first part of the news, and fill in the blanks with the words you hear.

1. ________ around the world took ________ on a ________ this week.

2. On Tuesday, ________ the health of Chinese markets and the United States economy helped send investors on a ________________.

3. A ________ that began on the Shanghai stock market quickly ________ Europe and the United States. Markets in Africa and Latin America also ________________.

4. China's main stock market in Shanghai ________ nine percent Tuesday. It was the ________ in Chinese stocks in ten years.

5. ________ hurried to sell their stocks as ______________ that the government might raise ______________.

6. There were also ________ of a possible new ______________. Chinese officials ________ those reports.

Ⅱ. Listen to the second part of the news, and translate it into Chinese.

Begin from "On Wall Street...".

Ⅲ. Listen to the third part of the news, and answer the following questions.

1. What happened to the system on Tuesday because of the biggest drop?

2. What happened to the traders?

3. What did some people blame? Does Dow Jones Company agree with them?

4. What did Alan Greenspan say?

5. Did Ben Bernanke agree with Alan Greenspan?

6. What will the US economy be like this year according to Ben Bernanke? Why did he say that?

Ⅳ. Listen to and repeat the last part of the news, then write it down.

From "a better-than-expected..." to the end.

Part Three　Keys to the Exercises

Ⅰ. Listen to the first part of the news, and fill in the blanks with the words you hear.

1. Financial markets around the world took investors on a shaky ride this week.

2. On Tuesday, concerns about the health of Chinese markets and the United States economy helped send investors on a flight from risk.

3. A selloff that began on the Shanghai stock market quickly spread to Europe and the United States. Markets in Africa and Latin America also suffered losses.

4. China's main stock market in Shanghai fell nine percent Tuesday. It was the worst drop in Chinese stocks in ten years.

5. Investors hurried to sell their stocks as concern spread that the government might raise

interest rates.

6. There were also unconfirmed reports of a possible new tax on capital gains. Chinese officials denied those reports.

Ⅱ. Listen to the second part of the news, and translate it into Chinese.

Begin from "On Wall Street..." .

1. On Wall Street, the Dow Jones Industrial Average of thirty major stocks dropped four hundred sixteen points, more than three percent.
   在华尔街，由三十个权重股组成的道琼斯工业平均指数下跌了416点，下跌幅度超过3%。
2. That was a loss about six billion dollars of shareholder value on the New York Stock Exchange.
   这个数字表示，纽约股市股东的股票价值缩水60亿美元。
3. It was the biggest one-day drop since the first day of trading after the terrorist attacks in September of two thousand and one.
   这是2001年9月恐怖袭击后第一个交易日以来最大的单日跌幅。
4. But at one point Tuesday, after a month of moving up, the Dow was down as much as five hundred forty-six points.
   但是，大盘上行一个月之后，道琼斯指数在周二的某个点位又下跌了546点。

Ⅲ. Listen to the third part of the news, and answer the following questions.

1. What happened to the systems on Tuesday because of the biggest drop?

The intense trading even overloaded the systems that continually compute the Dow Jones average.

2. What happened to the traders?

Traders had the wrong information for seventy minutes.

3. What did some people blame? Does Dow Jones Company agree with them?

People blame that the delay worsened the drop in the market. No, it doesn't.

4. What did Alan Greenspan say?

On Monday, the former chairman of the Federal Reserve said a recession was possible in the United States by the end of the year. Later, he said a recession is possible but not probable.

5. Did Ben Bernanke agree with Alan Greenspan?

No, the current Federal Reserve chairman told Congress that the markets in the United States seemed to be working well.

6. What will the US economy be like this year according to Ben Bernanke? Why did he say that?

Ben Bernanke said the central bank still expects "moderate growth" in the economy this year. His comments Wednesday seemed to help calm the markets.

Ⅳ. Listen to and repeat the last part of the news, then write it down.

1. A better-than-expected manufacturing report on Thursday also helped stock prices, after an early drop on Wall Street.

2. Another economic report had been blamed as one of the causes of Tuesday's big selloff.

3. On Tuesday the Commerce Department reported the biggest drop in three months in orders for durable goods in January.

4. These are higher-priced goods designed to last three years or more, like cars and computers.

5. There was also concern in the markets this week about companies that deal in "subprime" home loans.

6. These loans for people with weak credit histories have been popular in recent years.

7. But many people are now having trouble paying them back.

8. All together, it was one of the worst weeks in several years for financial markets that have recently hit new highs.

9. Investors hoped that their shaky ride was nothing more than a normal price correction.

Part Four Translation of the Text

Stock Market Investors Count Their Losses after a Bad Week Felt Near and Far

股市上周的惨跌可能引发下周的大跌，投资者们斩仓割肉

Tuesday's big selloff was blamed largely on concerns about China's markets and the US economy. Greenspan's comments may have also played a part.

有人指责对中国市场与美国经济的担忧导致了周二的大清仓。格林斯潘的评论对此也有一定的影响。

This is IN THE NEWS in VOA *Special English*.

这是美国之音《特别英语》新闻节目。

Financial markets around the world took investors on a shaky ride this week.

世界金融市场本周发生大震荡。

On Tuesday, concerns about the health of Chinese markets and the United States economy helped send investors on a flight from risk. A selloff that began on the Shanghai stock market quickly spread to Europe and the United States. Markets in Africa and Latin America also suffered losses.

周二，人们对中国市场与美国经济的担忧导致投资者逃离股市。开始于上海股市的大清仓行为迅速蔓延至欧洲和美国。非洲、拉美股市同样惨遭损失。

China's main stock market in Shanghai fell nine percent Tuesday. It was the worst drop in

Chinese stocks in ten years. Investors hurried to sell their stocks as concern spread that the government might raise interest rates. There were also unconfirmed reports of a possible new tax on capital gains. Chinese officials denied those reports.

中国的主要股票市场上海股市周二下跌了9%，是中国股市十年来跌幅最大的一次。投资者因为普遍担心政府提高利率而慌忙抛售股票。同时还有未经证实的报道说可能要征收资本收入税。中国官员否认了这些报道。

On Wall Street, the Dow Jones Industrial Average of thirty major stocks dropped four hundred sixteen points, more than three percent. That was a loss about six billion dollars of shareholder value on the New York Stock Exchange. It was the biggest one-day drop since the first day of trading after the terrorist attacks in September of two thousand and one.

在华尔街，由三十个权重股组成的道琼斯工业平均指数下跌了416点，下跌幅度超过3%。这个数字表示，纽约股市股东的股票价值缩水60亿美元。这是自2001年9月恐怖袭击后第一个交易日以来单日最大的跌幅。

But at one point Tuesday, after a month of moving up, the Dow was down as much as five hundred forty-six points.

但是，大盘上行一个月之后，道琼斯指数在周二的某个点位又下跌了546点。

The intense trading even overloaded the systems that continually compute the Dow Jones average. Traders had the wrong information for seventy minutes. But the Dow Jones Company says it does not believe that the delay worsened the drop in the market.

频繁的交易甚至使计算机系统因不断计算道琼斯平均指数而超负荷运行，以致交易者们在70分钟里看到的都是错误信息。但道琼斯公司否认系统的延搁导致市场跌势更趋严重的说法。

Investors may have also been influenced by comments from Alan Greenspan. On Monday, the former chairman of the Federal Reserve said a recession was possible in the United States by the end of the year. Later, he said a recession is possible but not probable.

投资者们还受了阿兰·格林斯潘评语的影响。这位美联储前主席周一说，美国年末有可能出现大萧条，后来他又说大萧条只是有可能发生，但不是很肯定。

The current Federal Reserve chairman told Congress that the markets in the United States seemed to be working well. Ben Bernanke said the central bank still expects "moderate growth" in the economy this year. His comments Wednesday seemed to help calm the markets.

现任美联储主席对国会说，美国的市场看来运行正常。伯南克说，央行期待本年经济有“适度增长”。他周三的发言似乎有助于稳定市场。

A better-than-expected manufacturing report on Thursday also helped stock prices, after an early drop on Wall Street. Another economic report had been blamed as one of the causes of Tuesday's big selloff.

周四出台的制造业报告比预期的要好，这也有助于华尔街股价在之前的大跌后止跌。另一个经济报告却被指责为引起周二股票大清仓的原因之一。

On Tuesday the Commerce Department reported the biggest drop in three months in orders for durable goods in January. These are higher-priced goods designed to last three years or more, like cars and computers.

商业部周二发布了耐用品在一月份的订单是三个月来跌幅最大的一次。这些耐用品是指那些使用期在三年或三年以上的高价商品，如汽车、电脑等。

There was also concern in the markets this week about companies that deal in “subprime” home loans. These loans for people with weak credit histories have been popular in recent years. But many people are now having trouble paying them back.

本周，市场还对参与“次级”家庭贷款的公司表示担忧。这类贷款近年来颇受那些有不良信用记录的人的欢迎，但现在许多人都处于还贷困境。

All together, it was one of the worst weeks in several years for financial markets that have recently hit new highs. Investors hoped that their shaky ride was nothing more than a normal price correction.

总而言之，这是金融市场近几年来冲击新高后最惨的几个星期之一。投资者希望这次的大震荡仅仅是正常的价格调整。

(And that's IN THE NEWS, written by Brianna Blake. I'm Steve Ember.)

Lesson 2 Similarities, but Also Big Differences, between Today's Crisis and 1930s

By Mario Ritter

November 29, 2008

Part One Background Information

金融危机与经济危机

2007 年 8 月，美国房地产次贷危机引发的金融危机导致大量金融机构破产或重组（如美国著名的投资银行雷曼公司）。人们对金融机构的不信任通常会蔓延至对本国货币的不信任，而美国政府为拯救金融市场疯狂增发美元，这又为未来美元货币的贬值埋下了祸根，最后可能导致其实体经济受到严重的冲击。可以说，金融危机是经济危机的前奏。

金融危机是指一个或几个国家与地区的全部或大部分金融指标（如短期利率、货币资产、证券、房地产、商业破产数和金融机构倒闭数）的急剧和超周期恶化。金融危机可以分为货币危机、债务危机、银行危机等类型，而且近年来的金融危机越来越呈现出某种混合形式的危机。2008 年发生在欧美大规模的投资银行、保险公司、商业银行等金融机构的倒闭就是明显的金融危机。

经济危机主要是指经济基本面发生极端恶化，大量企业倒闭，社会经济陷入极端萧条中。金融危机可能发展为经济危机，如 1929 年出现的世界经济大萧条就是由最初发生在华尔街的金融危机引发的①。本课新闻内容就是对两次金融危机进行比较。

Part Two Exercises

Ⅰ. Listen to the first part of the news, and fill in the blanks with the words you hear.

1. What began more than a year ago is often described as "the ____________ since the Great Depression".

2. The ____________ is bad, but it would have to get much worse to ____________ to the nineteen thirties.

3. Next October will mark the eightieth ____________ of what is generally considered the ____________ of the Depression.

① http://news.xinhuanet.com/fortune/2008-10/20/content_10222205.htm

4. In just two days the ____________ lost almost twenty-five percent of its ____________.

5. The ____________ continued to drop until July of nineteen thirty-two. By then, the Dow was about ninety percent ____________ in September of nineteen twenty-nine.

6. The Dow hit its ____________ in October of last year.

7. Since last year the Dow has lost about forty percent of its ____________ even more for the Standard & Poor's ____________ of five hundred ____________.

8. Like the Depression, the current crisis also ____________.

9. American ____________ fell by almost seventeen percent in the twelve months that ended in September.

Ⅱ. Listen to the second part of the news, and answer the following questions.

1. How much did the house price fall during the Depression? What happened to those who could not pay their mortgage loans (抵押贷款)?

2. Is it easy for people to borrow from the bank?

3. What will happen to the banks when those ten million Americans who owe more than their home is worth can not pay their mortgage loans?

4. Why do you think as many as an estimated nine thousand banks failed during the Depression?

5. What are the two recycled results of the banks failing?

6. What is the function of the Federal Deposit Insurance Corporation?

Ⅲ. Listen to the third part of the news, and translate it into Chinese.

From "Just twenty-two banks... this year" to the sentence before "President Franklin Roosevelt". (Washington Mutual 华盛顿互惠银行)

Ⅳ. Listen to and repeat the last part of the news, then write it down.

From "President Franklin Roosevelt..." to the end.

Ⅴ. Spoken English Practice.

Talk about the economic situation during the economic "downturn".

Part Three Keys to the Exercises

Ⅰ. Listen to the first part of the news, and fill in the blanks with the words you hear.

1. What began more than a year ago is often described as "the worst economic crisis since the Great Depression".

2. The downturn is bad, but it would have to get much worse to compare to the nineteen thirties.

3. Next October will mark the eightieth anniversary of what is generally considered the beginnings of the Depression.

4. In just two days the Dow Jones Industrial Average lost almost twenty-five percent of its value.

5. The stock market continued to drop until July of nineteen thirty-two. By then, the Dow was about ninety percent below its high reached in September of nineteen twenty-nine.

6. The Dow hit its all-time high in October of last year.

7. Since last year the Dow has lost about forty percent of its value even more for the Standard & Poor's index of five hundred stocks.

8. Like the Depression, the current crisis also involves falling property values.

9. American housing prices fell by almost seventeen percent in the twelve months that ended in September.

Ⅱ. Listen to the second part of the news, and answer the following questions.

1. How much did the house price fall during the Depression? What happened to those who

could not pay their mortgage loans（抵押贷款）?

Housing economist Robert Shiller at Yale University has found that home prices fell by about thirty percent during the Depression. Then, as now, many people lost their homes because they could not pay their mortgage loans.

2. Is it easy for people to borrow from the bank?

Yes. Today people borrow much more of the value of their homes than they used to.

3. What will happen to the banks when those ten million Americans who owe more than their home is worth can not pay their mortgage loans?

The banks will go bankrupted. In fact, Professor Shiller estimates that ten million Americans owe more than their home is worth.

4. Why do you think as many as an estimated nine thousand banks failed during the Depression?

Because Agencies that guarantee savings and supervise the financial system did not exist at the start.

5. What are the two recycled results of the banks failing?

When banks failed, people lost everything. Fear of bank failures led people to withdraw their money, leading to more failures.

6. What is the function of the Federal Deposit Insurance Corporation?

In nineteen thirty-three, Congress established the Federal Deposit Insurance Corporation. It currently guarantees bank deposits up to two hundred fifty thousand dollars.

Ⅲ. Listen to the third part of the news, and translate it into Chinese.

From "Just twenty-two banks... this year" to the sentence before "President Franklin Roosevelt". (Washington Mutual 华盛顿互惠银行)

1. Just twenty-two banks have failed this year.
   今年只有22家银行倒闭。
2. But among them was Washington Mutual, the biggest bank collapse in American history.
   但其中有华盛顿互惠银行，这是美国历史上倒闭的最大银行。
3. Possibly the best measure of an economic crisis is unemployment.
   也许最能衡量经济危机的是失业率。
4. The rate in October was reported at a fourteen-year high of six and one-half percent.
   据报道，10月份的失业率是14年来最高的，达6.5%。
5. Some think it could reach eight percent or higher.
   有人认为失业率可能会达到8%或更高。
6. During the Depression, however, one of every four workers was unemployed.
   然而在大萧条期间，每四个工人中有一个人失业。

Ⅳ. Listen to and repeat the last part of the news, and then write it down.

From "President Franklin Roosevelt..." to the end.

1. President Franklin Roosevelt and Congress established agencies to employ people in public works.

2. Yet employment did not completely recover until World War Two.

3. Policy mistakes increased the effects of the Depression.

4. For example, the Federal Reserve let the money supply shrink.

5. This meant there was less money available for lending to people and businesses.

6. In the current crisis, the government has been willing to spend freely; too freely for some critics.

7. On Tuesday the Federal Reserve and the Treasury announced a new plan to provide eight hundred billion dollars to increase credit availability.

8. Before the Thanksgiving holiday on Thursday, the Dow and the S&P rose four days in a row for the first time in months.

Part Four　Translation of the Text

Similarities, but Also Big Differences, between Today's 1930s
此次经济衰退与 20 世纪 30 年代大萧条之异同

This downturn is bad, but rates of unemployment and bank failures do not compare to the Great Depression.

经济衰退很严重，但失业率和银行坏账情况不比大萧条年代。

What began more than a year ago is often described as "the worst economic crisis since the Great Depression". The downturn is bad, but it would have to get much worse to compare to the nineteen thirties.

自一年多前开始的衰退通常被描述为“自大萧条以来最严重的经济危机”。衰退很严重，但比起 1930s 的大萧条来说还差得远。

Next October will mark the eightieth anniversary of what is generally considered the beginnings of the Depression.

明年十月被公认为大萧条的 80 周年纪念。

In just two days the Dow Jones Industrial Average lost almost twenty-five percent of its value. The stock market continued to drop until July of nineteen thirty-two. By then, the Dow was about ninety percent below its high reached in September of nineteen twenty-nine.

两天之内，道琼斯平均工业指数的股值下跌了近 25%。股市持续下跌至 1932 年 7 月。那时，道指已比 1929 年 9 月的最高点低了 90%。

The Dow hit its all-time high in October of last year. Since last year the Dow has lost about forty percent of its value even more for the Standard & Poor's index of five hundred stocks.

道指在去年 10 月达到历史最高值。自去年以来道指下跌了约 40%，比标准普尔 500 指数跌得还多。

Like the Depression, the current crisis also involves falling property values. American housing prices fell by almost seventeen percent in the twelve months that ended in September.

和大萧条一样，现在的危机也涉及房产价值的大跌。到9月份止，美国房市价格在12个月中下跌将近17%。

Housing economist Robert Shiller at Yale University has found that home prices fell by about thirty percent during the Depression. Then, as now, many people lost their homes because they could not pay their mortgage loans.

耶鲁大学的房市经济学专家罗伯特·希勒发现，在大萧条期间楼市价格下跌大约三成，那时候和现在一样，人们因为无法支付其抵押贷款而失去房产。

Today people borrow much more of the value of their homes than they used to. In fact, Professor Shiller estimates that ten million Americans owe more than their home is worth.

相比过去，人们现在购房借贷的钱大大超过了他们的房产价值。事实上，希勒教授估计有一千万美国人欠银行的钱超过了他们房产的价值。

An estimated nine thousand banks failed during the Depression. Agencies that guarantee savings and supervise the financial system did not exist at the start. When banks failed, people lost everything. Fear of bank failures led people to withdraw their money, leading to more failures.

估计有9 000家银行在大萧条期间倒闭。一开始并没有存款保证和监督金融系统的机构。当银行倒闭，人们就会失去他们所有的财产。对银行倒闭的担忧心理导致人们将钱从银行中取出，这又导致更多的银行倒闭。

In nineteen thirty-three, Congress established the Federal Deposit Insurance Corporation. It currently guarantees bank deposits up to two hundred fifty thousand dollars.

在1933年，国会设立联邦存款保险公司。其现在确保银行存有至少25万美元的保证金。

Just twenty-two banks have failed this year. But among them was Washington Mutual, the biggest bank collapse in American history.

今年只有22家银行倒闭，但其中包括华盛顿互惠银行，它是美国历史上倒闭的最大一家银行。

Possibly the best measure of an economic crisis is unemployment. The rate in October was reported at a fourteen-year high of six and one-half percent. Some think it could reach eight percent or higher. During the Depression, however, one of every four workers was unemployed.

经济危机最好的衡量指标是失业率。据报道，10月份的失业率是14年以来最高的，达6.5%。一些人认为失业率可能会攀升到8%或者更高。然而在大萧条时期，每四个人中就有一个失业。

President Franklin Roosevelt and Congress established agencies to employ people in public works. Yet employment did not completely recover until World War Two.

富兰克林·罗斯福总统和国会组织机构聘用民众从事公共工作。然而就业情况直至第二次世界大战期间才完全恢复。

Policy mistakes increased the effects of the Depression. For example, the Federal Reserve let the money supply shrink. This meant there was less money available for lending to people and businesses.

政策失误加重了大萧条的影响，比如美联储减少货币供应量，这意味着人们和公司能借到的钱更少。

In the current crisis, the government has been willing to spend freely; too freely for some critics. On Tuesday the Federal Reserve and the Treasury announced a new plan to provide eight hundred billion dollars to increase credit availability.

在目前的危机中，政府很乐意花钱，一些批评者认为太随意了。在周二，美联储和财政部宣布了一项新计划，可以提供 8 000 亿美元来提高信贷量。

Before the Thanksgiving holiday on Thursday, the Dow and the S&P rose four days in a row for the first time in months.

在周四的感恩节假期来临之前，道琼斯指数和标准普尔指数几个月以来首次连续四日攀升。

(And that's IN THE NEWS in VOA *Special English*, written by Mario Ritter. I'm Steve Ember.)

Lesson 3　World Wealth Report

By Mario Ritter

June 25, 2004

Part One　Background Information

贫富差距意味着什么?

贫富悬殊是如何产生的?贫富悬殊中的财富来自正当的渠道吗?在市场经济条件下,人人都想成为“最先富起来的人”。但现实告诉人们,只有一部分拥有某些资源的人才能“先富起来”。

“经济人追求自身利益最大化的欲望率先被唤醒,利润最大化理所当然地成为企业生产经营活动追求的目标,也成为一部分官员难以抵挡的诱惑;尤其是转型时期体制上的许多漏洞和空白,为权钱交易留下了大量的机会;个人收入来源、消费形式的多元化和让一部分人先富起来的政策,使寻租收入得以混同于正常的合法收入;经济法规不完善、法制不健全,使得对寻租活动的监督成本很高,监督难度很大。在这种特殊的历史条件下,某些缺乏制约的权力便毫无顾忌地恶性膨胀起来。一方面,寻求特殊政策和待遇、寻求批文和公章以获得非生产性利润推动着企业和个人寻租;另一方面,一部分直接掌握资源分配大权和行政执法权力的官员,将自己手中的公共权力视为一种稀缺资源,将前来办事的公民视为客户,以各种手段迫使客户进行权钱交易。”① 正是存在权力与资本结合的现象,使财富向少数人手中迅速集中,造成了社会贫富差距以超常规的速度迅速扩大。

任何一种社会变革,都不可能只是一种单纯的经济基础的变革,而是建立在经济基础之上的整个社会的综合性进化过程。比如,某些垄断行业凭借国家的特殊政策和特殊生产条件而获得垄断利润,不仅企业高管给自己发大量工资,也为职工发放额外收入,大大超过了他们所创造的经济和社会效益,部门分配基本失去控制。行业垄断造成的高收入,使社会分配不公的现象扩展到更广大的范围。

分配不公造成的直接后果是,在改革中收益最大的是掌握社会资源配置权力的官员及与其相关的人群,而他们付出的代价和承担的风险最小。与之相反,收益较小的普通老百姓却不得不付出最大的代价、承担最大的风险。有学者认为,贫富差距过大对一个国家的产业结构转换有着不可低估的不利影响。因为财富集中在少数富人手里,其必然结果是这个国家的产品和劳务将倾向于满足少数富人的需求,这将引导有限的资源流向满足富人的高档消费品和奢侈品生产部门,刺激这些部门的畸形扩张。民主社会以公平为制度标志,分配不公,毁坏的是社会公平,因而是对民主社会的损害,使一部分民众对政府失去信心。所有社会的人都向往共同富裕,一旦现实与理想存在差距,就会造成民众的信仰动

① http://ks.cn.yahoo.com/question/1307031301193.html

摇，其破坏性是对整个社会的生存发展产生根本性的影响。

Part Two Exercises

Ⅰ. Listen to the first part of the news, and fill in the blanks with the words you hear.

Two-thousand-three was a good year for wealthy people around the world.

Merrill Lynch and Capgemini have ______ their yearly World Wealth Report. Merrill Lynch is an American ______. Capgemini is a French company that gives ______.

______ people worldwide had ______ or more in wealth at the end of last year. The report says the number grew ______ from two-thousand-two. That year there were not many new ______.

But last year the ______ of the wealthy did well. Their wealth increased by almost ______. China, India, Spain and the United States were ______ in the creation of wealth.

Wealthy people around the world ______ last year. The report shows that their ______ as a share of their wealth increased from ______.

Ⅱ. Listen to the second part of the news, and translate it into Chinese, then repeat it in English.

Ⅲ. Listen to the third part of the news, and answer the following questions.

1. Among the continents, which one is easier for people to become millionaires last year?

2. Which place has more millionaires? The US, Europe or North America?

3. Is it true that less young people are millionaires? What is people's age for them to get most wealthy?

4. In the years from 2003 to 2008, how much will high-worth individuals'wealth increase?

5. How much do those richest of the rich have altogether?

Ⅳ. Spoken English Practice.

Tell which place has the most rich people and how the richest people do with their money.

Part Three Keys to the Exercises

Ⅰ. Listen to the first part of the news, and fill in the blanks with the words you hear.

Two-thousand-three was a good year for wealthy people around theworld.

Merrill Lynch and Capgemini have released their yearly World Wealth Report. Merrill Lynch is an American financial services company. Capgemini is a French company that gives business advice.

Seven-point-seven million people worldwide had one million dollars or more in wealth at the end of last year. The report says the number grew by seven and a half percent from two-thousand-two. That year there were not many new millionaires.

But last year the investments of the wealthy did well. Their wealth increased by almost eight percent. China, India, Spain and the United States were high performers in the creation of wealth.

Wealthy people around the world bought more stock last year. The report shows that their stock holdings as a share of their wealth increased from twenty percent to thirty-five percent.

Ⅱ. Listen to the second part of the news, and translate it into Chinese, then repeat it in English.

1. Last year, an economist at the Federal Reserve Board compared stock ownership rates among Americans.
去年，美联储委员会的一名经济学家对美国人的股票持有率进行了比较。
2. That report said the wealthiest one percent owned more than half of all stock held by individuals or families as of two-thousand-one.
报告称，最富有的1%人群拥有2001年全美国个人或家庭所有股票的一半以上。
3. The percentage was even higher for government-secured investments in bonds.
这一比率在政府发行的保值债券方面更高。
4. The top one percent owned sixty-four percent of the bonds.
顶层的1%人群拥有64%的债券。
5. Stocks and bonds are called liquid assets, just like money in the bank.
股票和债券被称为流动资产，就像银行里的钱一样。
6. Houses are less easy to sell.
房子难以出售。
7. So the World Wealth Report does not include the value of a personal home in its measure of wealth.
因此世界财富报告没有将个人的房产价值计入其所统计的财富总值。

Ⅲ. Listen to the third part of the news, and answer the following questions.

1. Among the continents, which one is easier for people to become millionaires last year?

The number of millionaires increased at the highest rates in Africa, North America and the Asia-Pacific areas.

2. Which place has more millionaires? The US, Europe or North America?

The United States had the largest increase in numbers of any country.

But Europe with its larger population continued to have the most millionaires, followed by North America. Both areas have over two million millionaires.

3. Is it true that less young people are millionaires? What is people's age for them to get most wealthy?

Right, the study says most very wealthy people are at or near retirement age. Seventy percent are over fifty-five years old.

4. In the years from 2003 to 2008, how much will high-worth individuals' wealth increase?

All together, high-worth individuals had twenty-nine-million-million dollars in wealth last year. The World Wealth Report says that is expected to reach forty-million-million dollars by two-thousand-eight.

40-million-million − 29-million-million = 11-million-million.

5. How much do those richest of the rich have altogether?

The report says a very small but fast growing group of seventy thousand people are worth more than thirty million dollars.

70, 000 ×30million = 210 billion.

Part Four Translation of the Text

World Wealth Report
世界财富报告

Two-thousand-three was a good year for wealthy people around the world.

Merrill Lynch and Capgemini have released their yearly World Wealth Report. Merrill Lynch is an American financial services company. Capgemini is a French company that gives business advice.

2003年对于全世界的富人来说是幸福的一年。美林投资银行和凯捷咨询公司联合公布其年度世界财富报告。美林投行是美国的一家金融服务公司，凯捷则是法国一家提供商业咨询的公司。

Seven-point-seven million people worldwide had one million dollars or more in wealth at the end of last year. The report says the number grew by seven and a half percent from two-thousand-two. That year there were not many new millionaires.

去年年底，全球有770万人拥有一百万美元或更多的财富。报告称该数字从2002年起以每年7.5%的比率增长。那年还没有产生这么多新百万富翁。

But last year the investments of the wealthy did well. Their wealth increased by almost eight percent. China, India, Spain and the United States were high performers in the creation of wealth.

但是上一年富人的投资收益很好。他们的财富增加了将近8%。中国、印度、西班牙和美国都是创造财富的"高手"。

Wealthy people around the world bought more stock last year. The report shows that their stock holdings as a share of their wealth increased from twenty percent to thirty-five percent.

全球的富人去年买的股票更多。报告显示，他们所持有的股票在其财富中的份额从20%增至35%。

Last year, an economist at the Federal Reserve Board compared stock ownership rates among Americans. That report said the wealthiest one percent owned more than half of all stock held by individuals or families as of two thousand and one. The percentage was even higher for government-secured investments in bonds. The top one percent owned sixty-four percent of the bonds.

去年，美联储委员会的一名经济学家对美国人的股票持有率进行了比较。报告称，以上最富有的百分之一人群拥有2001年全美国个人或家庭所有股票的一半以上。这一比率在政府发行的保值债券方面更高，项层的1%人群拥有64%的债券。

Stocks and bonds are called liquid assets, just like money in the bank. Houses are less easy to sell. So the World Wealth Report does not include the value of a personal home in its measure of wealth.

股票和债券被称为流动资产，就像银行里的钱一样。房产难以出售，因此世界财富报告没有将个人的房产价值计入其所统计的财富总值。

Last year, the number of millionaires increased at the highest rates in Africa, North America and the Asia-Pacific areas. The United States had the largest increase in numbers of any country.

去年，非洲、北美和亚太地区百万富翁的增长率最高。美国百万富翁在增长数量上比其他任何国家都多。

But Europe with its larger population continued to have the most millionaires, followed by North America. Both areas have over two million millionaires.

但是欧洲因其人口多而继续拥有最多的百万富翁，其次是北美。两个地区的百万富翁都超过了 200 万人。

The study says most very wealthy people are at or near retirement age. Seventy percent are over fifty-five years old.

相关研究显示，绝大部分非常富有的人到了或将到退休的年龄，其中有七成超过 55 岁。

All together, high-worth individuals had twenty-nine-million-million dollars in wealth last year. The World Wealth Report says that is expected to reach forty-million-million dollars by two-thousand-eight.

总的来说，去年的“首富们”总共拥有 29 万亿美元的财富。世界财富统计报告显示，这个数字有望在 2008 年达到 40 万亿美元。

And the richest of the rich are doing the best of all. The report says a very small but fast growing group of seventy thousand people are worth more than thirty million dollars.

而且富人中的“首富们”状况越来越好。报告显示，一个快速扩大的 7 万人的小团体拥有的财富超过 3 000 万美元。

(This VOA *Special English* Economics Report was written by Mario Ritter. This is Bob Doughty.)

Lesson 4　Nobel Recognizes Research into Economic Governance

By Mario Ritter

October 15, 2009

Part One　Background Information[①]

经济管理研究获得诺贝尔奖的承认

危机的出现是因为人们忘记了发展经济需要一个好的管理机制。所谓管理，就是通过一定的制度安排来合理界定各参与方的责任和权利，以期实现资源的最优配置。2009 年获得诺贝尔经济学奖的加州大学伯克利分校的奥利费·威廉姆森教授一直专注于经济组织的研究，并系统提出了经济组织的管理理论；印第安纳大学埃利诺·奥斯特罗姆教授则专注于公共治理的研究，试图提出公共领域的有效治理机制。所有这些都是为了让这个社会变得更富有效率。

这两个学者都不是学院派的，都关注现实。威廉姆森称得上是新制度经济学（NIE）的代表人物，正是得益于其系统化交易成本的概念，并且把这一概念应用于各种经济组织，才使得 NIE 的交易成本经济学分支得以建立和扩展，并且使得新制度经济学体系化，并顺利“入侵”其他社会科学。交易成本经济学甚至成为管理学当中的重要部分。

威廉姆森的理论是市场—各种中间组织—等级，即现实的组织状态，无论经济组织和其他类型的组织都是如此。他将不同的组织看成经济活动的治理机制。究竟在某个具体经济活动中选择哪类治理机制，取决其交易成本的大小，即一个被选出的治理机制必然是交易成本最低的机制！仅此而已。这大概可以说明威廉姆森理论之内核。而奥斯特罗姆的理论基本上是 NIE 的主要思想在公共领域中的应用，偏向于经济学和政治学以及公共行政的有机结合，因此对经济学领域基本没有太大影响。

Part Two　Exercises

Ⅰ. Listen to the first part of the news, and complete the following sentences with the words you hear.

1. Economists usually ____.

2. Now, two Americans have won ______________________________.

① http://zhouyean.blog.sohu.com/133809199.html

3. They will share almost one and a half million dollars ________________.

4. This is the study of how ________________________________.

5. The winners are Elinor Ostrom of ________________ in Bloomington and Oliver Williamson of the ________________________.

6. The prize in economic sciences has gone to sixty-three men ________________.

7. Elinor Ostrom is the first woman. And, like other winners over the years, ________________________________.

8. She is a professor of ________________________________.

Ⅱ. Listen to the second part of the news, and translate it into Chinese, then repeat it in English.

Ⅲ. Listen to the third part of the news, and answer the following questions.

1. What did Oliver Williamson study and find?

2. How do businesses solve conflicts according to Oliver Williamson's theory?

3. What are the suppliers' functions for companies to avoid disputes over prices?

4. What is Oliver Williamson's idea to make production more efficient?

Ⅳ. Listen to and repeat the last part of the news, then write it down.

V. Spoken English Practice.

Tell what Elinor Ostrom and Oliver William found in their researches.

Part Three Keys to the Exercises

I. Listen to the first part of the news, and complete the following sentences with the words you hear.

1. Economists usually study markets.
2. Now, two Americans have won the Nobel Prize in economics for not studying markets.
3. They will share almost one and a half million dollars for their analysis of economic governance.
4. This is the study of how economic activity is governed within companies, communities and other groups.
5. The winners are Elinor Ostrom of Indiana University in Bloomington and Oliver Williamson of the University of California, Berkeley.
6. The prize in economic sciences has gone to sixty-three men since it was first awarded forty years ago.
7. Elinor Ostrom is the first woman. And, like other winners over the years, her training is not limited to economics.
8. She is a professor of political science and of public and environmental affairs.

II. Listen to the second part of the news, and translate it into Chinese, then repeat it in English.

1. Today, economic theory suggests that good resource management requires ownership, either private or public.
   当今的经济理论认为，良好的资源管理需要以所有权为前提，无论是国营或私营。
2. If not, the thinking goes, then self-interest will lead to overuse and destruction of shared resources.
   该思潮认为，不是这样的话，自利动机将引发公有资源的滥用与破坏。
3. Ecologist Garrett Hardin described this idea in nineteen sixty-eight as "the tragedy of the commons".
   生态学家加勒特·哈定在1968年将这一现象描述为“共有的悲剧”。
4. Elinor Ostrom showed how local decision making can lessen the tragedy.

埃莉诺·奥斯特罗姆证明了地方决策可以减少这种“悲剧”。

5. Her research has deepened understanding of how people balance their needs with those of others who depend on the same resources.

   她的研究加深了人们对于依赖相同资源的人如何平衡彼此需求的理解。

6. She studied communities like farmers in Southern California who depended on a common water supply.

   她研究了诸如南加州社区的农民，他们都是依靠同一水源生活。

7. She documented how people who use resources often develop ways to share them. One example is forest management.

   她记录了人们如何在使用资源时设法分享资源。其中一个例子就是森林管理。

8. Elinor Ostrom："One of the absolutely key，most important variables as to whether or not a forest survives and continues is whether local people monitor each other and its use. Not officials，locals."

   埃莉诺·奥斯特罗姆说："其中决定一片森林能否幸存与持续的绝对答案和最重要变量之一，就是当地居民能否相互监督彼此使用森林的行为。不是官员，而是当地人。"

Ⅲ. Listen to the third part of the news，and answer the following questions.

1. What did Oliver Williamson study and find?

Oliver Williamson has studied big companies and found that they often are better than markets at doing complex jobs.

2. How do businesses solve conflicts according to Oliver Williamson's theory?

Under his theory，businesses act as structures for conflict resolution.

3. What are the suppliers' functions for companies to avoid disputes over prices?

For example，companies that own their suppliers can avoid long-term contracts and disputes over prices.

4. What is Oliver Williamson's idea to make production more efficient?

Companies own their suppliers. This can make production more efficient and make better use of limited resources.

Ⅳ. Listen to and repeat the last part of the news，then write it down.

But businesses can also abuse their power. Professor Williamson says the best way to deal with this is not by limiting the size of companies，but through industry regulation.

The Royal Swedish Academy of Sciences said economists need to do more than study markets and prices. The Nobel judges urged more research like the kind they recognized with this year's award.

Part Four Translation of the Text

Nobel Recognizes Research into Economic Governance
经济管理研究获得诺贝尔奖的承认

Economists usually study markets. Now, two Americans have won the Nobel Prize in economics for not studying markets.

经济学家通常是研究市场的。现在有两名美国人并不是因为研究市场而获得诺贝尔经济学奖。

They will share almost one and a half million dollars for their analysis of economic governance. This is the study of how economic activity is governed within companies, communities and other groups.

他们因为研究经济管理而可以分享近150万美元的奖金。此项研究是有关企业、社区及其他团体经济活动的管理问题。

The winners are Elinor Ostrom of Indiana University in Bloomington and Oliver Williamson of the University of California, Berkeley. The prize in economic sciences has gone to sixty-three men since it was first awarded forty years ago. Elinor Ostrom is the first woman. And, like other winners over the years, her training is not limited to economics. She is a professor of political science and of public and environmental affairs.

获奖者是布鲁明顿印第安纳大学的埃莉诺·奥斯特罗姆和加利福尼亚大学伯克利分校的奥利弗·威廉姆森。诺贝尔经济学奖自四十年前开始颁奖以来，已有六十三人获奖。而埃莉诺·奥斯特罗姆是第一位获奖的女性。与多年来的获奖者一样，她的教育背景不局限于经济学，她还是政治学以及公共与环境事务学教授。

Today, economic theory suggests that good resource management requires ownership, either private or public. If not, the thinking goes, then self-interest will lead to overuse and destruction of shared resources. Ecologist Garrett Hardin described this idea in nineteen sixty-eight as "the tragedy of the commons".

当今的经济理论认为，良好的资源管理需要以所有权为前提，无论是国营或私营。该思潮认为，不是这样的话，自利动机将引发公有资源的滥用与破坏。生态学家加勒特·哈定在1968年将这一现象描述为“共有的悲剧”。

Elinor Ostrom showed how local decision making can lessen the tragedy. Her research has deepened understanding of how people balance their needs with those of others who depend on the same resources.

埃莉诺·奥斯特罗姆证明了地方决策可以减少这种“悲剧”。她的研究加深了人们对于依赖相同资源的人如何平衡彼此需求的理解。

She studied communities like farmers in Southern California who depended on a common water supply. She documented how people who use resources often develop ways to share them.

One example is forest management.

她研究了诸如南加州社区的农民，他们都是依靠同一水源生活。她记录了人们如何在使用资源时设法分享资源。其中一个例子就是森林管理。

Elinor Ostrom："One of the absolutely key, most important variables as to whether or not a forest survives and continues is whether local people monitor each other and its use. Not officials, locals."

埃莉诺·奥斯特罗姆说："其中决定一片森林能否幸存与持续的绝对答案和最重要变量之一，就是当地居民是否能够相互监督彼此使用森林的行为。不是官员，而是当地人。"

Oliver Williamson has studied big companies and found that they often are better than markets at doing complex jobs. Under his theory, businesses act as structures for conflict resolution.

奥利弗·威廉姆森研究了大型企业，发现它们往往在完成复杂任务方面做得比市场好。根据他的理论，企业组织可作为整体结构来解决冲突。

For example, companies that own their suppliers can avoid long-term contracts and disputes over prices. This can make production more efficient and make better use of limited resources.

例如，供货方属于本公司就可以避免长期的合同以及价格方面的争端。这可以提高生产效率，更好地利用有限的资源。

But businesses can also abuse their power. Professor Williamson says the best way to deal with this is not by limiting the size of companies, but through industry regulation.

但是企业也可能滥用其权力。威廉姆森教授说，最好的解决方法不是限制公司的规模，而是通过行业规范。

The Royal Swedish Academy of Sciences said economists need to do more than study markets and prices. The Nobel judges urged more research like the kind they recognized with this year's award.

瑞典皇家科学院称，经济学家的研究应该超越市场和价格的研究范畴。诺贝尔奖评委通过本年度的颁奖来鼓励进行更多的此类研究。

(And that's the VOA *Special English* Economics Report, written by Mario Ritter. I'm Steve Ember.)

Lesson 5 Peter Drucker (1909 – 2005): A Thinker for Business Leaders

By Mario Ritter

November 25, 2005

Part One Background Information

现代管理学是研究什么的?

翻开诺贝尔经济学奖的得奖者名单，我们发现其中绝大部分得奖者来自美国。个中原因恐怕不能仅用瑞典皇家科学院评委的偏爱就可解释得清楚。笔者个人认为，它与美国经济学界拥有一批高屋建瓴的思想家有关。被誉为“现代管理学之父”的彼得·德鲁克就是其中之一，他虽然没有获得过诺贝尔经济学奖，但他建立于广泛实践基础之上的三十余部著作，“对后资本主义社会异常惊人的预见和行动指南，对未来社会的精辟洞见”[①] 不仅对美国微软总裁比尔·盖茨和通用电器公司首席执行官杰克·韦尔奇在企业实践方面产生了影响，也引领了美国半个世纪的企业发展道路。

甚至可以说，德鲁克对经济发展的高瞻远瞩无人能及：20 世纪 50 年代初，德鲁克预言，计算机终将彻底改变商业；1961 年，他提醒美国应关注日本工业的崛起；20 年后，又是他首先警告这个东亚国家可能陷入经济滞胀[②]。1977 年德鲁克在其如史书般的《旁观者》中明确宣告，250 年以来起源于欧洲的完美的社会拯救时代，即虚妄的世俗宗教的结束，他希望“以一个充裕、能让人忍受且自由的社会取而代之，而不是把历史完全交由自由的市场”。[③]

20 世纪 90 年代，他以八十多岁高龄学者的敏锐率先对“知识经济”进行了阐释，并首次提出具有深远意义的“组织”和目标管理的概念[④]。在德鲁克看来，“虽然社会不能被拯救，但社会是可以被管理的，当国家不能以权力来对社会进行管理时，承担最微观的社会管理责任的对象来自有赢利目标的组织——公司”[⑤]，而指导和控制管理者的是行动目标而不是他的老板。德鲁克对传统管理方法提出了最具挑战性的看法：公司变成了社会的代表性机构，要满足社会基本的信仰和承诺。

德鲁克的预言式经济理论对中国以世界工厂为标榜的崛起提出了“直击核心的告诫：现代化经济的真正力量，并不是建立在劳动力上。真正的经济力量来自许多受过教育的人才”。中国受过高等教育的人口比例仍相当小，其增长动力主要来自于制造而非创新[⑥]。

---

①② 杨帆. 德鲁克现代管理学之父. http://finance.sina.com.cn, 2004 – 07 – 14

③ 袁卫东. 中国为什么需要德鲁克. WSWire.com, 2005 – 11 – 30

④ 杨帆. 德鲁克现代管理学之父. http://finance.sina.com.cn, 2004 – 07 – 14

⑤⑥ 袁卫东. 中国为什么需要德鲁克. WSWire.com, 2005 – 11 – 30

德鲁克本人的智慧来源于自己的实践，而非用“数学公式”进行研究，因而始终未被学界主流认可。但是，2002 年，德鲁克荣获美国总统布什颁发的“总统自由勋章”，使他得到了与格林斯潘同等的官方认可。但很奇怪的是，在管理学风靡中国的今天，德鲁克的思想反而被埋没了，直至他逝世才唤起了中国经济学界对其理论的认识。

Part Two　Exercises

Ⅰ. Listen to the first part of the news, and fill in the blanks with the words you hear.

Peter Drucker was ______________________________ about social and business relations. He died in Claremont, California, on November eleventh ______________________________.

Peter Drucker was born ________________ in nineteen-o-nine. In the late nineteen twenties, he worked ________________ in Frankfurt, Germany. He also studied ________________.

He fled Germany as Adolf Hitler ________________ in nineteen thirty-three. Peter Drucker spent four years in Britain ______________________________. He then came to the United States.

Ⅱ. Listen to the second part of the news with the outlines given below, and translate it into Chinese orally.

1. Mister Drucker...
2. He developed this advice...
3. In the middle of the nineteen forties, Peter Drucker argued that...
4. He also warned that...
5. Mister Drucker...
6. He wrote about his experiences...
7. In it, he said that workers at all levels...

Ⅲ. Listen to the third part of the news, and answer the following questions.

1. What did critics say about Peter Drucker?

2. What did critics praise Peter Drucker for?

3. How did people call him? (guru 头面人物、专家、权威)

4. What is the change in Peter Drucker's thinking?

Ⅳ. Listen to and repeat the last two parts of the news, then write them down.

Part Three　Keys to the Exercises

Ⅰ. Listen to the first part of the news, and fill in the blanks with the words you hear.

Peter Drucker was a voice for change and new ways of thinking about social and business relations. He died in Claremont, California, on November eleventh at the age of ninety-five.

Peter Drucker was born in Austria in nineteen-o-nine. In the late nineteen twenties, he worked as a reporter in Frankfurt, Germany. He also studied international law.

He fled Germany as Adolf Hitler came to power in nineteen thirty-three. Peter Drucker spent four years in Britain as an adviser to investment banks. He then came to the United States.

Ⅱ. Listen to the second part of the news with the outlines given below, and translate it into Chinese.

1. Mister Drucker used his knowledge of international law to advise American businesses.
   彼得·德鲁克运用他的国际法知识为美国企业出谋划策。
2. He developed this advice into books on businesses methods and management.
   后来他将其策略撰写成经营方法与管理方面的书籍。
3. In the middle of the nineteen forties, Peter Drucker argued that the desire for profit was central to business efforts.
   在40年代中期，彼得·德鲁克认为对利润的渴求是企业取得成就的核心。
4. He also warned that rising wages were harming American business.
   同时他也警告，日渐提高的工资正在损害美国企业。
5. Mister Drucker was later invited to study General Motors.
   彼得·德鲁克先生随后被邀请研究通用汽车公司。
6. He wrote about his experiences in the book *The Concept of the Corporation*.
   他在《公司的概念》一书中总结了自己的经验。
7. In it, he said that workers at all levels should take part in decision-making, not just top managers.
   书中写到，不仅仅是高层经理，所有层次的员工都应参与决策过程。

Ⅲ. Listen to the third part of the news, and answer the following questions.

1. What did critics say about Peter Drucker?

Critics of Peter Drucker have said that he often included only information that supported his arguments.

2. What did critics praise Peter Drucker for?

But even his critics praised his clear reasoning and simple writing.

3. How did people call him?

He was called a management guru.

4. What is the change in Peter Drucker's thinking?

Peter Drucker changed his thinking as times changed. In nineteen ninety-three, he warned that seeking too much profit helped a business' competitors. That was almost fifty years after he had argued the importance of profits.

Ⅳ. Listen to and repeat the last two parts of the news, then write them down.

Mister Drucker taught at the Claremont Graduate School of Management for more than thirty years. He also advised companies. And he wrote for the *Wall Street Journal* opinion page for twenty years, until nineteen ninety-five. He commented on many economic and management issues.

Peter Drucker may be most famous not for answering questions but for asking them. He once said that business people must ask themselves not "what do we want to sell" but "what do people want to buy". Mister Drucker used terms like "knowledge workers" and "management goals". Many of his ideas have grown to be highly valued in business training and politics.

Part Four　Translation of the Text

Peter Drucker (1909 – 2005): A Thinker for Business Leaders
彼得·德鲁克（1909—2005）：引领企业的思想家

Peter Drucker was a voice for change and new ways of thinking about social and business relations. He died in Claremont, California, on November eleventh at the age of ninety-five.

彼得·德鲁克代表着社会与企业关系的转变和新思维。他（2005 年）11 月 11 日死于美国加州的克莱尔蒙特，终年 95 岁。

Peter Drucker was born in Austria in nineteen-o-nine. In the late nineteen twenties, he worked as a reporter in Frankfurt, Germany. He also studied international law.

彼得·德鲁克 1909 年生于奥地利。20 世纪 20 年代末，他在德国法兰克福当记者，曾经修读过国际法。

He fled Germany as Adolf Hitler came to power in nineteen thirty-three. Peter Drucker spent four years in Britain as an adviser to investment banks. He then came to the United States.

希特勒于1933年上台时彼得·德鲁克逃离了德国。他在英国的一家投资银行当了四年的顾问，然后便到了美国。

Mister Drucker used his knowledge of international law to advise American businesses. He developed this advice into books on businesses methods and management.

彼得·德鲁克运用他的国际法知识为美国企业出谋划策，后来他将其策略撰写成经营方法与管理方面的书籍。

In the middle of the nineteen forties, Peter Drucker argued that the desire for profit was central to business efforts. He also warned that rising wages were harming American business.

在40年代中期，彼得·德鲁克认为对利润的渴求是企业取得成就的核心。同时他也警告，日渐提高的工资正在损害美国企业。

Mister Drucker was later invited to study General Motors. He wrote about his experiences in the book *The Concept of the Corporation*. In it, he said that workers at all levels should take part in decision-making, not just top managers.

彼得·德鲁克随后被邀请研究通用汽车公司。他在《公司的概念》一书中总结了自己的经验。书中写到，不仅仅是高层经理，所有层次的员工都应参与决策过程。

Critics of Peter Drucker have said that he often included only information that supported his arguments. But even his critics praised his clear reasoning and simple writing. He was called a management guru.

批评彼得·德鲁克的人说，他在书中只提了一些支持自己论点的数据。但即便是批评他的人也称赞他清晰的推论和简洁明了的文笔。他被誉为管理界的宗师。

Peter Drucker changed his thinking as times changed. In nineteen ninety-three, he warned that seeking too much profit helped a business' competitors. That was almost fifty years after he had argued the importance of profits.

彼得·德鲁克随着时代的转变改变了他的思想。1993年他警告：企业追求高额的利润是在帮助自己的竞争对手。这是他在力辩利润的重要性近50年之后提出的。

Mister Drucker taught at the Claremont Graduate School of Management for more than thirty years. He also advised companies. And he wrote for the *Wall Street Journal* opinion page for twenty years, until nineteen ninety-five. He commented on many economic and management issues.

彼得·德鲁克在克莱尔蒙特研究生管理学院任教30多年。他也为公司作顾问。同时他也为《华尔街日报》撰写了20年的专栏评论，直至1995年。他的言论涉及许多经济和管理方面的问题。

Peter Drucker may be most famous not for answering questions but for asking them. He once said that business people must ask themselves not "what do we want to sell" but "what do people want to buy".

彼得·德鲁克不是因能够回答问题，而是因能够提出问题而享有盛名。他曾经说过，商人们不应该问“我们要卖什么”而应该问“人们要买什么”。

Mister Drucker used terms like "knowledge workers" and "management goals". Many of his ideas have grown to be highly valued in business training and politics.

彼得·德鲁克先生提出了一些专用名词如“知识工人”和“管理目标”。他的很多创意在企业培训和政治学中受到高度重视。

Lesson 6　Economic Conditions: Trying to Read the Future

By Mario Ritter

January 19, 2006

Part One　Background Information

经济指标及其含义

什么是经济指标？下面的表格①详细解释了各种经济指标的含义，以便我们对经济指标和它们的英语表达方法有一个基本了解。

经济指标	经济指标的含义
失业率 Unemployment	一国宏观经济发展的晴雨表，反映该国经济当前的发展与前景好坏，这势必影响货币政策的制定，并对汇率产生重大影响。
非农就业人口 Nonfarm Payroll Employment	美国的就业报告数据，与失业率一同公布。通常公布时间为每月第一周的周五。
国民生产总值 GNP	目前各国每季度公布一次，它以货币形式表示该国在一个时期内所有部门的生产与服务的总和，是不同经济数据的综合表现，反映了当前经济发展的状况。
国内生产总值 GDP	目前各国每季度公布一次，它显示了该国在一定时期境内的全部经济活动，包含外国公司在其境内投资建立子公司所产生的赢利。
生产价格（物价）指数 PPI	显示了商品生产的成本（生产原材料价格的变化）与未来商品价格的变化，从而影响商品以后的消费价格与人们的消费心理。
消费物价指数 CPI	根据与消费者生活有关的产品及劳务价格统计出来的物价变动指标，通常作为观察该国通货膨胀水平的一项重要指标。
个人收入 Personal Income	包括一切从工资及社会福利所取得的收入，反映了该国个人的实际购买力水平，预示着未来消费者对商品、服务等的需求变化。
个人消费支出 Personal Consumption Expenditures	包括个人购买商品和劳务两方面的支出，是衡量居民消费支出的重要指标。
消费信心指数 Consumer Confidence Index	反映国民对该国经济发展的看好程度，预示了未来消费支出的变化。

① 佚名. 经济指标详解. http: //fx. cmbchina. com/ForexKnowledge/k_2. htm

（续上表）

经济指标	经济指标的含义
工业生产指数 Industrial Production	反映该国生产和制造业的总体生产情况。
住房开工率 Housing Starts	衡量该国建筑业活跃程度的指标，由于建筑业为经济发展变化周期中的先导产业，故其可预示未来经济的变化。
采购经理人指数 PMI	反映制造业在生产、订单、价格、雇员、交货等方面综合发展状况的晴雨表，通常以50%为分界线，高于50%被认为是经济的扩张，低于50%则意味着经济的萎缩。
全美采购经理人协会指数 NAPM	美国的采购经理人指数，与芝加哥采购经理人指数在前后两天公布。
零售销售指数 Retail Sales Index	反映不包括服务业在内的零售业商品以现金、信用卡形式交易的情况。
批发物价指数 Wholesale Price Index	反映不包括劳务在内的大宗物资如原料、中间商品、最终产品和进出口商品等的批发价格的变动趋势与幅度。
贸易平衡（贸易收支） Trade Balance	反映该国在一个时期内对外贸易总额的收入与支出的对比，即货币流入、流出的情况。
工厂订单 Factory Order	反映消费者、厂商或政府对未来商品产出的需求。
耐久商品订单 Durable Goods Orders	指不易损耗商品如车辆、电器等的订购，反映了短期内制造商生产和投资支出情况。
设备使用率 Capacity Utilization	工业生产中对设备使用的比率。设备使用率超过95%，通货膨胀的压力将随产能无法应付而急速升高，低于90%，且持续下降，表示设备闲置过多，有经济衰退现象。
经常账目 Current Account	指该国与外国进行商品、劳务进出口，投资等所产生的资金流入、流出情况。
商业库存 Business Inventory	反映商业部门对短期信贷的需求。商业库存增加，可能带动短期利率的上升，使经济发展减缓，表明经济可能进入停滞状态。
综合经济领先指标 Leading Economic Indicators	指一系列引导经济循环的相关经济指标和经济变量的加权平均数。它主要用来预测整体经济的转变情况及衡量未来数月的经济发展趋势。

Part Two　Exercises

Ⅰ. Listen to the first part of the news, and fill in the blanks with the words you hear.

Economics and weather have a lot ________________. Knowing what ________________ will be like weeks or months in the future is not easy. One thing that helps economists predict the future is the index（指标）of leading economic ______________.

An index is a way to measure ____________________ in a group of numbers over time. In ____________________, for example, an index of ____________________ will rise or fall with changes in the wider market. The changes measured by an index can be represented with a ____________________.

The index may start at a ____________________ of time with a value of one hundred. Now say that a month later the value is ____________________ as one hundred one. That means it gained ____________________. If the index lost one percent, however, the value would be ninety-nine.

Ⅱ. Listen to the second part of the news, and answer the following questions.

1. What are the leading economic indicators composed of?

2. What do the ten indexes deal with?

3. What is the index of leading indicators（领先指标指数）?

4. What are business cycles（商业周期）?

5. What does coincident index（同步指数）provide? What does it include?

6. What is a lagging index（落后指数）? What does it include?

Ⅲ. Listen to the third part of the news and take it down, then translate it into Chinese.

Ⅳ. Try to talk about leading, lagging, coincident indicators and tell what they are composed of.

Part Three　Keys to the Exercises

Ⅰ. Listen to the first part of the news, and fill in the blanks with the words you hear.

Economics and weather have a lot in common. Knowing what conditions will be like weeks or months in the future is not easy. One thing that helps economists predict the future is the index of leading economic indicators.

An index is a way to measure changes in a group of numbers over time. In financial markets, for example, an index of stocks will rise or fall with changes in the wider market. The changes measured by an index can be represented with a single percentage.

The index may start at a base period of time with a value of one hundred. Now say that a month later the value is recorded as one hundred one. That means it gained one percent. If the index lost one percent, however, the value would be ninety-nine.

Ⅱ. Listen to the second part of the news, and answer the following questions.

1. What are the leading economic indicators composed of?
   The leading economic indicators are really ten indexes.
2. What do the ten indexes deal with?
   Four deal with manufacturing activity. One deals with unemployment claims. Another measures people's expectations of the economy. Still others involve financial information like the money supply and interest rates.
3. What is the index of leading indicators（领先指标指数）?
   The index of leading indicators is just one of the tools used to measure the business cycle.
4. What are business cycles（商业周期）?
   Business cycles are the normal changes that happen in economic growth over time.
5. What does coincident index（同步指数）provide? What does it include?
   A measure called the coincident index provides information about current conditions（现时经济状况）. Employment rates are an important part of it.
6. What is a lagging index（落后指数）? What does it include?
   There is also a lagging index. It helps confirm economic changes that currently appear to be taking place. Interest rates are an important lagging indicator.

Ⅲ. Listen to the third part of the news and take it down, then translate it into Chinese.

The Conference Board publishes economic indicators for the United States. The Conference Board is a non-profit organization based in New York. It brings together business leaders to learn new ideas from one another. It has member companies around the world.

经济协商会专门为美国公布经济指标。这是一家总部设在纽约的非营利性机构。它聚集了企业界的领导者，他们可以向对方学习新思想。它的会员公司遍布全世界。

The Conference Board also does economic research. Its work helps show business and government leaders what conditions might be ahead.

经济协商会亦进行经济研究，其研究有助于企业和政府领导者事先了解将要发生的情况。

But this group did not always produce the index of leading economic indicators. It took over the job in nineteen ninety-five from the Bureau of Economic Analysis, part of the Commerce Department.

该组织并非长期发布综合经济领先指标指数，该工作是其 1995 年从商业部经济分析处接管的。

The Conference Board also publishes economic indicators for Australia, France, Germany and Japan. Others are Britain, Mexico, South Korea and Spain.

经济协商会也为澳大利亚、法国、德国、日本及其他国家，包括英国、墨西哥、韩国和西班牙，提供经济指标。

Part Four Translation of the Text

Eoonomic Conditions: Trying to Read the Future
可以预测未来的经济局势

Economics and weather have a lot in common. Knowing what conditions will be like weeks or months in the future is not easy. One thing that helps economists predict the future is the index of leading economic indicators.

经济与天气有很多相同之处。要知道未来一个星期或一个月里的经济状况并不容易，而能帮助经济学家预测未来的是经济领先指数。

An index is a way to measure changes in a group of numbers over time. In financial markets, for example, an index of stocks will rise or fall with changes in the wider market. The changes measured by an index can be represented with a single percentage.

指数是用来估量一组数字在一段时间内变化的一种方法。例如，在金融市场中，股票的指数会随着外部市场的变动而有所升跌。这些由指数测量出来的变动能够以简单的百分比来表示。

The index may start at a base period of time with a value of one hundred. Now say that a month later the value is recorded as one hundred one. That means it gained one percent. If the index lost one percent, however, the value would be ninety-nine.

指数可以 100 为价值底线的一个周期开始，假设一个月后价格记录为 101，那就表示增加了 1%，如果指数下跌 1%，其价值就变成 99。

The leading economic indicators are really ten indexes. Four deal with manufacturing activity. One deals with unemployment claims. Another measures people's expectations of the economy. Still others involve financial information like the money supply and interest rates.

经济领先指标其实由十个指数组成。其中四个是指示制造业的生产活动，一个是关于失业率，一个测试人们对经济的期望，其余涉及如资金供应和利率等方面的财经信息。

The index of leading indicators is just one of the tools used to measure the business cycle. Business cycles are the normal changes that happen in economic growth over time.

综合经济领先指标中的指数就是其中一种用于测量经济发展周期的方法。经济发展周期是指在经济增长时期内所发生的正常变动。

A measure called the coincident index provides information about current conditions. Employment rates are an important part of it.

一种被称为同步指数的方法提供了现时经济状况信息，就业率是其中的一个重要部分。

There is also a lagging index. It helps confirm economic changes that currently appear to be taking place. Interest rates are an important lagging indicator.

落后指数明确显示当前正在发生的经济变化，利率就是一种重要的落后指标。

The Conference Board publishes economic indicators for the United States. The Conference Board is a non-profit organization based in New York. It brings together business leaders to learn new ideas from one another. It has member companies around the world.

经济协商会专门为美国公布经济指标。这是一家总部设在纽约的非营利性机构。它聚集了企业界的领导者，他们可以向对方学习新思想。它的会员公司遍布全世界。

The Conference Board also does economic research. Its work helps show business and government leaders what conditions might be ahead.

经济协商会亦进行经济研究，其研究有助于企业和政府领导者事先了解将要发生的情况。

But this group did not always produce the index of leading economic indicators. It took over the job in nineteen ninety-five from the Bureau of Economic Analysis, part of the Commerce Department.

该组织并非长期发布综合经济领先指标指数，该工作是其 1995 年从商业部经济分析处接管的。

The Conference Board also publishes economic indicators for Australia, France, Germany and Japan. Others are Britain, Mexico, South Korea and Spain.

经济协商会也为澳大利亚、法国、德国、日本及其他国家，包括英国、墨西哥、韩国和西班牙，提供经济指标。

Lesson 7　Work on Game Theory Wins Nobel Prize for Two Economists

By Mario Ritter

October 14，2005

Part One　Background Information

博弈论与现实生活的联系

随着经济建设成为人们社会生活的主题，“博弈”这个词被引用得热火朝天。博弈论是一种数学方法，可用于分析并决定在竞争环境下最适宜己方的策略，因此也被称为对策论，它决定“玩家”采取何种行动，大到政治、军事规划和企业管理，小到对弈和网球比赛，目的是免除损失，获得最佳结果。

人们常用来解释博弈论的例子是：两名纵火犯被分别关在不同的牢房中，狱方向他们发出最后通牒，若一人指证另一人，其中一人可获得自由，但另一人则要受到严重惩罚(如20年监禁)。如果双方都无人指证则共同被判5年监禁。根据一次性博弈理论，当两名罪犯首次面对这一种情况，都可能表示愿意指证对方，结果两人要一起受罚。按照奥曼的理论，如果是两名聪明的囚犯，他们应该意识到，最好的选择就是两人都保持沉默。这样虽然可能导致两人都被处以5年的监禁，其结果比起互相指证的结果来说，属于“双赢”局面。

还有人将博弈论用于恋爱中的两个人：如果双方都不变心，那是最好的结局，在天愿为比翼鸟，在地愿为连理枝；如果都变了心，效果也不坏，你走你的阳关道，我过我的独木桥；如果一方变了心，另外找到了更好的伴侣，一方却还傻乎乎地忠贞不二，那么，另觅新欢的一方是最幸福的，比两人都不变心的结果还幸福，因为他找到了更好的情人，而被抛弃的一方是最不幸的，比两人都变心的结果更不幸，因为他承担的压力来自于对方的太幸福和自己的太不幸福。①

由此可见，博弈论如果用于人际关系，有利于人们善待他人，减少人给人带来的伤害。换言之，博弈论改变了以道德或社会规范规劝人们向善的传统方法，而以不可辩驳的科学论证向人们展示了有利于自己，同时也不伤害他人的做人准则。这也许是为什么博弈论学者两次获得诺贝尔经济学奖的根本原因吧。1994年，美国数学家约翰·福布斯·纳什与另外两名学者一同获得了这一奖项。纳什的主要成果在于把数学理论应用到了“冷战”、国际贸易和商业拍卖场合。本课介绍2005年持有以色列和美国双重国籍的罗伯特·奥曼和美国公民托马斯·谢林以博弈论赢得诺贝尔经济学奖的情况。他们俩的主要贡献是将博弈论用于解释在冲突中如何合作的问题，即将博弈论应用于国际关系的斡旋，督促人们在

---

① 赵新月. 爱情博弈论. http：//www. jjxj. com. cn/news_ detail. jsp keyno＝3090，2004－04－05

战争和诸如价格战、贸易战之类的经济冲突中采取和平的方式，以减少双方的牺牲或损失。当然，在和平的环境中，博弈论也可用来管理社区共有资源，达成“双赢”的局面。

谢林对博弈论的研究尤其有趣，他使博弈论与人们的实际生活产生紧密联系，比如为何冰上曲棍球员要戴头盔？为何要坐在观众席欣赏音乐？人的性别及种族歧视如何影响行为等（见谢林的《微小动机与长远行为》，1978）。但他在《纠纷对策》（1980）一书中对当代社会的发展提出了可产生深远影响的策略，比如短期让步以赢得长期利益。

奥曼对博弈论进行数学分析，提出了“重复博弈”理论的平衡状态和不平衡状态。前者指对双方的短期利益冲突而言，和平合作通常是达到平衡的解决方法，后者指其中一方较另一方得知“游戏”中更多的资料，例如他国的军力或对手的实际利润等。

Part Two　Exercises

Ⅰ. Listen to the first part of the news，and fill in the blanks with the words you hear.

Thomas Schelling and Robert Aumann will share the ____________ this year. The two men are ____________ in developing an economic idea. It is called game theory.

Game theory began as the study of ____________ in competitive situations，like games. John von Neumann（pronounce：NOI-mahn）and Oskar Morgenstern ____________ of games with economic activity more than sixty years ago.

In the nineteen fifties，John Nash ____________ known as the “Nash equilibrium”. The Nash equilibrium is the point where all sides in a ____________ believe they have been given the best offer they will ever get. He proved this with ____________. Mister Nash won ____________ with two other men in nineteen ninety-four.

Ⅱ. Listen to the second part of the news，and answer the following questions.

1. What did Mister Schelling use the ideas of game theory to do?

2. What was Mister Schelling interested in?

3. What did Mister Schelling show in his studies?

4. Why divided societies can result even among persons mostly willing to live near people of another race?

5. What was Mister Aumann's work in game theory?

6. What did Mister Aumann show in his studies?

7. What is good for competitors with a temporary conflict?

8. What is important for people to make reasonable decisions?

Ⅲ. Listen to the last part of the news for only once, and try to take it down, then translate it into Chinese.

Ⅳ. Spoken English Practice.

Try to talk about Mr. Schelling and Mr. Aumann's findings in their research.

Part Three　Keys to the Exercises

Ⅰ. Listen to the first part of the news, and fill in the blanks with the words your hear.

Thomas Schelling and Robert Aumann will share the Nobel Prize in economics this year. The two men are being honored for their work in developing an economic idea. It is called game theory.

Game theory began as the study of decision-making in competitive situations, like games. John von Neumann (Pronounce: NOI-mahn) and Oskar Morgenstern linked the theory of games with economic activity more than sixty years ago.

In the nineteen fifties, John Nash developed an idea known as the "Nash equilibrium". The Nash equilibrium is the point where all sides in a competitive situation believe they have been given the best offer they will ever get. He proved this with mathematical methods. Mister Nash won the Nobel Prize in economics with two other men in nineteen ninety-four.

Ⅱ. Listen to the second part of the news, and answer the following questions.

1. What did Mister Schelling use the ideas of game theory to do?
   To study real-life problems, such as the arms competition between the United States and the Soviet Union forty years ago.
2. What was Mister Schelling interested in?
   He was interested in what influenced negotiating groups.
3. What did Mister Scelling show in his studies?
   He showed how one side might decide to harm its interests for a short period of time to make gains over a longer period.
   Mister Schelling also used game theory to show how people become divided by race.
4. Why divided societies can result even among persons mostly willing to live near people of another race?
   Because people of two sides have not chosen the best offer they can get. Or they can't reach a peaceful agreement.
5. What was Mister Aumann's work in game theory?
   He developed game theory mathematically so that it can be useful for different areas of study.
6. What did Mister Aumann show in his studies?
   He showed that peaceful cooperation can provide good results for all competitors in a game over a long period.
7. What is good for competitors with a temporary conflict?
   Peaceful corporation. This is true even among competitors with a temporary conflict of interest.
8. What is important for people to make reasonable decisions?
   Mister Auman also considered how reasonable decisions are made among groups. He showed that knowing what competitors know is important to decision-making.

Ⅲ. Listen to the last part of the news for only once, and try to take it down, then translate it into Chinese.

The work of both men has influenced areas of study other than economics. International negotiators, military planners, business leaders and biologists use methods developed by Misters Schelling and Auman.

两位科学家的理论已经影响到经济学以外的其他领域研究。国际谈判家、军事策略家、企业领导者和生物学家都可运用由谢林和奥曼所发展的研究方法。

Mister Schelling, an American, is a retired professor of the University of Maryland. Mister Aumann is a citizen of both the United States and Israel. He is a retired professor of the Hebrew University of Jerusalem.

美国人谢林先生是马里兰大学的一名退休教授。奥曼先生持有以色列和美国双重国籍，他是耶路撒冷希伯来大学的退休教授。

Part Four　Translation of the Text

Work on Game Theory Wins Nobel Prize for Two Economists
两经济学家博弈理论研究获诺贝尔经济学奖

Thomas Schelling and Robert Aumann will share the Nobel Prize in economics this year. The two men are being honored for their work in developing an economic idea. It is called game theory.

托马斯·谢林和罗伯特·奥曼将分享今年的诺贝尔经济学奖。他们两人因发展了一个经济理论而获得此荣誉，该理论被称为博弈论。

Game theory began as the study of decision-making in competitive situations, like games. John von Neumann (pronounce: NOI-mahn) and Oskar Morgenstern linked the theory of games with economic activity more than sixty years ago.

博弈论始于如何在竞争状态下作出决策的研究，如同游戏。早在60多年前，纽曼与摩根斯坦就将博弈理论与经济活动结合起来研究。

In the nineteen fifties, John Nash developed an idea known as the "Nash equilibrium". The Nash equilibrium is the point where all sides in a competitive situation believe they have been given the best offer they will ever get. He proved this with mathematical methods. Mister Nash won the Nobel Prize in economics with two other men in nineteen ninety-four.

20世纪50年代，约翰·纳什提出了"纳什均衡"理论。"纳什均衡"是指在某个"点位"上，参与竞争的所有人都相信，他们得到了前所未有的最好报价。他用数学方法证实了这一理论。纳什先生与另外两名科学家于1994年获得诺贝尔经济学奖。

Mister Schelling used the ideas of game theory to study real-life problems, such as the arms competition between the United States and the Soviet Union forty years ago. He was interested in what influenced negotiating groups. He showed how one side might decide to harm its interests for a short period of time to make gains over a longer period.

谢林先生运用博弈理论的观点去研究现实问题，例如40年前美苏两国的军备竞赛。他的研究兴趣在于，是什么因素影响着处于谈判中的人。他向人们展示，一方如何决定为了获得更长远利益而损害其短期利益。

Mister Schelling also used game theory to show how people become divided by race. He found that divided societies can result even among persons mostly willing to live near people of another race.

谢林先生还运用博弈论解释人们因为种族不同而处于分裂状态。他发现，即使愿意与另一个种族住在一起的人们之间也会产生社会分化。

Mister Aumann developed game theory mathematically so that it can be useful for different areas of study. He showed that peaceful cooperation can provide good results for all competitors in a game over a long period. This is true even among competitors with a temporary conflict of interest. Mister Auman also considered how reasonable decisions are made among groups. He showed that knowing what competitors know is important to decision-making.

奥曼先生利用数学发展了博弈论，使之能够被应用于不同领域的研究之中。他发现，和平合作对博弈中的竞争者来说可以产生长远利益。这个理论对于存在暂时利益冲突的竞争者同样有效。奥曼先生还对团队之间如何作出合理决策进行了研究。他指出，知己知彼对制定决策至关重要。

The work of both men has influenced areas of study other than economics. International negotiators, military planners, business leaders and biologists use methods developed by Misters Schelling and Auman.

两位科学家的理论已经影响到经济学以外的其他研究领域。国际谈判家、军事策略家、企业领导者和生物学家都可运用由谢林和奥曼所发展的研究方法。

Mister Schelling, an American, is a retired professor of the University of Maryland. Mister Aumann is a citizen of both the United States and Israel. He is a retired professor of the Hebrew University of Jerusalem.

美国人谢林先生是马里兰大学的一名退休教授。奥曼先生持有以色列和美国双重国籍，他是耶路撒冷希伯来大学的退休教授。

Lesson 8　NASDAQ：An Electronic Marketplace

By Mario Ritter
September 16，2005

Part One　Background Information

经济发展的新支柱——新经济

人们通常认为美国前总统克林顿的运气很好，在他的任期内，美国经济从战后的第 8 次经济危机中开始复苏，在他入主白宫后的第三年，即 1993 年，美国经济增长速度由慢转快，到 1994 年终于从缓慢爬行进入较为强劲的扩张阶段。

事实上这与克林顿采取的经济政策有很大的关系。1993 年 2 月，克林顿在硅谷发表了《为经济增长服务的技术——建立经济强国的新方向》的政策声明，其中主要包括建设面向 21 世纪、支撑和促进工商业的基础设施，即“国家信息技术设施计划”，又称“信息高速公路计划”。正是这一基础设施的开发建设引发了一场改变人们工作、生活和相互联系方式的信息革命，营造了一个以美国为发祥地的现代化大风暴——新经济。所谓“新经济”，实质上就是知识经济，它指“区别于以前的以传统工业为支柱产业、以自然资源为主要依托的新型经济。这种新型经济以高技术产业为支柱，以智力资源为主要依托”①。美国新经济的最大特征是，“计算机、软件和通信系统三个领域已结为一体。从 1990 年到 1996 年，美国信息产业的产值上升到了 8 660 亿美元，增长 57%，占国民生产总值的 6.2%，已超过基建、食品和汽车制造业，成为美国最大的产业。信息产业在美国经济中的地位日趋重要，同期内雇佣人员 1 426 万人，增加 7.2%”②。

本课所涉及的内容呈现了美国新经济发展的一个例证——在“新经济”形成的背后，美国政府及立法部门所进行的金融改革，使金融机构实现了分业经营向混业经营的转变。从本课美国纽约证券交易所和纳斯达克的扩张中，我们可以看到活跃、发达的美国风险投资和高资源配置效率的金融市场之一角。

道琼斯工业平均指数（DJIA）“是美国纽约证券交易所指数，于 1896 年 5 月 26 日问世，一直由道琼斯公司编制，并由该公司出版的《华尔街日报》发表。道琼斯工业平均指数问世当天收盘指数为 41.74 点，1906 年首度突破 100 点，1972 年首度突破 1 000 点，去年 3 月 16 日首度突破 1 万点。道琼斯指数于 2004 年底曾突破 11 000 点，此后时涨时跌。自问世以来，道琼斯指数曾断断续续有所修改，最近的两次修改分别在 1997 年和 1999 年，从头至尾一直待在这个指数里的只有通用电气公司。去年 11 月 1 日，该指数抛弃了联合碳化等 4 家工业时代的大公司，把信息时代的微软和英特尔等 4 家高科技公司吸收进来。道琼斯指数是美国经济百余年历史的见证，尽管它也在发生着重要变化，但人们仍把

①②　张锋．聚焦新经济．http：//www.shulu.net/zzjj/jjjj/001.htm

它视为美国传统经济的象征”。2005 年 4 月，纽约证券交易所宣布，它将与总部设在芝加哥的 Archipelago 控股公司合并，以增强纽约证交所在美国乃至世界证券交易市场的竞争力和主导地位。纽约证券交易所 1 366 个席位拥有人将获得 4 亿美元现金和新公司 70% 的股票，Archipelago 股东将持有新公司 30% 的股份。Archipelago 是一家电子证券交易公司，负责处理纳斯达克市场 25% 的股票交易，这起合并将有助于提高纽约证券交易所在与电子交易市场竞争中的地位，也有助于改善纽约证券交易所的市场形象。

纳斯达克（NASDAQ）全名为全国证券交易商协会自动报价系统，1971 年才问世。它通过计算机网络将全国证券经纪商组织在一起，及时准确地向其提供场外交易行情。它最初专门让投资者交易一些资本额很小的新创企业股票，但经过短短 20 多年的发展，本国上市公司数目、上市的外国公司数目、月交易额都已超过纽约证券交易所。纳斯达克综合指数包括 4 600 多种股票，主要由美国的数百家发展最快的先进技术、电信和生物公司组成，包括微软、英特尔、美国在线、雅虎这些家喻户晓的高科技公司，因而成为美国“新经济”的代名词。近年来，该指数一路猛涨，2003 年 12 月首度突破 3 000 点。2006 年 5 月，纽约股市三大股指全线上扬，其中标准普尔 500 种股票指数和纳斯达克综合指数均创 5 年来的最高水平。分析人士认为，投资者对公司第一财季赢利前景的良好预期是推动股市成长的主要原因。同样在 2005 年 4 月，纳斯达克证券市场宣布即将完成对 Instinet 电子市场和经纪子公司的收购，交易额约 18 亿美元。这笔交易完成后，纳斯达克将完全控制 Inet 电子通信网络和 Instinet 的经纪商——交易商分公司。这样一来，纳斯达克证券市场将夺回 20 世纪 90 年代末随着 Instinet 的 Inet 部门等电子通信网络崛起而丧失的订单流量，从而对纽约证券交易所构成很大威胁。

Instinet 原来由路透集团独资经营管理，是全球最大的电子证券经纪公司。“30 多年来一直从事于为投资者提供有价证券的电子交易解决方案和执行服务，并处理纳斯达克股市三分之一以上的交易量及全球其他 40 多个主要交易所的大宗机构交易。该集团也能够让其客户通过使用其销售—交易专有技术和复杂的技术工具而与全球证券市场形成互动，以此完善客户的交易投资行为并全面降低他们的交易成本。通过 Instinet 的电子平台，客户可以访问包括纳斯达克和纽约证券交易所在内的美国其他交易场所，以及法兰克福、香港、伦敦、巴黎、悉尼、东京、多伦多和苏黎世等近 30 个全球股票交易市场。”

纳斯达克股票交易所与纽约证交所进行的合并与收购行为证明了新经济对传统经济的冲击与挑战，也说明美国新经济之间的竞争已发展到白热化的程度。

Part Two　Exercises

Ⅰ. Listen to the news, and answer the following questions.

1. Why do many companies want to sell stock? What is stock?

2. Where can shares be bought and sold? Where else can shares be traded?

3. What kind of market is over-the-counter market?

4. When and why was the electronic system proposed? By whom ?

Ⅱ. Listen to the second part of the news, and repeat the missing part in the sentence.

1. The whole name of NASDAQ Stock Market: ______________________.
2. Traditionally, it has offered a home to smaller companies. It accepts ______________________ and traded less often than shares on the New York Stock Exchange.
3. But NASDAQ also ______________________.
4. Among them is Microsoft, ______________________.
5. NASDAQ provides ______________________ as well as many companies listed on the New York Stock Exchange. The prices are published in newspapers.

Ⅲ. Listen to the next two paragraphs separately for once, and try to remember one paragraph each time and repeat it.

Ⅳ. Listen to the fourth part of the news, and translate it into Chinese.

Ⅴ. Talk about NASDAQ's development, and over-the-counter market.

Part Three　Keys to the Exercises

Ⅰ. Listen to the news, and answer the following questions.

1. Why do many companies want to sell stock? What is stock?
   Many companies want to sell stock so they can get money to expand their business. Stock is shares of ownership.
2. Where can shares be bought and sold? Where else can shares be traded?
   Shares can be bought and sold on the trading floor of a stock exchange. Or they can be traded through an over-the-counter market.
3. What kind of market is over-the-counter market?
   Such a market links dealers directly by a computer or telephone system.
4. When and why was the electronic system proposed? By whom ?
   By nineteen sixty-one, Congress became concerned that the over-the-counter market was disorganized. So the Securities and Exchange Commission proposed that dealers use an electronic system to organize their sales.

Ⅱ. Listen to the second part of the news, and repeat the missing parts in the sentences.

1. the Whole name of Nasdaq Stock Market: The National Association of Securities Dealers Automated Quotations system began in nineteen seventy-one. Today it is known as the NASDAQ Stock Market or just NASDAQ.

2. Traditionally, it has offered a home to smaller companies. It accepts stocks that are lower in market value and traded less often than shares on the New York Stock Exchange.

3. But NASDAQ also trades big, active stocks.

4. Among them is Microsoft, maker of the operating system on most personal computers.

5. NASDAQ provides price information for over-the-counter stocks as well as many companies listed on the New York Stock Exchange. The prices are published in newspapers.

Ⅲ. Listen to the next two paragraphs separately for once, and try to remember one paragraph each time and repeat it.

On NASDAQ, each stock has a number of dealers called "market makers". They buy and sell shares for themselves and investors. Market makers use their own money as needed.

NASDAQ lists about three thousand three hundred companies. It points out that it lists more companies and trades more shares per day, on average, than any other market in the country.

Ⅳ. Listen to the fourth part of the news, and translate it into Chinese.

But the world's largest stock market is the New York Stock Exchange. Major activity still takes place on a trading floor. Each stock is handled by one "specialist" who acts as a market maker and has other duties. Specialists are expected to keep a "fair and orderly market".

但是世界上最大的股票市场是纽约股票市场。大型的交易活动仍然在交易大厅里进行。每只股票都由一个"专家"来负责，他既是股票交易员，也承担其他的职责。人们期望专家们能维护一个"公平有序的市场"。

Many people want a modern system of electronic trading. The exchange took a big step in April. It announced plans to combine with an electronic market, Archipelago. Two days later, competition grew when NASDAQ announced an agreement to buy Instinet, another electronic trading system.

许多人要求使用现代化的电子交易系统。交易所在四月采取了一项重大的措施，它宣布了与电子交易公司 Archipelago 合并的计划。两天之后，纳斯达克宣布收购另一家电子交易系统——极讯公司（Instinet），竞争由此更激烈了。

Part Four　Translation of the Text

NASDAQ: An Electronic Marketplale

纳斯达克：电子证券市场

A listener in China asks about the history of the world's largest electronic stock market, NASDAQ.

中国的一位听众询问关于世界上最大的电子证券市场——纳斯达克的历史。

Many companies want to sell stock so they can get money to expand their business. Stock is shares of ownership.

许多公司出售股票，以赚取更多的钱来扩展他们的生意。股票就是股权。

Shares can be bought and sold on the trading floor of a stock exchange. Or they can be traded through an over-the-counter market. Such a market links dealers directly by a computer or telephone system.

股份的买卖可以在股票交易所的大厅里进行，或者通过场外交易市场来进行。此类市场是通过电脑或电话系统将交易者直接联系起来的。

By nineteen sixty-one, Congress became concerned that the over-the-counter market was disorganized. So the Securities and Exchange Commission proposed that dealers use an electronic system to organize their sales.

1961 年，场外交易市场的混乱引起了议会的关注。因此证券交易委员会建议交易者们使用电子系统来买卖股票。

The National Association of Securities Dealers Automated Quotations system began in nineteen seventy-one. Today it is known as the NASDAQ Stock Market or just NASDAQ.

全美证券交易商协会自动报价系统始于 1971 年。今天，它被称为纳斯达克证券市场或者纳斯达克。

Traditionally, it has offered a home to smaller companies. It accepts stocks that are lower in market value and traded less often than shares on the New York Stock Exchange. But NASDAQ also trades big, active stocks. Among them is Microsoft, maker of the operating system on most personal computers.

传统上，它为小型的公司提供了场所。它接收那些市价较低的股票和在纽约证券市场交易频率低的股份。不过，纳斯达克中也有权重的活跃股。微软公司是其中之一，它是个人电脑操作系统的制造商。

NASDAQ provides price information for over-the-counter stocks as well as many companies listed on the New York Stock Exchange. The prices are published in newspapers.

纳斯达克提供场外交易股市的价格信息，也提供纽约证券所上市公司的信息。这些价格信息刊登在报纸上。

On NASDAQ, each stock has a number of dealers called "market makers". They buy and sell shares for themselves and investors. Market makers use their own money as needed.

在纳斯达克市场，每只股票都有数个经销商，称为"市场交易员（做市商）"。他们为自己或者投资者买卖股份。市场交易员在必要时也使用自己的钱。

NASDAQ lists about three thousand three hundred companies. It points out that it lists more companies and trades more shares per day, on average, than any other market in the country.

纳斯达克里有 3 300 个上市公司，它宣称，每天平均所列出的公司和成交的股份比美国任何其他股票市场都要多。

But the world's largest stock market is the New York Stock Exchange. Major activity still takes place on a trading floor. Each stock is handled by one "specialist" who acts as a market maker and has other duties. Specialists are expected to keep a "fair and orderly market".

但是世界上最大股票市场是纽约股票市场。大型的交易活动仍然在交易大厅里进行。每只股票都由一个"专家"来负责，他既是股票交易员，也承担其他的职责。人们期望专家们能维护一个"公平有序的市场"。

Many people want a modern system of electronic trading. The exchange took a big step in April. It announced plans to combine with an electronic market, Archipelago. Two days later, competition grew when NASDAQ announced an agreement to buy Instinet, another electronic trading system.

许多人要求使用现代化的电子交易系统。交易所在四月份采取了一项重大的措施，它宣布了与电子交易公司 Archipelago 合并的计划。两天之后，纳斯达克宣布收购另一家电子交易系统——极讯公司（Instinet），竞争由此更激烈了。

Lesson 9 Greenspan Retires and American Economy

By Mario Ritter

November 18, 2005

Part One Background Information

格林斯潘对美国新经济的影响

格林斯潘在美国经济领域的崇高地位实际上源于上一课中提到的“新经济”的发展，人们对他的崇拜之情来自他的“高瞻远瞩”对美国新经济起到了保驾护航的作用。一提到新经济，人们总是先想到克林顿，认为他创造了一个有利于私营企业创新和竞争的商业环境，增强了私营企业开发技术、把技术转化为产品和服务并迅速投入全球市场的能力。但一提到格林斯潘，人们便会想到已经被中国媒体引用过无数次美国一家媒体在1996年总统大选时说的一句话：“谁当总统都无所谓，只要让艾伦当联储主席就行。”① 格氏声望位居总统之上，其原因就在于他担任美联储主席的12年里，美国享受了连续8年经济增长的“黄金岁月”，同时也创造出“零通货膨胀型”经济的奇迹。因为，一旦各项经济指标过热，格氏就会作出调高利率的暗示，为过热的股市降温。所以更多的美国人认为，12年来一直为美国经济把脉的格林斯潘才是真正的英雄，正是由于他对美国“新经济”的关注，才使得美国经济高增长、低失业、低通胀，创下新纪录。

格林斯潘1987年上任后，经历了一系列大事件。例如，1987年10月19日，美国股市下跌了508点，这是自经济大萧条以来股指单日下跌最大的纪录，引起了美国及世界其他金融市场的巨大动荡。格林斯潘立即向市场提供了充沛的流动资金，以确保国家金融体系继续运转。之后还发生过两次经济萧条，但都因为格氏具有过人的判断力，采用灵活的利率调整等工具，引领美国经济走上了持续增长的道路。

人们将1987年8月格林斯潘上任至2006年卸任这近20年的时间称为“格林斯潘年代（Greenspan Years）”②。1998年7月，格林斯潘被授予美国“和平缔造者”奖。2002年8月，英国女王授予格林斯潘“爵士”荣誉称号，以表彰他对“全球经济稳定所作出的杰出贡献”。2005年11月10日，格林斯潘被授予“总统自由勋章”③。

不过，人们在普遍称赞格林斯潘的才能和成就的同时，也对他离任之际美国经济中存在的隐患感到担忧。美国知名经济学家，经济学网站ECONOMICS. COM的首席经济学家马克·赞迪表示，房地产泡沫的形成是格林斯潘的一个失误，也是他留给继任者的一大挑战。赞迪认为，超低的利率刺激了人们的投资和消费，一方面加速了房地产市场泡沫的扩

---

① 格林斯潘：两大失算为继任者留下业绩和挑战. http：//finance. people. com. cn/BIG5/42774/3653476. html，2005－08－30

② http：//www. bbc. co. uk/radio4/news/pip/q2rys/，2006－01－02

③ 美国联邦储备委员会前主席格林斯潘. http：//news. xinhuanet. com/ziliao/2002－10/15/content_ 597265. htm

大，另一方面助长了美国贸易赤字的持续扩大。果不其然，美国经济在2007年急转直下，由次贷引起的金融危机紧随格林斯潘的卸任而至，不知有没有人做过这样的猜测，如果格林斯潘晚离职一年，他能否预测甚至神奇地阻止此次经济灾难的发生？

什么是通货膨胀？

简单地说，通货膨胀指流通中货币量超过实际需要所引起的货币贬值，造成物价上涨的经济现象。换句话说，通货膨胀指物价水平在一定时期内持续普遍上升的过程，或者说货币价值在一定时期内持续下降的过程。政府有各种各样的理由多印钞票，比如，在一些税制不健全的国家，政府为了负担开支，就要通过增印钞票来暗中征税；另外，政府为了增加教育、基础建设或国防的开支，或为了援助灾民，也会增印钞票。

"通货膨胀分为需求拉动型通胀、工资和原料等成本推动型通胀以及进口通胀。英国伦敦经济学院的新西兰经济学家菲利普斯（A. W. Philips）通过整理英国1861—1957年近一个世纪的统计资料，发现货币工资增长率和失业率之间存在一种负相关的关系。就是说当政府增加经济中的货币量时，一个结果是通货膨胀，另一个结果是可在短期内降低失业水平。新凯恩斯主义认为通货膨胀与社会生产之间的关系是正相关的：随着通货膨胀的出现，物价水平上升，从而刺激供给量的增加。在这种情况下，如果企业出售产品的价格增长快于工资和其他资源价格的增长，那么企业获得超额经济利润，利润的增加又反过来刺激企业扩大生产规模，从而增加了产量，增加了劳务需求，拉动工资上升和增加就业。这也正是政府想看到的。"①

但我国经济学者认为："通货膨胀使价格上升快于工资增加，这就理所当然地减少了劳动者的实际购买力，从而减少了社会总需求。社会总供给远远大于社会总需求，企业的货存大大增加，而利润并没有增加，相反，随着供需关系的进一步恶化，企业利润必然减少，从而降低产量，增加了失业。"②

Part Two Exercises

I. Listen to the first part of the news, and fill in the blanks with the words you hear.

The Chairman of the United States ________________, Alan Greenspan, plans to retire at the end of January. Mister Greenspan is seventy-nine years old. He replaced Paul Volcker as chairman of the ____________________ on August eleventh, nineteen eighty-seven.

Less than one month later, Mister Greenspan announced an increase in an important ____________________________. The ____________________ is what ________________________ to borrow money. The increase showed that Mister Greenspan wanted to move quickly to fight __________________.

①② 梁兆国. 关于通货膨胀问题的几点思考. http://www.jjxj.com.cn/news_detail.jsp?keyno=4458，2004-09-24

Ⅱ. Listen to the second part of the news, and fill in the missing parts in the sentences.

1. Two months into his term, however, ______________________________.
2. On October nineteenth, nineteen eighty-seven, the stock market ______________.
3. The Dow Jones industrial average lost almost __________________________.
4. Mister Greenspan earned praise ______________________________.
5. ______________ climbed again.
6. In nineteen ninety-six, Alan Greenspan ______________________________.
7. He spoke of the risks of what he called "______________".

Ⅲ. Listen to the third part of the news, and answer the following questions.

1. Why do you think Greenspan surprised everyone when he raised interest only once until June of 1999?

2. What result will low unemployment and low interest rates cause?

3. Will low interest cause low unemployment?

4. Is it true that Mister Greenspan thought increase productivity can keep low inflation?

Ⅳ. Listen to the fourth part of the news, and translate it into Chinese.

V. Listen to the last part of the news, and repeat it sentence by sentence.

Part Three Keys to the Exercises

I. Listen to the first part of the news, and fill in the blanks with the words you hear.

The Chairman of the United States central bank, Alan Greenspan, plans to retire at the end of January. Mister Greenspan is seventy-nine years old. He replaced Paul Volcker as chairman of the Federal Reserve Board on August eleventh, nineteen eighty-seven.

Less than one month later, Mister Greenspan announced an increase in an important interest rate. The discount rate（贴现率）is what the Federal Reserve charges banks to borrow money. The increase showed that Mister Greenspan wanted to move quickly to fight inflation.

II. Listen to the second part of the news, and fill in the missing parts in the sentences.

1. Two months into his term, however, there was a shock: Black Monday.
2. On October nineteenth, nineteen eighty-seven, the stock market had the worst day in its history.
3. The Dow Jones industrial average lost almost one-fourth of its value.
4. Mister Greenspan earned praise for the way he dealt with the crisis.
5. Stock prices climbed again.
6. In nineteen ninety-six, Alan Greenspan warned that prices were too high.
7. He spoke of the risks of what he called "irrational exuberance（茂盛、丰富）".

III. Listen to the third part of the news, and answer the following questions.

1. Why do you think Greenspan surprised everyone when he raised interest only once until June of 1999?

Because people expect him to use interest rate to stop high inflation, while Greenspan used other ways against inflation.

2. What result will low unemployment and low interest rates cause?

Economists had worried that low unemployment and low interest rates would cause inflation.

3. Will low interest cause low unemployment?

Yes, business could get loan easily, so to increase people's chance to get work.

4. Is it true that Mister Greenspan thought increase productivity can keep low inflation?

Yes, because he thought inflation could remain low because of increased productivity. He was right. The economy had one of its longest expansions ever in peacetime.

Ⅳ. Listen to the fourth part of the news, and translate it into Chinese.

Today, stock prices are down from their record highs in two thousand. The United States suffered a moderate recession, made worse by the terrorist attacks of September eleventh, two thousand and one.

现在，股票价格已经从2000年的破纪录高位下跌。美国经济正处于一个轻缓适度衰退期，2001年的“9·11”恐怖袭击事件加速了经济的衰退。

And since June of two thousand and four the Federal Reserve has raised interest rates in a series of steps against inflation. Rates went up this month for the twelfth time, to the highest level in more than four years.

自2004年6月以来，美联储在一系列对付通货膨胀的步骤中已经上调利率。这个月利率是第12次上调，为四年多来的最高水平。

Recently Alan Greenspan has warned about high home prices, trade barriers and budget deficits. But what has marked his eighteen years as chairman is trust in the ability of the economy to recover from shocks.

最近，艾伦·格林斯潘警告说美国国内物价、贸易壁垒、预算赤字过高。但正是人们对经济复苏的信心，成就了他18年美联储主席的光辉生涯。

Ⅴ. Listen to the last part of the news, and repeat it sentence by sentence.

President Bush chose his top economic adviser, Ben Bernanke, to replace Alan Greenspan. On Wednesday, the Senate Banking Committee approved the nomination for a vote in the full Senate. Mister Bernanke says he will seek to continue the policies established during the Greenspan years.

Part Four Translation of the Text

US Central Banker Alan Greenspan Prepares to Retire
美国中央银行主席格林斯潘即将退休

The chairman of the United States central bank, Alan Greenspan, plans to retire at the end of January. Mister Greenspan is seventy-nine years old. He replaced Paul Volcker as chairman of the Federal Reserve Board on August eleventh, nineteen eighty-seven.

美国中央银行主席格林斯潘计划在明年1月底退休。现年79岁的格林斯潘是在1987

年8月接替保罗·沃尔克担任美联储主席的。

Less than one month later, Mister Greenspan announced an increase in an important interest rate. The discount rate is what the Federal Reserve charges banks to borrow money. The increase showed that Mister Greenspan wanted to move quickly to fight inflation.

上任后不到一个月，格林斯潘宣布提高一项重要的利率。贴现率是美联储在银行发生借款业务时向银行收取一定的利率。加息表明格林斯潘想以最快的速度抗击通货膨胀。

Two months into his term, however, there was a shock: Black Monday. On October nineteenth, nineteen eighty-seven, the stock market had the worst day in its history. The Dow Jones industrial average lost almost one-fourth of its value. Mister Greenspan earned praise for the way he dealt with the crisis.

然而，在他上任后的两个月，发生了令人震惊的大事：黑色星期一。在1987年10月19日，股票市场遭遇了历史上最糟糕的一天。道琼斯工业平均指数下跌了近四分之一。格林斯潘处理该危机时赢得了赞誉。

Stock prices climbed again. In nineteen ninety-six, Alan Greenspan warned that prices were too high. He spoke of the risks of what he called "irrational exuberance."

股票价格再次攀升。1996年，艾伦·格林斯潘就警告股票价位太高。他将这种风险称为"非理性繁荣"。

Yet after that, he surprised everyone when the central bank raised interest rates only once until June of nineteen ninety-nine. Economists had worried that low unemployment and low interest rates would cause inflation.

但此后，他让每一个人都感到震惊，美国中央银行到1999年6月只提高了一次利率。经济学家曾担心低失业率和低利率会造成通货膨胀。

But Mister Greenspan thought inflation could remain low because of increased productivity. He was right. The economy had one of its longest expansions ever in peacetime.

但格林斯潘认为，由于生产力在增长，通货膨胀可以保持在低位。实践证明他是对的，经济获得了和平年代里最长时期的扩张。

Today, stock prices are down from their record highs in two thousand. The United States suffered a moderate recession, made worse by the terrorist attacks of September eleventh, two thousand and one.

现在，股票价格已经从2000年的破纪录高位下跌。美国经济正处于一个轻缓适度衰退期，2001年的"9·11"恐怖袭击事件加速了经济的衰退。

And since June of two thousand and four the Federal Reserve has raised interest rates in a series of steps against inflation. Rates went up this month for the twelfth time, to the highest level in more than four years.

自2004年6月以来，美联储在一系列对付通货膨胀的步骤中已经上调利率。这个月利率是第12次上调，为四年多来的最高水平。

Recently Alan Greenspan has warned about high home prices, trade barriers and budget deficits. But what has marked his eighteen years as chairman is trust in the ability of the economy to recover from shocks.

最近，艾伦·格林斯潘警告说美国国内物价、贸易壁垒、预算赤字过高。但正是人们对经济复苏的信心，成就了他 18 年美联储主席的光辉生涯。

President Bush chose his top economic adviser, Ben Bernanke, to replace Alan Greenspan. On Wednesday, the Senate Banking Committee approved the nomination for a vote in the full Senate. Mister Bernanke says he will seek to continue the policies established during the Greenspan Years.

美国总统布什提名白宫首席经济顾问本·伯南克将接替艾伦·格林斯潘。星期三，参议院银行委员会批准对此项提名进行全体投票。伯南克表示，他将致力于贯彻在“格林斯潘年代”期间制定的政策。

Lesson 10　Americans and Their Credit Reports

By Mario Ritter

August 18, 2005

Part One　Background Information

市场经济是一种信用经济

信用体系中包含了个人信用、企业信用、社会信用和政府信用等。其中，个人信用的内涵体现在个人信用信息征信的概念之中，依照德国加氏经济辞典（Gabler's Wirtschaftslexikon）之定义，个人信用信息征信“系以提供顾客所需有关第三者之资讯，特别是有关营利事业之信用资讯为主要业务。信用资讯业从事收集自然人或法人收集之有关资讯，加以整理、归类、分析、存档，并作主观之评断，将其结果提供给客户”。比如，“‘消费者信用报告’是指由信用报告机构提供的有关消费者信用可靠度、信用的名声、信用能力、性格、一般名誉、个人特点或生活方式的任何书面、口头及其他联系方式的信息。它被部分或全部用于或准备用于作为确定一个消费者某种资格的因素”①。

一、个人信用与经济发展的关系

“市场经济是一种信用经济、契约经济、法制经济。信用是市场经济的基础，而法律是契约、信用得以实现的保障。个人信用系统在整个信用系统中与企业信用有着同等的重要性。”②

“个人信用通过降低市场交易成本、优化资源配置、促进消费需求等途径促进经济发展。个人信用可降低经济系统中的交易成本，表现在：交易前，可减少为获得交易机会而收集信息的时间和金钱；交易过程中，使交易省时省力；交易后，不用为防止对方违约而继续关注，并增加人力物力。有了良好的个人信用，自然省去了因为违约而带来的退货等时间的浪费和物质的损失，甚至发生诉讼的成本。失去了个人信用，我们的交易难度将很大。”③

20 世纪 90 年代中，我国经济界冒出了牟其中“标的”总额高达 2.4 亿元人民币的逾期不还案和其他经济纠纷案。牟其中的口号是“银行的钱，不用白不用”④。像他这种“有借不还，再借不难”的奇迹得以发生，就是因为当时缺少一种有效的个人信用报告制度，或者说当时的信用征信制度没有能够准确地反映牟其中企业的信用“黑洞”，致使银行的巨额贷款被这个黑洞持续不断地吞噬，它给金融业和地方经济带来了直接的损害。由此可见，要发展经济、拉动消费需求，就得建立良好的个人信用征信制度，使拥有良好个

---

① 张鹏. 论个人信用信息征信体系的概念. http://www.pbcti.cn/main/show.php id = 15049，2006 - 12 - 20

② 杨承训，乔法容. 市场经济是信用经济. 人民日报，2001 - 01 - 18

③ 刘建江. 论个人信用与经济发展的相关性（上）. http://www.globrand.com/2009/216812.shtml

④ 方进玉. 牟其中其人其骗. 南方周末，1999 - 01 - 29

人信用和稳定工作或其他固定收入的人可以用分期付款等方式，增加即期消费倾向，依靠他们创造新的消费热点。相反，如果像牟其中那样的人层出不穷，就会出现银行资金积压，资源利用率不足，市场投资机会减少的情况，从而造成恶性循环，严重阻碍经济的正常的发展。

二、如何建立个人信用制度

"个人信用信息征信体系的主要内容涉及银行、公检法、海关、税务、保险等许多方面。它包括：①征信机构的设置，征信机构的职能范围，征信机构、信用信息提供人和相关监督管理部门三者之间的关系；②信用信息的真实、完整、保密机制，防止因此而对个人隐私造成侵害；③当事人的权利，指当事人就自己的信用信息而言，可以要求法律为其提供哪些法律救济；④对征信行业的监督和管理；⑤信用信息争议解决机制，指在个人就自己的信用信息提出异议的时候能够建立起一套高效的争端解决机制，迅速、公正地处理纠纷；⑥信用等级评定制度，是指如何规范信用等级评定机构，科学、合理地对个人信用等级作出公正的判定，从而为市场交易人提供准确的风险信息；⑦征信机构的法律责任等。"①

Part Two Exercises

Ⅰ. Listen to the first part of the news, and complete the following sentences.

1. More and more Americans are ____________________________.
2. Credit reports are used by lenders to decide ____________________________.
3. The report holds information about a person's ____________________________.
4. It records ____________________________.
5. It all adds up to a ____________________________.

Ⅱ. Listen to the second part of the news, and answer the following questions.

1. Why do lenders welcome people with bad credit histories these days?

2. Why do Some Americans want to read their credit report?

3. What is the change in policy about the right to see the credit report?

① 张鹏. 论个人信用信息征信体系的概念. http://www. pbcti. cn/main/show. php id = 15049, 2006 - 12 - 20

4. What have been the new rights added to the Fair Credit Reporting Act?

5. What is FICO? What kind of company is FICO? Where do the numbers they use come from?

6. Who and what for do people use Fair Isaac's technology?

Ⅲ. Listen to the last two parts of the news, and translate them into Chinese, then repeat them in English.

Ⅳ. Spoken English Practice.

Tell what is an individual's credit report composed of.

Part Three　Keys to the Exercises

Ⅰ. Listen to the first part of the news, completing the following sentences.

1. More and more Americans are <u>reading their own credit report</u>.

2. Credit reports are used by lenders to decide <u>how risky it would be to offer a loan or credit to an individual</u>.

3. The report holds information about a person's <u>current loans and credit-card debt</u>.

4. It records late payments of bills and any unpaid loans.

5. It all adds up to a credit history.

Ⅱ. Listen to the second part of the news, and answer the following questions.

1. Why do lenders often welcome people with bad credit histories these days?

They are charged higher interest rates and other loan costs.

2. Why do Some Americans want to read their credit report?

1) To know if they have been a victim of identity theft.

2) They can see if any loans or credit cards have been opened in their name with stolen personal information.

3) Another reason is that credit reports are not always correct. They might contain wrong information or old information.

3. What is the change in policy about the right to see the credit report?

Before nineteen seventy-one, Americans could not see any of this information. Then Congress passed a law to give citizens the right to see and dispute their credit reports.

4. What have been the new rights added to the Fair Credit Reporting Act?

One change, in two thousand and one, permits people to see their FICO score.

5. What is FICO? What kind of company is FICO? Where do the numbers they use come from?

FICO is short for the Fair Isaac Corporation.

That company developed a way to represent credit risk with a number.

The number is based on information gathered by credit reporting agencies.

6. Who and what for do people use Fair Isaac's technology?

Fair Isaac says many lenders not just in the United States but around the world use its technology to create credit scores. But lenders are not the only ones interested in these numbers. As of May, the company says it sold ten million credit scores to individuals.

Ⅲ. Listen to the last two parts of the news, and translate them into Chinese, then repeat them in English.

People with high scores can expect lower interest rates for loans. The idea is that the higher the score, the lower the risk. Paying bills on time and paying off credit-card debt improves credit scores.

以五月为例，公司称，它向私人出售了一千万个信用分数。评分高的人能享有较低的贷款利息。理由是得分逾高，风险逾低。账单准时付清和还清信用卡债务会改善信用评分。

There are three main credit reporting agencies. Two companies are Equifax, in Atlanta, Georgia, and Trans Union in Chicago, Illinois. The third, Experian, is owned by a British company.

有三个主要的信用报告代理机构。其中两家公司分别是在佐治亚州亚特兰大的 Equifax

和在伊利诺伊州芝加哥市的 Trans Union。第三家公司是英国的 Experian。

These agencies will sell people a copy of their credit report. But Congress last year again amended the Fair Credit Reporting Act. As of this September first, all Americans can receive one free credit report per year from each of the three agencies.

这些机构给人们出售信用报告的副本。但是国会去年再一次修正了公平信用报告法案。从今年 9 月 1 日起，所有的美国人每年都能免费得到分别来自这三家代理公司的信用报告。

Part Four Translation of the Text

Americans and Their Credit Reports
国民信用报告制度

More and more Americans are reading their own credit report. Credit reports are used by lenders to decide how risky it would be to offer a loan or credit to an individual.

越来越多的美国人关注自己的信用报告。信用报告是被借贷人用来评估个人贷款或借贷风险时用的。

The report holds information about a person's current loans and credit-card debt. It records late payments of bills and any unpaid loans. It all adds up to a credit history. These days, though, lenders often welcome people with bad credit histories. They are charged higher interest rates and other loan costs.

报告中包括关于个人贷款现状和信用卡债务的资讯。它记录迟付款的账单和所有未还清的贷款。它们累计成为一个人的信用记录。但最近以来，借贷人欢迎信用档案不佳的人，因为可以向这些人收取较高的借贷利息和其他贷款费用。

Some Americans want to read their credit report to know if they have been a victim of identity theft. They can see if any loans or credit cards have been opened in their name with stolen personal information.

美国人阅读信用报告是想知道自己的身份是否已经被盗。他们要了解是否有人用自己的名义和盗窃来的个人资料办理贷款或信用卡。

Another reason is that credit reports are not always correct. They might contain wrong information or old information.

另一个原因是信用报告并不总是正确的。其中可能包含错误的或过时的信息。

Before nineteen seventy-one, Americans could not see any of this information. Then Congress passed a law to give citizens the right to see and dispute their credit reports. Over the years, new rights have been added to the Fair Credit Reporting Act.

在 1971 年以前，美国人无法看到这些数据。之后国会通过了一项法律，授予市民查阅并争辩本人信用报告的权利。这些年来，公平信贷报告法案中增加了一些新的权利。

One change, in two thousand and one, permits people to see their FICO score. FICO is short for the Fair Isaac Corporation. That company developed a way to represent credit risk with a number. The number is based on information gathered by credit reporting agencies.

其中的一个变化是，2001 年开始允许人们查阅自己的 FICO 分数。FICO 是伊萨克公正信用报告公司的简称。这家公司发明了使用数字代表信用风险的方法。该数字是以信用报告代理机构收集的数据为基础计算出来。

Fair Isaac says many lenders not just in the United States but around the world use its technology to create credit scores. But lenders are not the only ones interested in these numbers.

伊萨克公正信用报告公司说，不仅仅是美国，全世界都使用该公司的技术计算信用分数。但是借贷人并不是唯一对这些数字感兴趣的人。

As of May，the company says it sold ten million credit scores to individuals. People with high scores can expect lower interest rates for loans. The idea is that the higher the score，the lower the risk. Paying bills on time and paying off credit-card debt improves credit scores.

以五月为例，公司称，它向私人出售了一千万个信用分数。评分高的人能享有较低的贷款利息。理由是得分逾高，风险逾低。账单准时付清和还清信用卡债务会改善信用评分。

There are three main credit reporting agencies. Two companies are Equifax，in Atlanta，Georgia，and Trans Union in Chicago，Illinois. The third，Experian，is owned by a British company.

有三个主要的信用报告代理机构。其中两家公司是在佐治亚州亚特兰大市的 Equifax 和在伊利诺伊州芝加哥市的 Trans Union。第三家公司是英国的 Experian。

These agencies will sell people a copy of their credit report. But Congress last year again amended the Fair Credit Reporting Act. As of this September first，all Americans can receive one free credit report per year from each of the three agencies.

这些机构给人们出售信用报告的副本。但是国会去年再一次修正了公平信用报告法案。从今年 9 月 1 日起，所有的美国人每年都能免费得到分别来自这三家代理公司的信用报告。

（This VOA *Special English* Economics Report was written by Mario Ritter. I'm Barbara klein.）

Lesson 11 On the Job, at Minimum Wage

By Mario Ritter
January 13, 2006

Part One Background Information

最低工资制的利弊

中国的劳动力资源供过于求，在劳资双方谈判博弈时占不到优势，资方往往无原则地压榨员工，克扣工人工资，使处于弱势的劳动力价值被严重低估。例如，“在珠三角地区的最低工资标准中，广州为510元，甚至低于山西、江西520元的标准；东莞为450元；深圳特区最低工资扣除个人应承担的社会保险费后为388元。福建莆田和泉州的最低工资是350元。而不少企业，特别是‘三来一补’等劳动密集型加工企业，常常以最低工资作为员工的底薪，加班也不按标准支付加班工资”①。针对此种严重违反劳动者权益的情况，欧美一些国家甚至对存在拖欠与克扣工资、最低工资标准实施不充分、工时长、工作条件差、劳动事故多的企业（“血汗”工厂）的产品实行进口限制。在他们看来，设定最低工资制是文明社会维护社会公平与正义的一个手段，它保证在职的劳动者通过劳动获得报酬以满足其基本生活需要。当然，它也可化解劳资矛盾，保护弱者利益。但是，千万别天真地以为设定了最低工资制度，就一定可以保护弱者。事实上，所设定的最低工资制在市场均衡工资之上，用工单位就会为了降低工资成本而削减用工数量（岗位短缺），通常被裁减的都是无技术特长者。如此一来，有生产能力但迫于生计而不得不接受低于最低工资的人将被排斥在劳动力市场的大门之外，导致不熟练劳动者的失业增加。中国拥有65%左右的农村劳动力，他们在农村中的微薄收入决定了他们愿意接受城市里低于最低工资制的工资。设定最低工资制将使他们被排斥在“打工”队伍之外，实际上等于让他们失去了改善生活的一个途径。

对此，哈耶克在《自由秩序原理》中提出：“工资的形成还是应该遵循自由市场原则，由劳资双方谈判决定，政府制定的最低工资标准，背离了充分就业的均衡价格，只会将愿意接受更低工资的劳动者排斥在就业市场之外，而名义上的高工资也不可能真正实现，因为高于均衡价格的工资水平会推动通货膨胀，长期内劳动者根本拿不到实际的高工资。”②

2006年7月12日，广东省劳动保障厅公布了广东最新的最低工资标准方案，将广州市的最低工资标准由684元上涨到780元③。近年广东省发生“劳工荒”，广东省人力资源

---

① 佚名. 劳动保障部调查表明：待遇偏低直接酿出“民工荒”. http://job.cixi.cn，2005-09-14

② 邓聿. 最低工资制度的另一面. http://www.lm.gov.cn/gb/salary/2005-06/23/content_76875.htm，2005-06-23

③ 严利. 广东大幅调高最低工资幕后. 广州日报，2006-07-22

和社会保障厅再次宣布调高企业职工最低工资标准。调整后，广东省广州市最低工资标准为每月 1 030 元，东莞市为每月 920 元，中山市为每月 920 元，惠州市为每月 810 元，高于京苏而低于沪浙。①②

此举使广东 2 300 万农民工成为最主要的受惠群体。但它对技术含量较低的企业形成冲击，因此，如果无法支付最低工资就意味着企业效益偏低，这就迫使企业进行技术升级，同时也逼迫广大的农民工参加技术学习和行业培训，以提高自身的就业竞争能力。

Part Two Exercises

Ⅰ. Listen to the first part of the news, and answer the following questions.

1. What is Minimum Wage?

2. What is federal minimum wage like in the US?

3. Who earn only $2.30 per hour?

4. Is it possible for workers of small companies to receive less than $5.15?

5. What is the use of State laws in setting the minimum pay?

Ⅱ. Listen to the second part of the news, and complete the following sentences.

1. The ________________ says about two million workers earn the minimum wage or less.

2. That is about three percent of all workers ________________.

3. Ohio and Kansas have lower minimum wages for some workers ________________.

4. But ________________ and the District of Columbia have minimum wages higher than the federal one.

---

① 严利．广东大幅调高最低工资幕后．广州日报，2006－07－22

② 王俊萍．珠三角地区调高最低工资标准．河南科技报，2010－03－30

5. In California, Republican Governor Arnold Schwarzenegger has just proposed ________________.

6. California's minimum wage would rise one dollar, to seven dollars and seventy-five cents an hour, ________________.

7. ________________ last year to add a dollar to the minimum wage.

8. But Mister Schwarzenegger ________________ because it would have also required ________________.

Ⅲ. Listen to the third part of the news, and translate it into Chinese sentence by sentence.

Ⅳ. Listen to the last part of the news for three times, and try to repeat the whole paragraph with the subjects（主语）of the sentences given below.

1. Some economists and lawmakers ________________.
2. They ________________.
3. Employers ________________.
3. But labor activists ________________.
4. They ________________.

Part Three Keys to the Exercises

Ⅰ. Listen to the first part of the news, and answer the following questions.

1. What is Minimum Wage?

Minimum Wage is the lowest hourly pay rate permitted by law.

2. What is federal minimum wage like in the US?

a) In the United States, the federal minimum wage is five dollars and fifteen cents an hour.

b) It has not changed since nineteen ninety-seven.

c) And it does not include all jobs.

3. Who earn only $2. 30 per hour?

For example, workers who receive extra money in the form of tips can be paid two dollars and thirteen cents an hour.

4. Is it possible for workers of small companies to receive less than $5. 15?

Yes. Also, the federal rate may not cover some workers for small companies.

5. What is the use of State laws in setting the minimum pay?

State laws often set minimum pay in these cases (where the federal rate does not cover).

Ⅱ. Listen to the second part of the news, and complete the following sentences.

1. The Department of Labor says about two million workers earn the minimum wage or less.

2. That is about three percent of all workers paid by the hour.

3. Ohio and Kansas have lower minimum wages for some workers than under federal law.

4. But sixteen of the fifty states and the District of Columbia have minimum wages higher than the federal one.

5. In California, Republican Governor Arnold Schwarzenegger has just proposed what he says is a much-needed raise.

6. California's minimum wage would rise one dollar, to seven dollars and seventy-five cents an hour, over the next year and a half.

7. State lawmakers passed a bill last year to add a dollar to the minimum wage.

8. But Mister Schwarzenegger vetoed it because it would have also required yearly increases for inflation.

Ⅲ. Listen to the third part of the news, and translate it into Chinese.

State governments led the way in the history of the minimum wage in America. Massachusetts passed a law for women and children in nineteen twelve. But in nineteen twenty-three, the Supreme Court found wage requirements for private employers unconstitutional. It ruled that states could not interfere with pay agreements.

州政府是美国历史上实行最低工资的先行者。1912 年马萨诸塞州通过了保障妇女和儿童的法律。但在 1923 年，最高法院作出裁决，对私人雇主提出工资最低规定属于违宪，继而规定州政府不能干涉薪酬协议。

In nineteen thirty-eight, however, the Fair Labor Standards Act established a federal minimum wage. At that time, it was twenty-five cents.

但到 1938 年，公平劳工标准法案设立了联邦最低工资，那时是每小时 25 美分。

Ⅳ. Listen to the last part of the news for three times, and try to repeat the whole paragraph with the subjects of the sentences given below.

1. Some economists and lawmakers argue that markets, and not the government, should set prices for labor.

2. They say minimum wage laws reduce the number of jobs for unskilled workers and young people.

3. Employers might not be happy with higher labor costs.

4. But labor activists warn that inflation has reduced the buying power of today's minimum wage.

5. They say a minimum wage must be a "living wage". That is, it must be enough for

workers and their families to live on.

Part Four Translation of the Text

On the Job，at Minimum Wage

美国最低工资制

Minimum wage is the lowest hourly pay rate permitted by law. In the United States，the federal minimum wage is five dollars and fifteen cents an hour. It has not changed since nineteen ninety-seven. And it does not include all jobs.

最低工资即法律上规定的每小时的最低工资。在美国，联邦最低工资是每小时5.15美元。自从1997年后，这项规定就没有改变过。这还不包括所有的工作。

For example，workers who receive extra money in the form of tips can be paid two dollars and thirteen cents an hour. Also，the federal rate may not cover some workers for small companies. State laws often set minimum pay in these cases.

举个例子，可以收取小费而有额外收入的工人每小时甚至只有2.13美元。同时，联邦最低工资制并不保护为小型公司工作的工人。各州法律为这种情况设置法定最低工资。

The Department of Labor says about two million workers earn the minimum wage or less. That is about three percent of all workers paid by the hour.

劳工部表示大约有200万个工人每小时只能赚取最低或者更少的工资。这部分人大约占所有收取“时薪”工人的百分之三。

Ohio and Kansas have lower minimum wages for some workers than under federal law. But sixteen of the fifty states and the District of Columbia have minimum wages higher than the federal one.

美国的俄亥俄州和堪萨斯州某些工人的最低工资比联邦法律规定的要少。但全国50个州中的16个以及哥伦比亚特区的最低工资比联邦政府规定的要高。

In California，Republican Governor Arnold Schwarzenegger has just proposed what he says is a much-needed raise. California's minimum wage would rise one dollar，to seven dollars and seventy-five cents an hour，over the next year and a half.

在加利福尼亚州，共和党的州长施瓦辛格不久前提出了他认为急需的加薪提案。加州的最低工资在接下来的一年半中将增加1美元，即提升至每小时7.75美元。

State lawmakers passed a bill last year to add a dollar to the minimum wage. But Mister Schwarzenegger vetoed it because it would have also required yearly increases for inflation.

州立法者上年通过了给最低工资增加1美元的议案。但施瓦辛格先生否决了这个议案，因为这样一来就需考虑年通货膨胀率的增长。

State governments led the way in the history of the minimum wage in America. Massachusetts passed a law for women and children in nineteen twelve. But in nineteen twenty-three，the Supreme Court found wage requirements for private employers unconstitutional. It ruled that states could not interfere with pay agreements.

州政府是美国历史上实行最低工资的先行者。1912 年马萨诸塞州通过了保障妇女和儿童的法律。但在 1923 年，最高法院作出裁决，对私人雇主提出工资最低规定属于违宪，继而规定州政府不能干涉薪酬协议。

In nineteen thirty-eight, however, the Fair Labor Standards Act established a federal minimum wage. At that time, it was twenty-five cents.

但到 1938 年，公平劳工标准法案设立了联邦最低工资，那时是每小时 25 美分。

Some economists and lawmakers argue that markets, and not the government, should set prices for labor. They say minimum wage laws reduce the number of jobs for unskilled workers and young people.

一些经济学家和立法者主张，应该由市场而非政府来确定劳工价格。他们表示最低工资法减少了没有技能的工人和年轻人的工作机会。

Employers might not be happy with higher labor costs. But labor activists warn that inflation has reduced the buying power of today's minimum wage. They say a minimum wage must be a "living wage". That is, it must be enough for workers and their families to live on.

雇主可能不愿意增加劳工成本。但工会活动分子警告说，通货膨胀已经减少了现今最低工资的购买能力。他们认为，最低工资必须是"生存工资"，也就是说，最低工资必须足以维持工人们及其家庭的生活。

Lesson 12 Gold Prices Reach Their Highest Levels in Years

By Mario Ritter

January 5, 2006

Part One Background Information

黄金价格为什么会大涨

黄金这种金属人见人爱，谁都想与它沾点边儿，但它与国际政治、经济、美元、石油以及通货膨胀的关系更“密切”、更玄妙。学者白萌认为，美元贬值时，黄金价格就会上涨，“由于黄金是用美元计价，即美元指数下跌时，使用其他货币例如欧元的投资者就会发现他们使用欧元购买黄金时，等量资金可以买到更多的黄金，从而刺激需求，导致黄金的需求量增加，进而推动金价走高”①。2002 年，欧元正式流通，标志着布雷顿森林体系建立起来的美元独霸的国际货币体系出现了真正强有力的竞争者。2004 年，美国贸易赤字再创新高，使消费者对美元的信心被摧毁，也导致黄金价格的持续走高。但当美国经济发展过猛之时，黄金价格就会下跌。例如，20 世纪八九十年代，美国新经济突飞猛进，大量海外资金流入美国，这段时期由于其他市场的投资回报率远远大于投资黄金，投资者大规模地撤出黄金市场，导致黄金价格经历了连续 20 年的下挫②。相反，国际政治形势发生动荡，例如，“9·11”事件和阿富汗战争与伊拉克战争，就导致投资者为了规避通货膨胀和货币贬值而重新回到黄金市场，使黄金价格再次走高。另一个与黄金齐头并进的“宝贝”是被称为“黑金”的石油，故油价通常被人们当作金价升降的信号指标。因为一方面，油价的升降同样受国际局势和美元的影响，另一方面，国际市场上石油通常以美元来结算，“石油价格上涨后，产油国所持有的美元（用石油换来的美元）会迅速膨胀，于是这些国家就会提高黄金在其国际储备中的比例，从而增加了对黄金的需求。由于石油换来的美元数额巨大，石油输出国操作集中性强，推动了黄金价格的上涨”③。过去，一盎司黄金的价格大概相当于 16 桶原油，到 2005 年每盎司黄金只能换 7 桶左右的原油。

正是以上各种因素使黄金价格从 2001 年的 250 美元左右的低点开始上涨，一直涨到 2006 年 5 月份的 730 美元的高点。随后黄金价格开始大幅下跌，最低跌 542 美元。到 2007 年 2 月份，纽约市场的黄金期货价格每盎司上升 1．1 美元，收于 638 美元；黄金现货价格每盎司上升 1．1 美元，收于 635．2 美元。

---

①② 白萌．美元指数与黄金走势相关性分析．http：//www.forex.com.cn/news/newscontent.asp newsid = 20060428174006498&classid = 292513，2006 - 04 - 28

③ 杨叶．黄金和石油的价格关系及原因分析．中国黄金报，2006 - 7 - 25

Part Two　Exercises

Ⅰ. Listen to the first part of the news, and complete the sentences.

1. Gold has long been ____.

2. The metal is also valuable for its ____________________________, and for its electrical qualities.

3. But some people have always valued gold most as an investment, even without ____.

4. For years, ____.

5. Now gold is in the news because prices have risen _______________________ since the early nineteen eighties.

6. Gold is trading above ________________ a troy ounce（金衡制盎司）, about __________________________________（克）.

Ⅱ. Listen to the second part of the news, and answer the following questions.

1. What is the experts' explanation for the increase in gold prices?

2. What led people to buy gold traditionally?

3. What is the common belief for gold?

4. What does it mean that money was based on gold?

5. What is the result when the link between gold and money was cut? (President Franklin Roosevelt, Legal Tender Act)

6. What was the Gold Reserve Act in nineteen thirty-four about?

7. What do you think is the "gold standard" about?

Ⅲ. Listen to the third part of the news, and translate it into Chinese sentence by sentence, then repeat it in English.

From "In nineteen forty-four..." to "until the late nineteen sixties".

Part Three Keys to the Exercises

Ⅰ. Listen to the first part of the news, and complete the sentences.

1. Gold has long been valued, and not just for its beauty.

2. The metal is also valuable for its resistance to chemical reactions, and for its electrical qualities.

3. But some people have always valued gold most as an investment, even without any guarantee of growth in its value.

4. For years, gold prices fell.

5. Now gold is in the news because prices have risen to their highest levels since the early nineteen eighties.

6. Gold is trading above five hundred dollars a troy ounce (金衡制盎司), about thirty-one grams (克).

Ⅱ. Listen to the second part of the news, and answer the following questions.

1. What is the experts' explanation for the increase in gold prices?

There seems to be no simple explanation for the increase in gold prices. Experts say investments in precious metals have increased in general.

2. What led people to buy gold traditionally?

This is true even without the economic warning signs that have traditionally led many investors to buy gold.

3. What is the common belief for gold?

In any case, the common belief in the security of gold has a long history.

4. What does it mean that money was based on gold?

From nineteen hundred to nineteen thirty-three, United States money was fully based on gold. In fact, under the gold standard, anyone who wanted could exchange paper money for gold coins.

5. What is the result when the link between gold and money was cut?

But President Franklin Roosevelt and Congress began to cut the link between gold and money. Congress passed the Legal Tender Act of nineteen thirty-three. All United States money, paper or metal, became acceptable as payment for all debts, public and private.

6. What was the Gold Reserve Act in nineteen thirty-four about?

The Gold Reserve Act made it illegal to use gold as a form of currency within the United States.

7. What do you think is the "gold standard" about?

But the gold standard remained important to international trade. It allows to use gold as currency in international trade.

Ⅲ. Listen to the third part of the news, and translate it into Chinese sentence by sentence, then repeat it in English.

In nineteen forty-four, the United Nations held a meeting at a hotel in Bretton Woods, New Hampshire. The Bretton Woods conference established a new international monetary system. Other currencies were linked to the value of the American dollar, and the dollar remained linked to the value of gold.

1944 年，联合国在新罕布什尔州布雷顿森林的一家酒店召开了一次会议。布雷顿森林会议设立了一项新的国际货币制度，将其他国家的货币与美元币值“挂钩”，而美元则保持与黄金价值“挂钩”。

The official price of gold was controlled. It stayed at about thirty-five dollars an ounce until the late nineteen sixties.

黄金的官价是受到控制的，直至 20 世纪 60 年代后期，黄金价格被控制在每盎司 35 美元左右。

Ⅳ. Listen to the last part of news for three times, and write it down.

In nineteen seventy-one, the gold standard ended in the United States. By nineteen seventy-six, the International Monetary Fund agreed to a new system of exchange rates. But the process did not go smoothly. Gold prices reached record levels in the early eighties, at a time when inflation also jumped.

Today, gold remains important to the wealth of nations. But money supplies and gold supplies no longer have the relationship they had in the past.

Part Four　Translation of the Text

Gold Prices Reach Their Highest Levels in Years

黄金价格创近年新高

Gold has long been valued, and not just for its beauty. The metal is also valuable for its resistance to chemical reactions, and for its electrical qualities. But some people have always valued gold most as an investment, even without any guarantee of growth in its value.

长期以来，黄金受到追捧，不仅仅因为其美丽，还因为其抵抗化学反应的能力及良好的导电性能。许多人总把黄金当作一项有价值的投资，即使黄金价格没有增长的任何保证。

For years, gold prices fell. Now gold is in the news because prices have risen to their highest levels since the early nineteen eighties. Gold is trading above five hundred dollars a troy ounce, about thirty-one gram.

多年来，黄金的价格一直在下跌。现在，黄金之所以又成为新闻焦点，是因为自20世纪80年代初期以来，黄金价格升至巅峰。黄金的交易价已上涨至每盎司（约31克）500美金。

There seems to be no simple explanation for the increase in gold prices. Experts say investments in precious metals have increased in general. This is true even without the economic warning signs that have traditionally led many investors to buy gold.

有关黄金价值上涨的原因很难解释。专家们认为，贵重金属方面的投资在整体上是增加了。即使没有任何经济警示，情况也是如此，传统上，经济发生危险的征兆导致投资者购买黄金。

In any case, the common belief in the security of gold has a long history.

无论如何，人们对黄金安全度的普遍信赖已经有一段漫长的历史。

From nineteen hundred to nineteen thirty-three, United States money was fully based on gold. In fact, under the gold standard, anyone who wanted could exchange paper money for gold coins.

从1900年至1933年，美国货币完全以黄金为基准。事实上，在黄金汇率制中，任何人只要愿意，都可以把纸币兑换成金币。

But President Franklin Roosevelt and Congress began to cut the link between gold and money. Congress passed the Legal Tender Act of nineteen thirty-three. All United States money, paper or metal, became acceptable as payment for all debts, public and private.

但是，美国前总统富兰克林·罗斯福和国会着手消除黄金和货币之间的“挂钩”关系。国会1933年通过了租借法案，规定美国货币无论是纸币还是金属，都可支付任何公私债务。

In nineteen thirty-four, the Gold Reserve Act made it illegal to use gold as a form of currency within the United States. But the gold standard remained important to international trade.

1934 年，黄金储备法案规定，在美国把黄金当作流通货币属于非法行为。但是，黄金汇率制在国际贸易上依然保持着重要的地位。

In nineteen forty-four, the United Nations held a meeting at a hotel in Bretton Woods, New Hampshire. The Bretton Woods conference established a new international monetary system. Other currencies were linked to the value of the American dollar, and the dollar remained linked to the value of gold.

1944 年，联合国在新罕布什尔州布雷顿森林的一家酒店召开了一次会议。布雷顿森林会议设立了一项新的国际货币制度，将其他国家的货币与美元币值“挂钩”，而美元则保持与黄金价值“挂钩”。

The official price of gold was controlled. It stayed at about thirty-five dollars an ounce until the late nineteen sixties. In nineteen seventy-one, the gold standard ended in the United States. By nineteen seventy-six, the International Monetary Fund agreed to a new system of exchange rates. But the process did not go smoothly. Gold prices reached record levels in the early eighties, at a time when inflation also jumped.

黄金的官价是受到控制的，直至 20 世纪 60 年代后期，黄金价格被控制在每盎司 35 美元左右。1971 年，黄金汇率制在美国被终止。1976 年，国际货币基金组织通过了一项新的货币兑换率系统。但是这个过程并不十分顺利。黄金的价格在 80 年代初通货膨胀高涨时再创新高。

Today, gold remains important to the wealth of nations. But money supplies and gold supplies no longer have the relationship they had in the past.

如今，黄金仍然是国家的重要财富。但货币和黄金供应的关系已不再像以前那样了。

(This VOA *Special English* Economics Report was written by Mario Ritter. I'm Steve Ember.)

Lesson 13　High Oil Prices and the World Economy

By Jill Moss
August 27, 2005

Part One　Background Information

石油与经济发展的关系

石油被誉为经济发展的血液和命脉，因为在现代化建设的浪潮中，交通、建筑、机械、汽车、钢铁等重工业增加了对能源的需求。尤其是世界加工制造业中心向第三世界国家转移，那里城市化水平的提高和城市人口的增长都使能源消耗大幅增加。以中国对石油的需求为例，“在过去 10 年的总增长达 112.5%，2004 年中国共进口 1.23 亿吨，即 8.73 亿桶原油，增长 34.8%。2005 年的头 5 个月，中国的原油进口量比 2004 年同期增加 5.1%。但 2004 年中国的原油产量只有每日 349 万桶，比 2003 年仅增长 2.9%。经过 10 年的发展，中国原油产量的增长不足 20%”①。所以能源专家大多认为，全球石油需求增加是油价上涨的原因之一。另外，炼油能力不足也是国际油价上涨不可忽视的重要因素。“从 1993 年至 2003 年的 10 年间，国际原油消耗量增加了 17%，而世界炼油能力仅增长 2.6%，2003 年世界原油需求增长 24%，但当年的全球炼油能力仅增长 0.4%。两者之间差幅极大，不成比例。炼油能力不足在美国尤为突出。由于环保等压力逐渐增大，美国炼油商 1976 年以来就没有新建炼油厂，这直接导致美成品石油进口激增。”②

可以想象，石油作为战略物资，不仅影响国家经济的发展，也是遏制他国军事及经济发展的外交策略之一。比如，“美国是全球第一大石油消耗国。据国际能源机构估计，目前美国的石油消耗量约占全球石油产量的 1/4。长期以来，美国深深地卷入中东政治之中，并极力向拉美和非洲扩张，拓展其政治经济利益。这些政策很多都贴着‘保障石油供应’的标签。但是，今天看来，无论是在中东，还是在拉美，美国的一些政策并没有取得预期的效果。将石油资源国有化、维护国家经济主权，正成为一些产油国的政策潮流，以致成为美国干涉与扩张的阻力”③。但是，石油资源国有化后，其中很大一部分石油的销售权被授予给如英国石油公司、埃克森—美孚公司、英荷壳牌公司、德士古—雪佛龙这四大石油寡头。而“石油作为一种价格弹性较低的商品，它的主要利润不是来自于产量，而是来自于价格。国际上的一些大银行、投机基金和其他金融投资者，通过远期商品交易，以一种非常隐秘的方式来决定商品的价格。据估计，目前世界上 2/3 的原油交易是在伦敦国际石油交易市场以投机下赌注的方式决定价格的。那些被称为现货市场的交易活动，更是限

① 佚名．剖析石油与中国经济的关系．http：//www. hkcd. com. hk/node_ 27737. htm，2005 - 07 - 19

② 吴建友．石油价格波动冲击世界经济．http：//news. xinhuanet. com/world/2005 - 07/04/content_ 3171617. htm，2005 - 07 - 04

③ 宿景祥．错综复杂的石油政治．人民日报，2006 - 04 - 11

定在一个很小的圈子里，局外人几乎一无所知”①。这样一来石油价格暴涨中真正受益的是那些垄断中东石油市场的石油寡头，另外是那些石油投机商。

高价石油令美国政府十分担忧，首先是石油高价会增强伊朗的国力，“据美国剑桥能源咨询公司估计，石油价格每上升5美元，伊朗每周的石油输出所得将增加8 500万美元，如此一来，伊朗的领导人就会更加大胆，即使危机有扩散之势，他们也能更加轻而易举地对真主党提供资助”②。其次，“俄罗斯会对中亚国家施加压力，让它们反对美国的能源计划，并反对美国将该地区作为军事基地。因为俄罗斯已经联合中国成立了上海合作组织，该组织成立5年以来，吸纳了一些中亚国家作为其成员国，美国国防部甚至由此而担心该集团会从最初的以能源为重点发展成与北大西洋公约组织相抗衡的军事联盟”③。

Part Two　Exercises

Ⅰ. Listen to the first part of the news, and fill in the blanks with the words you hear.

This week, ________________ traded briefly at a ____________________ dollars a barrel on the New York Mercantile Exchange. Prices are up about ____________________ from last year. ______________________________, prices are still below what they were in the early nineteen eighties. Then, __________ sold for well above eighty dollars a barrel.

But, ____________________, this is the most that the world's ________________ has ever had to pay. In some areas, prices at ________________ are almost as high as Americans have ever paid, ____________________.

Ⅱ. Listen to the second part of the news, and answer the following questions.

1. Is it because that there are no supplies of oil, so the prices are high?

2. Was the demand for oil at this time of the year very high? Why did oil supplies decrease at this time of the year?

3. What is the role of the "buildup" according to officials? What will happen without the buildup?

---

①　宿景祥. 错综复杂的石油政治. 人民日报, 2006 - 04 - 11

②③　佚名. 石油影响国际政治局势的能力骤增. http://www.china.com.cn/international/txt/2006 - 08/11/content_7070377_2.htm, 2006 - 08 - 11

4. Who is Alan Greenspan? What's his opinion about the economy?

Ⅲ. Listen to the third part of the news, and try to repeat every sentence, then write them down.

the Managing Director's name: Rodrigo de Rato

Ⅳ. Listen to the last part of the news, and translate it into Chinese sentence by sentence.

Sabotage 破坏，妨碍　　Katrina 卡特尼娜

Part Three　Keys to the Exercises

Ⅰ. Listen to the first part of the news, and fill in the blanks with the words you hear.

This week, crude oil traded briefly at a record sixty-eight dollars a barrel on the New York Mercantile Exchange. Prices are up about fifty percent from last year. With inflation considered, prices are still below what they were in the early nineteen eighties. Then, crude oil sold for well above eighty dollars a barrel.

But, in dollar terms, this is the most that the world's largest economy has ever had to pay.

In some areas, prices at fuel stations are almost as high as Americans have ever paid, even with inflation.

Ⅱ. Listen to the second part of the news, and answer the following questions.

1. Is it because that there are no supplies of oil, so the prices are high?

The Energy Department said this week that crude oil prices remain very high even though supplies in the United States are growing.

2. Was the demand for oil at this time of the year very high? Why did oil supplies decrease at this time of the year?

Yes. Oil supplies generally decrease at this time of year because of seasonal demand.

3. What is the role of the "buildup" according to officials? What will happen without the buildup?

Officials say the recent buildup should keep prices from being as high this winter as they might be without it.

4. Who is Alan Greenspan? What's his opinion about the economy?

On Friday, central bank chairman Alan Greenspan had praised for the way the economy has dealt with high energy costs. So far, he says, it has handled the sharp rise in prices for oil and natural gas over the past two years "reasonably well".

Ⅲ. Listen to the third part of the news, and try to repeat every sentence, then write them down.

But economists at the International Monetary Fund in Washington have voiced concerns about the world economy. On Thursday, the Managing Director warned about the risk to economic growth in Asia. Rodrigo de Rato urged Asian central banks to use monetary policies to fight inflationary pressures caused by high oil prices. He directed his comments especially to Indonesia and the Philippines. The high cost of oil has slowed Indonesia's economic growth.

Ⅳ. Listen to the last part of the news, and translate it into Chinese sentence by sentence.

Many issues can affect oil prices. For example, on Friday, Nigerian officials ordered increases in the price of fuel. There were fears of general strikes. Nigeria is the world's eighth larger exporter of oil.

计多方面的问题都可能对油价产生影响。例如，尼日利亚官方命令在周五提高燃料价格。人们担心会发生全国性的大罢工。尼日利亚是世界第八大石油出口国。

Terrorism is another concern for oil traders. But even the weather can sabotage the industry. This week, there were concerns about the possible risk to oil production in the Gulf of Mexico from the ocean storm Katrina.

恐怖主义是石油贸易商担忧的另一个隐患。天气甚至可能会毁掉石油产业。本周，人们担心墨西哥湾的卡特尼娜风暴可能对石油生产带来风险。

However, industry experts say the biggest concern is the growing world demand for oil. The United States and China are the top two users. A report this week said China imported fifteen percent more crude oil in July than a year ago. Crude oil becomes fuel and other products.

然而，该产业专家说最大的风险是世界对石油的需求越来越大。美国和中国是名列前茅的两大用户。本周有报告说，中国在7月份进口的原油比一年前增加了15%。原油可以加工成燃料和其他产品。

There are questions about the ability of oil-producing nations to meet growing demand. Some experts believe that Saudi Arabia's oil fields may have reached peak production. This is when more than half of the recoverable crude oil has already been pumped out. Saudi Arabia denies that. Earlier this year, the International Monetary Fund called for more openness to confirm the supplies of the world's top oil producer.

人们对石油生产国是否能够满足对石油日益增长的需求表示怀疑。有些专家认为沙特阿拉伯的油田也许已经达到了生产极限。这就意味着可找到的原油已经被抽掉了一半多。沙特阿拉伯否认了这一说法。今年初，国际货币基金组织要求提高透明度，以确定世界顶级石油生产国的供应量。

Currently Saudi Arabia produces more than ten million barrels of crude a day. It says it expects to produce more than twelve million barrels daily by two thousand and nine.

目前沙特阿拉伯每天的产量超过1 000万桶原油。沙特阿拉伯预计，到2009年，每天产油量将超过1 200万桶。

Part Four　Translation of the Text

High Oil Prices and the World Economy
居高不下的石油价格与世界经济

This week, crude oil traded briefly at a record sixty-eight dollars a barrel on the New York Mercantile Exchange. Prices are up about fifty percent from last year. With inflation considered, prices are still below what they were in the early nineteen eighties. Then, crude oil sold for well above eighty dollars a barrel.

纽约商品交易所原油交易本周创下每桶68美元的新纪录。其价格从去年至今上涨了约50%。考虑到通货膨胀的因素，原油价格仍然低于20世纪80年代初的价格。那个时候，原油价格远高于每桶80美元。

But, in dollar terms, this is the most that the world's largest economy has ever had to pay. In some areas, prices at fuel stations are almost as high as Americans have ever paid, even with inflation.

但是，按美元计，这是世界最大经济体所付出的最大代价。在一些地区，加油站的油价已上升到美国人从没支付过的高价，即使是考虑通货膨胀因素。

The Energy Department said this week that crude oil prices remain very high even though supplies in the United States are growing. Oil supplies generally decrease at this time of year because of seasonal demand. Officials say the recent buildup should keep prices from being as high this winter as they might be without it.

能源部本周说，即使美国的供应在增长，原油价格依然保持高位。石油供应一般来说在每年的这个时候因季节性需求而减少。官方称，最近的原油库存将避免使今冬的油价因无存货而高涨。

On Friday, central bank chairman Alan Greenspan had praised for the way the economy has dealt with high energy costs. So far, he says, it has handled the sharp rise in prices for oil and natural gas over the past two years "reasonably well".

中央银行主席格林斯潘本周五称赞美国经济应付高能源成本的方式。他说，到目前为止，美国经济在过去的两年里"非常理性"地应对了石油和天然气价格的急剧上涨。

But economists at the International Monetary Fund in Washington have voiced concerns about the world economy. On Thursday, the managing director warned about the risk to economic growth in Asia. Rodrigo de Rato urged Asian central banks to use monetary policies to fight inflationary pressures caused by high oil prices. He directed his comments especially to Indonesia and the Philippines. The high cost of oil has slowed Indonesia's economic growth.

但国际货币基金组织的经济学家在华盛顿表示对世界经济感到担忧。总裁周四警告说亚洲经济增长蕴含着风险。罗德里戈·德·拉托敦促亚洲中央银行使用货币政策来应对因石油价格带来的通货膨胀压力。他的评论特指印度尼西亚和菲律宾。石油成本增高减缓了印度尼西亚的经济增长速度。

Many issues can affect oil prices. For example, on Friday, Nigerian officials ordered increases in the price of fuel. There were fears of general strikes. Nigeria is the world's eighth larger exporter of oil.

许多方面的问题都可能对油价产生影响。例如，尼日利亚官方命令在周五提高燃料的价格。人们担心会发生全国性的大罢工。尼日利亚是世界第八大石油出口国。

Terrorism is another concern for oil traders. But even the weather can sabotage the industry. This week, there were concerns about the possible risk to oil production in the Gulf of Mexico from the ocean storm Katrina.

恐怖主义是石油贸易商担忧的另一个隐患。天气甚至可能会毁掉石油产业。本周，人们担心墨西哥湾的卡特尼娜风暴可能对石油生产带来风险。

However, industry experts say the biggest concern is the growing world demand for oil. The United States and China are the top two users. A report this week said China imported fifteen percent more crude oil in July than a year ago. Crude oil becomes fuel and other products.

然而，该产业专家说最大的风险是世界对石油的需求越来越大。美国和中国是名列前茅的两大用户。本周有报告说，中国在 7 月份进口的原油比一年前增加了 15%。原油可以加工成燃料和其他产品。

There are questions about the ability of oil-producing nations to meet growing demand. Some experts believe that Saudi Arabia's oil fields may have reached peak production. This is when more than half of the recoverable crude oil has already been pumped out. Saudi Arabia denies that.

Earlier this year, the International Monetary Fund called for more openness to confirm the supplies of the world's top oil producer.

人们对石油生产国是否能够满足对石油日益增长的需求表示怀疑。有些专家认为沙特阿拉伯的油田也许已经达到了生产极限。这就意味着可找到的原油已经被抽掉了一半多。沙特阿拉伯否认了这一说法。今年初，国际货币基金组织要求提高透明度，以确定世界顶级石油生产国的供应量。

Currently Saudi Arabia produces more than ten million barrels of crude a day. It says it expects to produce more than twelve million barrels daily by two thousand and nine.

目前沙特阿拉伯每天的产量超过1 000万桶原油。沙特阿拉伯预计，到2009年，每天产油量将超过1 200万桶。

Lesson 14 International Monetary Fund

By Caty Weaver

January 12, 2002

Part One Background Information

国际货币基金组织是西方国家的“聚宝箱”

国际货币基金组织属于联合国的专门机构，于1945年12月27日成立，是政府间国际金融组织，共有185个成员国。该组织的宗旨是“稳定国际汇率，在成员国之间保持有秩序的汇价安排，避免竞争性的汇价贬值；协助成员国建立经常性交易的多边支付制度，消除妨碍世界贸易的外汇管制；在有适当保证的条件下，基金组织向成员国临时提供普通资金，使其有信心利用此机会纠正国际收支的失调，而不采取危害本国或国际繁荣的措施”①。

在第十二课，我们提到由于布雷顿森林体系使美元得以独霸国际货币体系的问题，国际货币基金组织（IMF）的建立就涉及此体系的形成过程。IMF和世界银行被称为布雷顿森林货币体系，这两个金融组织与关贸总协定在20世纪后半叶的50年中成为支撑着世界经贸和金融格局的三大支柱，它们都源于1944年召开的布雷顿森林会议。

1944年7月，在美国新罕布什尔州的布雷顿森林召开了由44个国家参加的联合国与联盟国家国际货币金融会议，通过了以美国财政部官员命名的“怀特计划”中提出的“联合国家货币金融会议的最后决议书”以及“国际货币基金组织协定”和“国际复兴开发银行协定”两个附件，总称为“布雷顿森林协定”②。“‘怀特计划’主张取消外汇管制和各国对国际资金转移的限制，设立一个国际稳定基金组织，发行一种国际货币，使各国货币与之保持固定汇率，也就是基金货币与美元和黄金挂钩。会员国货币都要与‘尤尼它’保持固定汇率，不经‘基金’会员国四分之三的投票权通过，会员国货币不得贬值。”③而“国际复兴开发银行协定是根据英国财政部顾问凯恩斯从当时英国黄金储备缺乏而提出建立一个世界性中央银行的建议而设立的，它将各国的债权、债务通过它的存款账户转账进行清算”。

“美国经济实力在‘二战’后急剧增长，它根据‘租借法案’向盟国提供了价值500多亿美元的货物和劳务，得到了源源不断的黄金，美国的黄金储备从1938年的145.1亿美元增加到1945年的200.8亿美元，约占世界黄金储备的59%，美元的国际地位因其国

---

① 杨立杰. 国际货币基金组织. http：//news. xinhuanet. com/ziliao/2003 -01/27/content_ 709580. htm

②③ 吴剑芸. 布雷顿森林体系建立的历史背景、作用及其崩溃. http：//space. cenet. org. cn/user1/375/archives/2006/888. html

际黄金储备的巨大实力而空前稳固。”① 而 IMF 就是一个以美元为支柱的有利于美国对外经济扩张的国际货币体系，首先是美元与黄金挂钩。各国政府或中央银行都可按官价用美元向美国兑换黄金（每一美元的含金量为 0.888671 克黄金）。其次，其他国家货币与美元挂钩。其他国家政府规定各自货币的含金量，通过含金量的比例确定同美元的汇率，并且 IMF 规定，各国货币对美元的汇率，一般只能在法定汇率上下各 1% 的幅度内波动，以维持汇率稳定。

选择固定汇率对本国的货币政策加以限制，可以使本币的利率及通胀与国际主要货币的利率与通胀不会相差太多，特别是对“开放型、以国际贸易及资本市场为主的经济体，固定汇率有利于营造一个相对稳定及容易预测的宏观经济环境。对于像中国这样的发展中国家，当中央银行的货币政策制定及执行能力还不成熟时，固定汇率也有利于稳定通胀预期及宏观经济环境”②。但固定汇率的缺点是在货币政策上没有自主性，比如，“如果美国提高利率以遏制通货膨胀，发展中国家即使需要降低利率以刺激经济增长时也不得不跟上，这样就会造成内部目标和外部目标的尖锐冲突。而如果放弃汇率稳定实现货币政策的自主性则要求资本可以在国际间转移，没有任何人为的和自然的限制，也要求国际间资本完全替代、套利、资本无穷大等条件”③。一般来说，发展中国家资本相对短缺，境内利率水平较高，一旦开放资本账户，就会吸引资金的流入。结果，涌入发展中国家的资金远远超过当地的需求。所以国内金融体系不完善的多数发展中国家往往选择盯住美元的汇率制度。

Part Two　Exercises

Ⅰ. Listen to the first part of the news, and fill in the blanks with the words you hear.

A team from the International Monetary Fund completed ____________________ to Argentina this week. The ____________________ were there to examine the country's ____________________ and how the new government is ____________________.

Argentina __________ other countries more than ____________________ dollars. The country is in the fourth year of a __________. It has an eighteen percent __________. The economic troubles have led to a ________________ and violent protests in Argentina.

The Argentine Economy Minister, Jorge Remes Lenicov, said the government is seeking as much as ____________________ dollars in new aid. He said Argentine officials would negotiate with the IMF to ____________________ the country's debt.

---

① 吴剑芸. 布雷顿森林体系建立的历史背景、作用及其崩溃. http://space.cenet.org.cn/user1/375/archives/2006/888.html

② 肖耿. 固定汇率与浮动汇率各有利弊. 南方周末，2006-06-15

③ 何帆. 美元霸权对世界经济的影响. 中国宏观经济信息网，2004-12-01

Ⅱ. Listen to the second part of the news, and answer the following questions.

1. What kind problems is the IMF expected to help solve?

2. What did the twenty nine countries do to create the IMF?

3. What was the IMF's purpose when it was established?

4. How does the IMF help countries with economic problems?

5. What should governments do to get IMF's help?

Ⅲ. Listen to the third part of the news, and take it down.

From "The IMF lends money..." to "...the country honors the arrangement".

Ⅳ. Listen to the last three parts of the news, and translate them into Chinese.

From "The IMF has created..." to the end.

Part Three Keys to the Exercises

Ⅰ. Listen to the first part of the news, and fill in the blanks with the words you hear.

A team from the International Monetary Fund completed a two-day visit to Argentina this week. The financial experts were there to examine the country's economic crisis and how the new government is dealing with it.

Argentina owes other countries more than one-hundred-forty-thousand-million dollars. The country is in the fourth year of a recession. It has an eighteen percent unemployment rate. The economic troubles have led to a political crisis and violent protests in Argentina.

The Argentine Economy Minister, Jorge Remes Lenicov, said the government is seeking as much as twenty-thousand-million dollars in new aid. He said Argentine officials would negotiate with the IMF to re-structure the country's debt.

Ⅱ. Listen to the second part of the news, and answer the following questions.

1. What kind problems is the IMF expected to help solve?

The International Monetary Fund was created in part to deal with problems of unemployment, debt, and political crisis.

2. What did the twenty-nine countries do to create the IMF?

In nineteen forty-five, twenty-nine countries signed an agreement establishing the organization.

3. What was the IMF's purpose when it was established?

They promised to cooperate on international financial issues and to help expand international trade.

4. How does the IMF help countries with economic problems?

The IMF also seeks to help countries pay their debts when they are experiencing economic problems.

5. What should governments do to get IMF's help?

In return, governments usually must take action that the IMF thinks will help solve the problems.

Ⅲ. Listen to the third part of the news, and take it down.

The IMF lends money under an "arrangement". The arrangement states the conditions the country must meet in order to receive the loan. Officials of the country and the IMF develop the arrangement together. Then it is presented to the IMF Executive Board. The Board represents the IMF's one hundred eighty-three member countries.

If the Board approves the arrangement, then the loan is released in a series of payments. IMF officials periodically re-consider the loan. Loan payments continue as long as the country honors the arrangement.

Ⅳ. Listen to the last three parts of the news, and translate them into Chinese.

The IMF has created a number of loan programs to deal with special situations among its members. The most common loan program is called a Stand-By Arrangement. It is for countries experiencing short-term debt problems. Payments usually are made for twelve to eighteen months. Countries generally are expected to repay the loan within two to four years.

IMF 为解决成员国的特殊情况而设立了数种贷款项目。最常见的贷款项目称为应急协议。其目的是解决短期债务问题。贷款分 12 至 18 个月发放。借债国一般在两到四年内返还贷款。

The IMF has another program for poor countries. The Poverty Reduction and Growth Facility permits poor countries to borrow money at a very low rate of interest. All other IMF programs have interest rates linked to the open market. The Poverty Reduction and Growth Facility also gives countries as long as ten years to repay loans.

IMF 还为贫穷国家设立了另一个项目——“减少贫困，促进发展”，目的是让贫穷的国家以非常低的利率借贷。IMF 其他项目的借贷利息都与开放市场挂钩。“减少贫困，促进发展”项目的还款期是 10 年。

Many people around the world oppose the IMF. In recent years, thousands of demonstrators have protested outside meetings of the IMF and similar organizations. Many of these activists say IMF policies make industrial nations richer and developing nations poorer. They also say the organization's activities result in damage to the environment.

世界上有很多人反对 IMF。近几年来，IMF 和同类国际组织的会场外发生了数以千计的游行示威活动。很多示威者说，IMF 的政策使工业国家更富，发展中国家更穷。他们还认为该组织的行为导致了对环境的破坏。

Part Four　Translation of the Text

International Monetary Fund
国际货币基金会

A team from the International Monetary Fund completed a two-day visit to Argentina this week. The financial experts were there to examine the country's economic crisis and how the new government is dealing with it.

国际货币基金组织的一个小组在本周完成了对阿根廷为期两天的访问。金融专家们到阿根廷是为了视察该国经济危机的情况，以及新政府是怎样应对经济危机的。

Argentina owes other countries more than one-hundred-forty-thousand-million dollars. The country is in the fourth year of a recession. It has an eighteen percent unemployment rate. The economic troubles have led to a political crisis and violent protests in Argentina.

阿根廷负债 1 400 亿美元。这个国家正处于经济衰退的第四年，其失业率达 18%。阿根廷的经济困境导致该国发生政治危机和暴力抗议。

The Argentine Economy Minister, Jorge Remes Lenicov, said the government is seeking as much as twenty-thousand-million dollars in new aid. He said Argentine officials would negotiate with the IMF to re-structure the country's debt.

阿根廷的经济部长勒尼柯夫说，其政府还想寻求200亿美元的新援助。他说，阿根廷官方将与IMF协商重新整顿该国的账务。

The International Monetary Fund was created in part to deal with problems like this. In nineteen forty-five, twenty-nine countries signed an agreement establishing the organization. They promised to cooperate on international financial issues and to help expand international trade.

建立国际基金组织部分原因是为了解决此类问题。1945年，20个国家参与签约，建立了该组织。他们承诺共同合作解决国际金融问题，以促进国际贸易。

The IMF also seeks to help countries pay their debts when they are experiencing economic problems. In return, governments usually must take action that the IMF thinks will help solve the problems.

IMF同时协助处于经济困境的国家偿还债务。作为回报，这些国家的政府必须按照IMF认为能够解决问题的方案采取措施。

The IMF lends money under an "arrangement". The arrangement states the conditions the country must meet in order to receive the loan. Officials of the country and the IMF develop the arrangement together. Then it is presented to the IMF Executive Board. The Board represents the IMF's one hundred eighty-three member countries.

IMF按"协议"的方式贷款。协议中列明了该国必须具备的贷款条件。由该国官员和IMF一起制定这个协议，并提交给IMF的执行委员会。该委员会代表着IMF183个成员国。

If the Board approves the arrangement, then the loan is released in a series of payments. IMF officials periodically re-consider the loan. Loan payments continue as long as the country honors the arrangement.

如果委员会批准了该协议，贷款将分期发放，IMF官员定期重审贷款。该国只要遵照协议办事，就能继续获得贷款的分次付款。

The IMF has created a number of loan programs to deal with special situations among its members. The most common loan program is called a Stand-By Arrangement. It is for countries experiencing short-term debt problems. Payments usually are made for twelve to eighteen months. Countries generally are expected to repay the loan within two to four years.

IMF为解决成员国的特殊情况而设立了数种贷款项目。最常见的贷款项目称为应急协议。其目的是解决短期债务问题。贷款分12至18个月发放。债务国一般在两到四年内返还贷款。

The IMF has another program for poor countries. The Poverty Reduction and Growth Facility permits poor countries to borrow money at a very low rate of interest. All other IMF programs have interest rates linked to the open market. The Poverty Reduction and Growth Facility also gives countries as long as ten years to repay loans.

IMF还为贫穷国家设立了另一个项目——"减少贫困，促进发展"，目的是让贫穷的国家以非常低的利率借贷。IMF其他项目的借贷利息都与开放市场挂钩。"减少贫困，促进发展”项目的还款期长达 10 年。

Many people around the world oppose the IMF. In recent years, thousands of demonstrators have protested outside meetings of the IMF and similar organizations. Many of these activists say IMF policies make industrial nations richer and developing nations poorer. They also say the organization's activities result in damage to the environment.

世界上有很多人反对 IMF。近几年来，IMF 和同类国际组织的会场外发生了数以千计的游行示威活动。很多示威者说，IMF 的政策使工业国家更富，发展中国家更穷。他们还认为该组织的行为导致了对环境的破坏。

Lesson 15 US States Fight Back to Protect Rights of Property Owners

By Brianna Blake

December 2, 2006

Part One Background Information

公共利益，有多少罪恶假汝之名而行

在城市建设中，房屋拆迁往往反映出官商之间的利益同盟关系。2005 年 6 月 23 日，美国最高法院竟然在凯洛诉康涅狄格州就新伦敦市一案作出判决，赋予地方政府为发展经济而征用私有房产所在土地的权力。而我国政府在拆迁方面迈出了一大步，于 2010 年 1 月 29 日公布了《国有土地上房屋征收与补偿条例（征求意见稿）》。之前实行的《城市房屋拆迁管理条例》被认为是“一项和血泪冲突的社会惨剧相伴相生的公共政策”①。新条例共五章四十一条，其立法理念与设计思路努力平衡公权与私权，对公共利益与私人利益的保障同等重视。多年来，城市拆迁肆虐，与政府公权在房屋拆迁上的不当作为密切相关。由于公共利益明显缺乏界定，行政权力于公于私均可畅行无阻，以致出现拆迁过程中令人惊骇的官商合谋。新条例首次以列举方式界定了“公共利益的需要”所包含的内容，明确了政府是公共利益征收的唯一补偿主体。除此之外，政府完全退出非公共利益项目的拆迁环节。这就使政府角色回到了公共机构的应有立场，官商之间的利益同盟至少在条例上得到了切割和厘清。这势必形成城市开发领域中政府、开发商与征收对象之间的新图景。

新条例还规定，如果政府出于公共利益的需要征收国有土地上的私人房屋，必须履行一系列法定程序，并且充分保证私产利益，比如必须两次公告相关信息，以不低于市场价格的补偿征收，在拆迁周转环节提供住房保障，不得使用非法、暴力手段等。虽然新条例附则部分有关非公共利益需要的拆迁规定不是很完善，令人忧心忡忡，但新条例毕竟是政府为杜绝公权、扶持商业开发而作出的首次努力。公民权益保障已然成为房屋拆迁中的关注焦点。

---

① http：//www. lawbase. com. cn/law_ info/lawbase_ @45281. htm，2010 - 04 - 06

Part Two Exercises

Ⅰ. Listen to the first part of the news, and complete the following sentences with the words you hear.

1. Local governments in the United States have always had a ______________________________.

2. This right is called eminent domain (土地征用权). Eminent domain has traditionally been limited to ______________________________.

3. But on June twenty-third of two thousand and five, ______________________________ of Kelo (凯洛案) versus the City of New London, Connecticut.

4. The decision gave local governments ______________________________.

5. That means a ______________________ not only for reasons of public use, but also for private use.

6. Owners could have their property condemned ______________________________.

7. ______________________ supported the decision. Four opposed it.

Ⅱ. Listen to the second part of the news, and answer the following questions.

1. Why do supporters support the eminent domain?

2. Do most people feel the decision fair? What's the source?

3. What kind of group is the Castle Coalition?

4. What has been greatly increased over the past year according to the coalition's report?

5. When did the group publish a report?

6. What did local governments do in one year according to the report?

7. How many properties did local government condemn for the five-year period between 1998 and 2002?

8. Interpret the two words: threats and condemn, and say the difference between them.

9. What did local officials do following the Kelo decision?

10. What do most owners do when their properties are condemned and why?

Ⅲ. Listen to the third part of the news, and translate it into Chinese, then repeat it in English.

Part Three Keys to the Exercises

Ⅰ. Listen to the first part of the news, and complete the following sentences with the words you hear.

1. Local governments in the United States have always had a constitutional right to seize private property, with fair payment.

2. This right is called eminent domain（土地征用权）. Eminent domain has traditionally been limited to the taking of land for public uses like roads, schools or bridges.

3. But on June twenty-third of two thousand and five, the Supreme Court decided the case of Kelo（凯洛案）versus the City of New London, Connecticut.

4. The decision gave local governments the right to take private property for the purpose of

economic development.

5. That means a homeowner or business owner could be forced to move not only for reasons of public use, but also for private use.

6. Owners could have their property condemned if officials decide that another owner could make more money on that property.

7. Five of the nine justices on the Supreme Court supported the decision. Four opposed it.

Ⅱ. Listen to the second part of the news, and answer the following questions.

1. Why do supporters support the eminent domain?

Supporters say eminent domain is needed to improve economically depressed areas and create growth and new jobs.

2. Do most people feel the decision fair? What's the source?

No, all across the country, opinion studies showed that most people did not feel the decision was fair.

3. What kind of group is the Castle Coalition?

The Castle Coalition is a nonprofit group that is part of the Institute for Justice, which fought the Kelo case before the Supreme Court.

4. What has been greatly increased over the past year according to the coalition's report?

The coalition says the threatened use of eminent domain for private development has greatly increased over the past year.

5. When did the group publish a report?

The group published a report in June, the anniversary of the Kelo decision.

6. What did local governments do in one year according to the report?

It said that in one year, local governments had threatened or condemned nearly six thousand properties for private development.

7. How many properties did local government condemn for the five-year period between 1998 and 2002?

Less than 12, 000 (6, 000 × 2). It said that in one year, local goverments had threatened or condemned nearly six thousand properties for private development. That, it said, was equal to more than half the number for the five-year period between nineteen ninety-eight and two thousand and two.

8. Interpret the two words: threats and condemn, and say the difference between them.

Condemn refers to: to take (private property) for public use by the power of eminent domain; expropriate;

Threat refers to: possibility to be expropriated.

But, while the number of threats increased sharply, officials rarely had to act on their threats. Officials must act on their condemn.

9. What did local officials do following the Kelo decision?

The report said local officials took steps to condemn three hundred fifty-four properties for private use in the year following the Kelo decision.

10. What do most owners do when their properties are condemned and why?

The coalition says owners largely choose not to fight what they believe will be a hopeless battle.

Ⅲ. Listen to the third part of the news, and translate it into Chinese, then repeat it in English.

1. Under the ruling, no one's property is safe unless individual states pass their own laws to restrict eminent domain.
按此判断，谁的房产都不安全，除非各州制定自己的法律限制土地征用权。
2. And that is just what they have done.
这正是许多州的做法。
3. The Castle Coalition reported last month that thirty-four of the fifty states have passed laws that aim to restrict eminent domain.
城堡联盟上个月一报告说，50 个州已有 34 个通过了旨在限制土地征用权的法律。
4. That includes nine states where voters passed ballot measures in the November seventh elections.
它们当中有九个州在 11 月 7 日的选举中通过了差额投票。
5. Some state laws do more to protect the rights of property owners than others.
有的州比其他州有更多的立法来保护业主的权利。
6. Lisa Knepper of the Institute for Justice says it is still too soon to tell the effects of these new laws.
正义研究所的李萨·内柏说，现在谈论这些新法的效果还为时过早。
7. But efforts are also being made to pass federal legislation to protect all property owners from eminent domain for private development.
但有人正在努力通过联邦立法来保护业主，使其财产免受因私人发展的目的而被强制征用。

Part Four　Translation of the Text

US States Fight Back to Protect Rights of Property Owners
美国各州为保护业主权利而奋战

Local governments in the United States have always had a constitutional right to seize private property, with fair payment. This right is called eminent domain. Eminent domain has traditionally been limited to the taking of land for public uses like roads, schools or bridges.

在美国，地方政府始终有宪法赋予的在合理补偿情况下征用私有房产的权力。这一权利被称为征用权。传统上，征用权被限制在只能征用作为公共用途，比如公路、学校和桥梁的土地。

But on June twenty-third of two thousand and five, the Supreme Court decided the case of Kelo versus the City of New London, Connecticut. The decision gave local governments the right to take private property for the purpose of economic development.

但在 2005 年 6 月 23 日，最高法院对凯洛诉康涅狄格州新伦敦市一案作出判决。这一判决赋予地方政府为发展经济的目的而征用私有房产的权力。

That means a homeowner or business owner could be forced to move not only for reasons of public use, but also for private use. Owners could have their property condemned if officials decide that another owner could make more money on that property.

这意味着房屋或企业的所有者不仅仅是因公共用途的原因，因私人用途也可能被强迫搬出。一旦官员们认为另一拥有者可以利用该房产赚取更多的钱，所有者的产业就可能被强迫征收。

Five of the nine justices on the Supreme Court supported the decision. Four opposed it.

最高法院的九名大法官中有五人赞成该判决，四人反对。

Supporters say eminent domain is needed to improve economically depressed areas and create growth and new jobs.

支持者认为需要使用征用权在经济萧条地区刺激经济增长和增加新的就业。

But all across the country, opinion studies showed that most people did not feel the decision was fair.

但在全国来说，民意调查显示大部分民众认为这一判决不公平。

The Castle Coalition is a nonprofit group that is part of the Institute for Justice, which fought the Kelo case before the Supreme Court. The coalition says the threatened use of eminent domain for private development has greatly increased over the past year. The group published a report in June, the anniversary of the Kelo decision.

城堡联盟是正义研究所旗下的一个非营利性组织。正义研究所在最高法院为凯洛辩护。联盟称，在过去一年中，因私人的发展目的而威胁使用征用权的案例大大增加。该组织在凯洛案判决一周年即六月份发布了一份研究报告。

It said that in one year, local governments had threatened or condemned nearly six thousand properties for private development. That, it said, was equal to more than half the number for the five-year period between nineteen ninety-eight and two thousand and two.

报告称在一年的时间里，地方政府对将近六千所房产因私人目的威胁式使用征用权。据说，这一数字超过了 1998 到 2002 年这 5 年间数量的一半。

But, while the number of threats increased sharply, officials rarely had to act on their threats. The report said local officials took steps to condemn three hundred fifty-four properties for private use in the year following the Kelo decision. The coalition says owners largely choose not to fight what they believe will be a hopeless battle.

不过，虽然迫拆迁的情况急剧增多，官员却极少真正付诸行动。报告称，在凯洛案判决后的一年，地方官员因私人用途采取措施征用了 354 处房产。联盟称，业主对这种被认为没有胜利希望的斗争大都选择不反抗。

Under the ruling, no one's property is safe unless individual states pass their own laws to restrict eminent domain. And that is just what they have done.

按此判决，谁的房产都不安全，除非各州制定自己的法律限制土地征用权。这正是许多州的做法。

The Castle Coalition reported last month that thirty-four of the fifty states have passed laws that aim to restrict eminent domain. That includes nine states where voters passed ballot measures in the November seventh elections.

城堡联盟上个月一报告说，50 个州已有 34 个州通过了旨在限制土地征用权的法律。它们当中有九个州在 11 月 7 日的选举中通过了差额投票。

Some state laws do more to protect the rights of property owners than others. Lisa Knepper of the Institute for Justice says it is still too soon to tell the effects of these new laws. But efforts are also being made to pass federal legislation to protect all property owners from eminent domain for private development.

有的州比其他州有更多的立法来保护业主的权利。正义研究所的李萨·内柏说，现在谈论这些新法的效果还为时过早。但有人正在努力通过联邦立法来保护业主，使其财产免受因私人发展的目的而被强制征用。

(This is IN THE NEWS in VOA *Special English*, written by Brianna Blake. I'm Steve Ember.)

第二部分　区域性新闻热点

Lesson 16　East Asian Leaders Form New Group to Improve the Area's Future

By Nancy Steinbach

December 17，2005

Part One　Background Information

亚洲如果团结起来就能充分显示其“人多势众”的优势，这主要表现在前面有关博弈论一课中提到的“合作带来的政治利益”，另一方面则表现在世界最大的四个经济区域中，亚洲就占三个，他们在经济上的合作将决定世界贸易的发展趋势。2005 年 12 月 14 日，在马来西亚首都吉隆坡召开的首届东亚峰会就证明了这一点。峰会当天发表的《吉隆坡宣言》明确了东亚峰会的性质和东盟的主导作用，并决定将定期举行东亚峰会。此前，它与每年的东盟首脑会议同期举行，目的在于加快东亚地区在政治、经济和安全等领域的合作。

东亚峰会参加国都表示愿意本着平等的伙伴精神和协商一致的原则，加强合作，增进友谊，创造一个和平的环境，为本地区及世界的和平、安全与经济繁荣作出贡献。各国领导人都认识到将东亚峰会建成一个以东盟为主导的开放、包容、透明和外向型的论坛，就共同关注的战略、政治和经济问题进行对话，才能使东亚在贸易和影响力方面不至于输给美国和欧洲。

第一届东亚峰会发布了《关于预防、控制和应对禽流感的东亚峰会宣言》，参与国表示“要加强联系，与所有相关方建立伙伴关系，分享信息，协调地区性倡议等”，同时“进一步认识到预防和控制禽流感是全球的责任，需要政府、社区和商界之间的紧密配合和共同努力以及相关地区和国际组织及机制的积极参与”①。

第二届东亚峰会于 2007 年 1 月 15 日在菲律宾宿务国际会议中心闭幕。针对全球所面临的能源问题，出席会议的东盟十国和中国、日本、韩国、印度、澳大利亚和新西兰的国家元首或政府首脑签署了《东亚能源安全宿务宣言》，提出了东亚地区能源合作的具体目标和措施。与会领导人宣布将共同合作改善能源的使用效率和环境效应；通过强化有关能效和节能计划，利用水力，扩大可再生能源系统和生物燃料的生产和利用，开发民用核能，减少对传统能源的依赖；营造开放和具有竞争力的地区和国际市场，致力于在各个经济层面提供价格上可承受的能源；减少温室气体排放；通过私营部门的更多参与，寻求和

---

① 关于预防、控制和应对禽流感的东亚峰会宣言. www. moh. gov. cn，2005 - 12 - 21

鼓励针对能源及基础设施开发的投资。

东亚峰会的重大意义在于，它为东亚人民提供了新的合作平台，为各国应对共同面临的问题设定了共同的目标，并制订相应的行动计划。比如在能源问题上，东亚各国通过创新融资机制，增加对东盟电网和跨东盟天然气管道等能源基础设施的投资，从而确保稳定的能源供应，改善能源供应的国际合作环境。至于这个新组织能否在未来具有与欧盟一样的经济实力，还要看将来其内部的合作与发展。

Part Two　Exercises

Ⅰ. Listen to the first part of the news, and fill in the blanks with the words you hear.

1. Two meetings this week in Asia could set ________________________________, and the future of Asia itself.
2. In Kuala Lumpur, leaders of sixteen countries held ________________________.
3. The leaders met Wednesday in ____________________ to plan for a united future.
4. They agreed to create a group that will work together to improve ________________.

Ⅱ. Listen to the second part of the news, and answer the following questions.

1. Can you name the countries in the new group in Asia?

2. How important is this group in terms of population?

3. How important is this group in terms of world trade?

4. What is this trend in the future?

5. What is the significance of the new group?

Ⅲ. Listen to the third and fourth part of the news, and translate them into Chinese sentence by sentence, then repeat them in English.

From "For now, the sixteen leaders. . . " to ". . . that negotiates trade rules".

Ⅳ. Listen to the last part of the news for three times according to the following order, and repeat it in English, then write it down.

1. The last ministerial conference (Cancun, Mexico) . . .
2. Objections by poor countries. . .
3. The United States, the European Union and Japan. . .
4. They announced. . .
5. They also announced plans. . .
6. Some officials, however, said. . .
7. The WTO had hoped. . .
8. Now the hope is to have. . .
9. But in Hong Kong Friday, Reuters news agency. . .
10. And developing countries. . .
11. European Union Trade Commissioner Peter Mandelson said. . .
12. The meeting. . .

Part Three　Keys to the Exercises

Ⅰ. Listen to the first part of the news, and fill in blanks with the words you hear.

1. Two meetings this week in Asia could set the direction for the future of world trade, and the future of Asia itself.

2. In Kuala Lumpur, leaders of sixteen countries held the first East Asia Summit.

3. The leaders met Wednesday in the Malaysian capital to plan for a united future.

4. They agreed to create a group that will work together to improve economic, security and political conditions in Asia.

Ⅱ. Listen to the second part of the news, and answer the following questions.

1. Can you name the countries in the group in Asia?

The new sixteen-member group will include both China and India. The leaders represented the ten members of ASEAN, the Association of Southeast Asian Nations. They also represented Australia, China, India, Japan, New Zealand and South Korea including ten countries in ASEAN.

2. How important is this group in terms of population?

1) The sixteen-member group will represent about three thousand million people

2) Half the world's population.

3. How important is this group in terms of world trade?

It will represent about twenty percent of world trade.

4. What is this trend in the future?

Both numbers are expected to increase in the future. An expert on Asia says it will have three of the four largest economies in the world by two thousand fifty.

5. What is the significance of the new group?

Some Asian leaders say the new group is needed because East Asia does not want to lose trade and influence to the Americas and Europe. Supporters say the new group could become an economic force like the European Union in the future.

Ⅲ. Listen the third and fourth part of the news, and translate them into Chinese sentence by sentence, then repeat them in English.

For now, the sixteen leaders from Asia and the Pacific have agreed to meet again next year. They plan to meet in the Philippine capital, Manila, just after the next ASEAN meeting.

目前，来自亚洲及太平洋地区的16位领导人已经同意明年再次召开会议，地点选在菲律宾首都——马尼拉，就在下一届的东盟会议之后召开。

The other big meeting in Asia this week is the ministerial conference of the World Trade Organization. There are protests outside, as at earlier meetings.

本星期于亚洲举行的另一会议是世界贸易组织的部长会议，正如其他早期举行的会议一样，会场外有人举行抗议。

The WTO has one hundred forty-eight members. It is the only international organization that negotiates trade rules.

WTO有148位成员国，是唯一一个可以协商贸易规则的国际性组织。

Ⅳ. Listen to the last part of the news for three times according to the following order, and repeat it in English, then write it down.

1. The last ministerial conference two years ago in Cancun, Mexico, ended without a new trade agreement.

2. Objections by poor countries to agricultural support programs and trade barriers in wealthy ones were major issues.

3. The United States, the European Union and Japan said they have been trying to avoid such problems in Hong Kong.

4. They announced plans for thousands of millions of dollars in aid to poor countries.

5. They also announced plans to end import taxes on goods from some of these nations.

6. Some officials, however, said the proposals came with too many conditions.

7. The WTO had hoped for a free trade agreement by the end of last year on trade in farm and industrial goods and services.

8. Now the hope is to have one completed by the end of two thousand six.

9. But in Hong Kong Friday, Reuters news agency said rich nations were arguing over protected farm markets.

10. And developing countries threatened to block any deal that did not give them better prices for bananas, sugar and cotton.

11. European Union Trade Commissioner Peter Mandelson said the talks were, if anything, "going backwards".

12. The meeting is to end on Sunday.

Part Four Translation of the Text

East Asian Leaders Form New Group to Improve the Area's Future
东亚领袖们为促进未来发展建构新的组织

Two meetings this week in Asia could set the direction for the future of world trade, and the future of Asia itself.

本星期于亚洲举行的两次会议将有可能确定世界贸易和亚洲自身未来的发展方向。

In Kuala Lumpur, leaders of sixteen countries held the first East Asia Summit. The leaders met Wednesday in the Malaysian capital to plan for a united future. They agreed to create a group that will work together to improve economic, security and political conditions in Asia.

16位国家领导人于吉隆坡举行第一次东亚峰会。各国领导星期三在马来西亚首都商讨未来合作计划。他们同意成立一个组织，共同合作，促进亚洲经济、国防及政治局势。

The new sixteen-member group will include both China and India. The leaders represented the ten members of ASEAN, the Association of Southeast Asian Nations. They also represented Australia, China, India, Japan, New Zealand and South Korea.

由16个国家组成的新组织将包括印度与中国这两个国家。这些领导人代表着东盟（东南亚国家联盟）的十个成员国，也代表了澳大利亚、中国、印度、日本、新西兰和韩国。

The sixteen-member group will represent about three thousand million people, half the world's population. And it will represent about twenty percent of world trade.

这个16个成员国组织将代表着占世界半数人口的约30亿人民，其贸易占世界贸易的百分之二十。

Both numbers are expected to increase in the future. An expert on Asia says it will have three of the four largest economies in the world by two thousand fifty. Some Asian leaders say the new group is needed because East Asia does not want to lose trade and influence to the Americas and Europe. Supporters say the new group could become an economic force like the European Union in the future.

以上两组数据在未来都将增加。一位亚洲专家认为，到 2050 年，该地区将占有四个世界最大经济区域中的三个。部分亚洲领导人认为，成立这个新组织是很有必要的，因为东亚不想在贸易和国家影响力方面输给美国和欧洲。支持者认为，这个新组织未来可能具有与欧盟一样的经济实力。

But that will take work. For now, the sixteen leaders from Asia and the Pacific have agreed to meet again next year. They plan to meet in the Philippine capital, Manila, just after the next ASEAN meeting.

但那尚需努力。目前，来自亚洲及太平洋地区的 16 位领导人已经同意明年再次召开会议，地点选在菲律宾首都——马尼拉，就在下一届的东盟会议之后召开。

The other big meeting in Asia this week is the ministerial conference of the World Trade Organization. There are protests outside, as at earlier meetings.

本星期于亚洲举行的另一会议是世界贸易组织的部长会议，正如其他早期举行的会议一样，会场外有人举行抗议。

The WTO has one hundred forty-eight members. It is the only international organization that negotiates trade rules. The last ministerial conference two years ago in Cancun, Mexico, ended without a new trade agreement. Objections by poor countries to agricultural support programs and trade barriers in wealthy ones were major issues.

WTO 有 148 位成员国，是唯一一个可以协商贸易规则的国际性组织。上一次部长会议于两年前在墨西哥的康城举行，结束时没有达成新的贸易协定。其中最大的问题是贫困国家反对富裕国家的农业津贴计划与贸易壁垒。

The United States, the European Union and Japan said they have been trying to avoid such problems in Hong Kong. They announced plans for thousands of millions of dollars in aid to poor countries. They also announced plans to end import taxes on goods from some of these nations. Some officials, however, said the proposals came with too many conditions.

美国、欧盟和日本反映，他们一直试图努力阻止此类事件在香港发生。他们宣布拨款数十亿美元资助穷困国家与取消其中一些国家商品进口税的计划。但有官员认为这些提议所附带的条件太多。

The WTO had hoped for a free trade agreement by the end of last year on trade in farm and industrial goods and services. Now the hope is to have one completed by the end of two thousand six. But in Hong Kong Friday, Reuters news agency said rich nations were arguing over protected farm markets. And developing countries threatened to block any deal that did not give them better prices for bananas, sugar and cotton.

WTO 希望在去年年底达成农产品、工业用品和服务业的贸易协定。目前的期望是在 2006 年底能够达成一项协议。路透社星期五在香港报道说，富裕国家不断争论要保护农业市场，而发展中国家则威胁说，如果世贸组织不给香蕉、白糖、棉花较好的价格，他们将抵制任何协定。

European Union Trade Commissioner Peter Mandelson said the talks were, if anything, "going backwards". The meeting is to end on Sunday.

欧盟贸易委员会委员彼德·曼迪逊认为，如果说谈判有什么成效的话，就是"倒退"，会议将于本周日结束。

Lesson 17　After French and Dutch Reject EU Constitution, What Now?

By Jerilyn Watson

June 4, 2005

Part One　Background Information

欧　盟[①]

一、欧洲联盟（简称欧盟）发展简史

欧盟，由欧洲共同体演变而来，其总部设在比利时首都布鲁塞尔。

20 世纪 40 年代，美苏争霸令全球动荡不安，西欧国家感到，要在美苏两大国之间保证自己的安全，提高国际地位，加快经济发展，必须联合起来。因而 1951 年，在法国经济学家和外交家莫内的建议下，法国、联邦德国、意大利、比利时、荷兰和卢森堡六国签署了《罗马条约》，决定把各自的煤钢工业置于共同管理之下，建立欧洲煤钢联营。1965 年 4 月 8 日，六国又签订了《布鲁塞尔条约》，决定将欧洲煤钢共同体、欧洲原子能共同体、欧洲经济共同体的机构合并，统称欧洲共同体，但三个组织仍各自存在，具有独立法人资格。《布鲁塞尔条约》于 1967 年 7 月 1 日生效，欧洲共同体正式成立。1967 年，三个机构合并为欧洲共同体，争取在成员国之间逐步实现商品、人员、劳务和资本的自由交流，并于 1968 年 7 月 1 日实现了关税同盟。英国、丹麦、爱尔兰、希腊、西班牙和葡萄牙先后加入欧共体，其成员国扩大到 12 个。欧共体 12 国间建立起了关税同盟，统一了外贸政策和农业政策，创立了欧洲货币体系，并建立了统一预算和政治合作制度，逐步发展成为欧洲国家经济、政治利益的代言人。

1991 年 12 月 11 日，欧共体马斯特里赫特首脑会议通过了以建立欧洲经济货币联盟和欧洲政治联盟为目标的《欧洲联盟条约》（通称《马斯特里赫特条约》，简称《马约》）。1993 年 11 月 1 日《马约》生效，欧洲联盟成立，标志着欧共体从经济实体向着经济政治实体的过渡。《马约》生效后，欧共体未就其称谓的变更问题作出决定，但欧共体内和国际上越来越广泛地使用"欧洲联盟"（简称"欧盟"），目前"欧共体"和"欧盟"两种称谓均可使用，但法律文件和对外签署协议仍需用"欧共体"。

1995 年 1 月 1 日，奥地利、瑞典和芬兰三国正式加入欧洲联盟，其成员国扩大到 15 个。1997 年 7 月 16 日，欧盟委员会提出首批东扩名单。1999 年 1 月 1 日欧元（euro）正式启用。

二、欧盟的宗旨

早期的《罗马条约》申明，各成员国"决心在欧洲各国人民之间建立愈益密切的联

---

① http://www.cistc.gov.cn/embassymember/browse.asp id=47593&site=6220

合基础，逐步废止国际交流的限制”，“保证它们国家的经济和社会进步，执行共同的贸易政策”。1986 年 2 月签署的《欧洲单一文化》强调，“欧洲共同体及欧洲政治合作旨在促进欧洲的团结发展”，“共同为维护世界和平与安全作出应有的贡献”。1991 年 12 月，欧共体签署的具有历史意义的《马斯特里赫特条约》，正式确立了欧洲经货联盟和政治联盟的目标，勾画出经济和货币联盟的前景。2002 年 1 月 1 日欧元开始流通，三个月后区内各国货币将停止使用。单一货币将成为推动欧盟进一步融合和经济政治化的核心力量。

欧盟将在经货联盟的基础上结成政治联盟，最高目标是成立泛欧联邦式合众国。2005 年以后欧盟开始组建自己的防御力量。2010 年，欧盟拟建“联邦”警察部队和检察机构。

三、欧盟宪章

《欧盟宪章》是欧盟的首部宪法，其宗旨是保证欧盟的有效运作以及欧洲一体化进程的顺利发展。《欧盟宪法条约》由欧盟宪法、欧盟公民基本权利宪章、欧盟政策和欧盟条约基本规定 4 个部分组成。其主要内容包括：设立欧洲理事会主席和欧盟外交部长，组建欧盟外交部，以保持欧盟工作的连续性。欧洲理事会主席的主要职能是为欧盟首脑会议做准备，并主持首脑会议。主席由欧洲理事会（由各成员国国家元首或政府首脑、欧洲理事会主席、欧盟委员会主席和欧盟外长组成，后三者没有表决权）以有效多数表决方式选举产生，任期为两年半，可连选连任一次，主席不能同时在成员国任职。欧盟外交部长由欧洲理事会以有效多数表决方式选举产生，主要负责欧盟共同外交与安全政策，同时也是欧盟委员会副主席。改革欧盟委员会，扩大欧洲议会的权力；改革欧盟理事会和欧盟部长理事会的表决机制；欧盟成员国加强在共同防务政策方面的合作。

《欧盟宪章》草案于 2004 年 6 月 18 日在欧盟布鲁塞尔首脑会议上通过。同年 10 月 29 日，欧盟 25 个成员国的领导人在意大利首都罗马签署了这项条约。根据有关规定，宪法条约签署后还需要欧洲议会以及欧盟各成员国根据本国的法律规定予以认可方可生效。如果顺利得到各成员国认可，《欧盟宪法条约》将于 2006 年 11 月 1 日正式生效。

目前已有 9 个国家通过了《欧盟宪法条约》，但《欧盟宪法条约》必须得到全部 25 个欧盟成员国通过才能生效。宪法条约规定，条约生效后产生的第一届欧盟委员会仍然实行现行的一个成员国一名委员的制度。从第二届起，欧盟委员会委员的人数将是欧盟成员国数目的三分之二，由各成员国轮流提名。宪法条约拓宽了欧洲议会同欧盟部长理事会在立法和预算方面进行“共同决策”的领域，赋予欧洲议会在欧洲理事会提名的前提下选举欧盟委员会主席的权力。为保障人口少的成员国的权益，条约规定欧洲议会的议员人数不能超过 750 名，每个成员国至少拥有 6 个名额，最多不能超过 96 个名额。

欧盟成员国必须尽其所有的军事和民用能力用于欧盟共同防务政策的实施，最终目标是发展欧盟共同防务。条约规定，一旦某一个成员国受到外来侵略或恐怖袭击，其他成员国必须提供一切资源进行援助，包括军事资源。

Part Two Exercises

Ⅰ. Listen to the first part of the news, and fill in the table that shows what European countries or country officials did for the EU Constitution.

European Countries or Country Officials	Approve or Reject	Time or Place
French President		
Voters in France and Netherlands		Earlier this week.
Parliament of Latvia		
British Foreign Minister Jack Straw		
The government of Prime Minister Tony Blair		
Leaders of all member nations		June16 – 17 in Brussels

Ⅱ. Listen to the second part of the news, and take down what is missing in the following sentences.

1 The constitution ______________________________.

2. It would ______________________________.

3. ______________________ are several hundred pages.

4. The goal is to increase ______________________________.

5. ______________ of French voters, and ______________ of Dutch voters, said "no".

6. France and the Netherlands ______________________________.

7. In nineteen fifty-one they were among six nations ______________________.

8. That led to the ______________________________.

9. Last year the union admitted ______________________________.

10. ______________ hope to join next year. ______________ is to begin membership talks in October.

Ⅲ. Listen to the third part of the news, and answer the following questions.

1. Why did the French opponents reject the EU constitution?

2. Who is Jean-Pierre Raffarin? And who is Dominique de Villepin ? Why do you think the former prime minister was dismissed?

3. Why did the Dutch voters reject the EU constitution?

Ⅳ. Listen to the last part of the news, and translate it into Chinese.

Part Three Keys to the Exercises

Ⅰ. Listen to the first part of the news, and fill in the table that shows what European countries or country officials did for the EU Constitution.

European Countries or Country Officials	Approve or Reject	Time or Place
French President	Could not gain enough support to approve the EU Constitution.	
Voters in France and Netherlands	Rejected it.	Earlier this week
Parliament of Latvia	Approved it.	
British Foreign Minister Jack Straw	Is expected to discuss the issue Monday in Parliament.	
The government of Prime Minister Tony Blair	Has not said if it will hold a national vote.	
Leaders of all member nations	Could decide to re-negotiate the document and concider what to do when they meet.	June16 – 17 in Brussels

Ⅱ. Listen to the second part of the news, and take down what is missing in the following sentences.

1. The constitution took two years to negotiate.
2. It would replace several treaties.
3. Versions in different languages are several hundred pages.
4. The goal is to increase the influence of the European Union with its more than four hundred fifty million people.
5. But fifty-five percent of French voters, and sixty-two percent of Dutch voters, said "no".

6. France and the Netherlands hold important places in European Union history.

7. In nineteen fifty-one they were among six nations that established the European Steel and Coal Community.

8. That led to the European Economic Community and, in nineteen ninety-three, the European Union.

9. Last year the union admitted ten more countries to reach twenty-five.

10. Bulgaria and Romania hope to join next year. Turkey is to begin membership talks in October.

Ⅲ. Listen to the third part of the news, and answer the following questions.

1. Why did the French opponents reject the EU constitution?

1) They argued that France would lose power and influence if a central EU government gained strength.

2) Economic problems for the French, and popularity problems for Jacques Chirac, may have also influenced voters.

3) Mister Chirac says the rejection means France will have trouble defending its interests in Europe.

2. Who is Jean-Pierre Raffarin? And who is Dominique de Villepin ? Why do you think the former prime minister was dismissed?

He was the former Prime Minister. This week, Mister Chirac dismissed Jean-Pierre Raffarin. The new prime minister is Dominique de Villepin.

So , that may be because the president want to campaign for the constitution together with the new PM.

3. Why did the Dutch voters reject the EU constitution?

1) The Dutch government also campaigned for the constitution. But some voters said the EU administration in Brussels was getting too big and powerful.

2) Observers say concerns about the Dutch economy and EU immigration policies only added to the opposition.

Ⅳ. Listen to the last part of the news, and translate it into Chinese.

The constitutional crisis has affected the euro. Twelve EU nations created a single money system in nineteen ninety-nine. In recent days the euro fell to eight-month lows against the dollar.

欧盟的宪章危机已经影响了欧元。欧元是12个欧盟国家于1999年创立的一种独立货币系统。最近几天，欧元兑美元的汇率降到了8个月里的最低点。

Besides Latvia, the nations that have ratified the constitution include Lithuania, Hungary, Slovenia, Italy and Greece. The others are Austria, Slovakia, Spain and Germany. Of the ten, only Spain held a national vote; the others approved it in their parliaments.

除了拉脱维亚，还有立陶宛、匈牙利、斯洛文尼亚、意大利和希腊批准了欧盟宪章。

其他国家是奥地利、捷克斯洛伐克、西班牙和德国。但在这十个国家中，只有西班牙通过全民投票的方式进行决议，其他几个国家是由议会通过的。

Part Four　Translation of the Text

After French and Dutch Reject EU Constitution What Now?
法国与荷兰否决了欧盟宪章，下步如何走？

French President Jacques Chirac could not gain enough support to approve the EU Constitution.

法国总统希拉克无法获得足够的支持以通过欧盟宪章。

Leaders of the European Union are trying to rescue the proposed EU constitution. Voters in France and the Netherlands rejected it earlier this week. However, the parliament of Latvia approved it. Ten countries now have accepted the constitution.

欧盟的领导人们正试图挽救欧盟宪章提案。本周早些时候法国和荷兰选民否决了该宪章。但拉脱维亚国会通过了此宪章。到目前为止，有十个国家接受了欧盟宪章。

German Chancellor Gerhard Schroeder says all twenty-five should have a chance to say "yes" or "no". Mister Schroeder and French President Jacques Chirac set up a meeting Saturday in Berlin to discuss the situation.

德国总理施罗德说，所有 25 个欧盟成员国都有机会对欧盟宪章表示同意或者反对。施罗德和法国总统希拉克将于本周六在柏林进行一次会晤来讨论目前的情况。

British Foreign Minister Jack Straw is expected to discuss the issue Monday in Parliament. The government of Prime Minister Tony Blair has not said if it will hold a national vote.

英国外务大臣杰克·斯特劳将在周一的英国议会上讨论欧盟宪章的问题。布莱尔政府还没有确定是否要举行一场全民投票表决。

All member nations must approve the constitution. But leaders could decide to re-negotiate the document. They will consider what to do when they meet June sixteenth and seventeenth in Brussels.

该宪章必须获得所有成员国的赞成（才能生效）。但是各国领导人都可决定是否就宪章内容进行重新谈判。他们将于 6 月 16 日、17 日在布鲁塞尔的会晤中探讨下一步行动。

The constitution took two years to negotiate. It would replace several treaties. Versions in different languages are several hundred pages. The goal is to increase the influence of the European Union with its more than four hundred fifty million people.

欧盟宪章的谈判已历经两年，它将取代几个条约。其不同语言的版本达数百页，目的在于提高有着 4. 5 亿人口的欧盟的影响力。

But fifty-five percent of French voters, and sixty-two percent of Dutch voters, said "no". France and the Netherlands hold important places in European Union history. In nineteen fifty-one they were among six nations that established the European Steel and Coal Community. That led to the European Economic Community and, in nineteen ninety-three, the European Union.

但是55%的法国投票者和62%的荷兰投票者对这部宪章说“不”。法国和荷兰两国在欧盟的发展史上举足轻重。1951年，他们是六个组建欧洲钢铁和煤炭联盟国家中的成员。钢铁煤炭联盟后来演变成欧洲经济共同体，1993年成为现在的欧盟。

Last year the union admitted ten more countries to reach twenty-five. Bulgaria and Romania hope to join next year. Turkey is to begin membership talks in October.

去年，欧盟吸纳了10个国家，目前已有25个成员国。保加利亚和罗马尼亚希望明年能够加入（欧盟）。土耳其的入盟谈判将在10月份开始。

French opponents of the constitution argued that France would lose power and influence if a central EU government gained strength. Economic problems for the French, and popularity problems for Jacques Chirac, may have also influenced voters. Mister Chirac says the rejection means France will have trouble defending its interests in Europe.

法国欧盟宪章的反对者们认为，如果以欧盟为中心的政府权力过大，法国将失去它（在欧洲）的权力和影响力。法国面临的经济问题和希拉克本人的声望都是影响本次投票的因素。希拉克声称，对欧盟宪章的拒绝意味着法国在欧洲的利益很难得到保障。

The president had campaigned for the constitution. So had the prime minister. This week, Mister Chirac dismissed Jean-Pierre Raffarin. The new prime minister is Dominique de Villepin.

法国总统大力推行欧盟宪章运动。总理也是倡导者。本周希拉克解除了让-皮埃尔·拉法兰的总理职务，新总理由多米尼克·德维尔潘担任。

The Dutch government also campaigned for the constitution. But some voters said the EU administration in Brussels was getting too big and powerful. Observers say concerns about the Dutch economy and EU immigration policies only added to the opposition.

荷兰政府也极力推崇欧盟宪章。但是一部分投票者认为布鲁塞尔的欧盟行政机构庞大，权力过大。观察家们认为对荷兰本国经济和欧洲移民政策的关注恰恰强化了人们（对欧盟宪章）的反对意见。

The constitutional crisis has affected the euro. Twelve EU nations created a single money system in nineteen ninety-nine. In recent days the euro fell to eight-month lows against the dollar.

欧盟的宪章危机已经影响了欧元。欧元是12个欧盟国家于1999年创立的一种独立货币系统。最近几天，欧元兑美元的汇率降到了8个月里的最低点。

Besides Latvia, the nations that have ratified the constitution include Lithuania, Hungary, Slovenia, Italy and Greece. The others are Austria, Slovakia, Spain and Germany. Of the ten, only Spain held a national vote; the others approved it in their parliaments.

除了拉脱维亚，还有立陶宛、匈牙利、斯洛文尼亚、意大利和希腊批准了欧盟宪章。其他国家是奥地利、捷克斯洛伐克、西班牙和德国。但在这十个国家中，只有西班牙通过全民投票的方式进行决议，其他几个国家是由议会通过的。

Lesson 18　Israel Withdrawing from Gaza after 38 Years

By Nancy Steinbach
August 12，2005

Part One　Background Information

一、巴勒斯坦与以色列冲突的渊源

2005 年，加沙被占领 38 年之后，终于回归巴勒斯坦人民的怀抱。巴勒斯坦被认为是一块“流着蜜与油”的土地，这片沃土上的人们却让它伤痕累累、满目疮痍，这一切源于不同种族在这里“创造”的历史事件。早在公元前 20 世纪前后，闪米特族的迦南人定居在巴勒斯坦的沿海和平原。公元前 13 世纪腓力斯人也来到沿海建立国家，公元前 13 世纪末希伯来各部落迁入定居，公元前 11 世纪犹太人建立希伯来王国。之后亚述、巴比伦、波斯等外族都曾占领过巴勒斯坦。公元前 1 世纪罗马帝国入侵，绝大部分犹太人被迫流往世界各地，为以后的犹太复国运动埋下了“伏笔”。到公元 7 世纪，巴勒斯坦成为阿拉伯帝国的一部分。此后阿拉伯人不断移入，并和当地土著居民同化，逐步形成了现代巴勒斯坦阿拉伯人。19 世纪末在“犹太复国运动”者的策动下，大批犹太人从世界各地移入巴勒斯坦，因为移民人数一开始没有限制，与当地阿拉伯人发生了多次流血冲突事件。

1920 年获得巴勒斯坦统治权的英国以约旦河为界把巴勒斯坦分为东西两部分，东部称外约旦（即今约旦王国），西部仍称巴勒斯坦（今以色列、约旦河西岸和加沙地带）为英国委任统治地。

二、联合国大会 181 号决议案

1947 年 11 月，联合国大会投票，以 33 票赞成，13 票反对，10 票弃权的结果，通过了巴勒斯坦分割案，即规定巴勒斯坦在 1948 年结束英国的委任统治后建立犹太国（约 1. 52 万平方千米）和阿拉伯国（约 1. 15 万平方千米），耶路撒冷（176 平方千米）国际化。此决议遭到所有阿拉伯人的极力反对。因为，在联合国大会 181 号决议发布时，巴勒斯坦境内居住的阿拉伯人占总人口的 68%，阿拉伯人拥有的土地占巴勒斯坦总面积的 94%。可是 181 号决议却规定把巴勒斯坦总面积的 57% 划给只占三分之一人口的犹太人，占三分之二人口的阿拉伯人只得到 43% 的土地。为什么要把近 60% 的土地分给只占三分之一人口的犹太人？联合国大会的决议案中没有任何解释①。不管从哪个角度来看，联合国大会 181 号决议明显偏向犹太人。

1948 年 5 月，以色列建国后推行扩张主义政策，在 1948 年、1956 年、1967 年、1973 年四次对阿拉伯国家的大规模战争中，100 多万巴勒斯坦阿拉伯人被赶出世代居住的家园，沦为难民。

① 佚名. 犹太复国主义政权——西方殖民的产物. http：//chinese. irib. ir/qudus/01. htm

三、巴以冲突之源——圣殿山

巴以半个多世纪的流血冲突，最大的症结就在于圣城耶路撒冷的地位，而耶路撒冷城争夺的根源或焦点，则集中在圣殿山的归属。2000年，当时的利库德领导人沙龙就是因为闯入这里，引燃了延续至今的巴以冲突。犹太人认为，巴勒斯坦是上帝“赠予”犹太人的土地，因为圣殿山还是古犹太人流传下来的称呼。犹太教古经典就曾记载，上帝为考验犹太始祖亚伯拉罕，让他在圣殿山一巨石上献祭独子以撒，后把这片土地分给了亚伯拉罕及其子孙。在基督教传说中，这块石头也被视为上帝用泥土捏成人类始祖亚当的地方。

公元前10世纪，雄才大略的犹太国王所罗门在这里建了第一圣殿，存放约柜、诺亚方舟等圣物。圣殿后来被毁，重建，但最终于公元2世纪被彻底毁灭，犹太人也被驱逐出故土，浪迹天涯。圣殿山的巴勒斯坦人，称此地为“圣地”。因为在这个当年的犹太圣殿遗址上矗立着有千百年历史的阿克萨清真寺和金顶清真寺，所以耶路撒冷也成为伊斯兰教继麦加和麦地那后的第三大胜地。原来的犹太圣殿遗迹几乎荡然无存。

四、阿以间的四次大规模战争

第一次中东战争又称巴勒斯坦战争。1948年5月15日（以色列建国第二天），约旦、埃及、叙利亚、黎巴嫩和伊拉克等国为反对以色列建国，组织了阿拉伯军团对以色列发动圣战。此次战争以以色列胜利告终。结果是，以色列不仅保住了分治决议划定的1.52万平方千米，还占领了划给巴勒斯坦人建国的6 700平方千米土地和耶路撒冷西区；约旦占领了约旦河西岸的4 800平方千米土地和耶路撒冷老城，埃及控制了加沙350平方千米的土地①。

第二次中东战争，又称苏伊士运河战争。1956年7月26日，埃及总统纳赛尔宣布将英、法投资修建的苏伊士运河收归国有，英、法、以向埃及发动侵略战争，占领西奈半岛，后于1957年3月撤出。

第三次中东战争又称“六·五”战争。随着阿以对峙加剧，埃及于1967年5月向西奈半岛增兵，并要求联合国驻西奈部队撤出，同时派兵占据加沙地带，封锁蒂朗海峡，禁止以色列船只和向以运送战略物资的船只在亚喀巴湾航行，以色列于6月5日突然出动所有作战飞机对埃及、叙利亚、约旦三国机场进行轰炸，同日以出动装甲部队分三路向西奈半岛推进，在第四天到达苏伊士运河东岸后，埃及被迫接受停火协议；6日以军重创约旦驻约旦河西岸部队，并于7日占领了约旦河西岸；9日，以军进攻叙利亚的戈兰高地，叙利亚于11日宣布接受停火协议。以色列在这次战争中占领了近7万平方公里的阿拉伯土地。

第四次中东战争又称“十月战争”或“赎罪日战争”。为打破不战不和状态，收复失地，埃及与叙利亚等阿拉伯国家于1973年10月6日同时向以军发动袭击。阿拉伯产油国以“石油武器”支持交战国。但由于美全力支持以色列，阿拉伯国家未能获胜②。

---

① 四次中东战争内幕. http：//zh. wikipedia. org

② 王春生. 军枭——以色列军情内幕. 新华出版社，2002

Part Two Exercises

Ⅰ. Listen to the first part of the news about the history of Gaza, and repeat it, then write it down.

Ⅱ. Listen to the second part of the news, and write down what Israel and America do to help move away settlers.

1. Thousands of Israeli troops and police ____________________________________.
2. After Wednesday ____.
3. Soldiers will ____________________. The Palestinians ______________________.
4. However, on Friday, an Israeli economic cooperation group _______________. Officials say the settlers ____.
5. American special representative James Wolfensohn ______________________. He is the former president of the World Bank.

Ⅲ. Listen to the third and forth part of the news, and fill in the following table.

About what is happening after the withdrawal	
Who oppose the withdrawal	Their reasons and the protested way...
Benjamin Netanyahu	
Opponents	
Yet sixty percent of the people in Israel support the withdraw. After the withdrawal...	
Who will govern Gaza	
Who will keep order	
The biggest change is	

（续上表）

What is still controlled by Israel	
PM Ariel Sharon	
The reason for the withdrawal according to Ariel Sharon	
The real peace negotiation according to Israelis is	

Ⅳ. Listen to the last part of the news, and translate it into Chinese, then repeat it in English.

Part Two　Keys to the Exercises

Ⅰ. Listen to the first part of the news about the history of Gaza, and repeat it, then write it down.

1. Gaza is a small area on the Mediterranean coast.
2. It is long but narrow.
3. Israel captured the Gaza Strip from Egypt in the nineteen sixty-seven war.
4. It also captured the West Bank from Jordan.
5. The war lasted six days.
6. It began when Arab countries attacked Israel.
7. More than one million Palestinians live in Gaza.
8. So do around eight thousand five hundred Jewish settlers.
9. Next week, the Israeli government wants them to leave their twenty-one settlements.

Ⅱ. Listen to the second part of the news, and write down what Israel and America do to help move away settlers.

1. Thousands of Israeli troops and police will help the settlers move out.

2. After Wednesday, the troops will use force to remove any who stay.

3. Soldiers will destroy all of the houses. The Palestinians want to build their own.

4. However, on Friday, an Israeli economic cooperation group announced a deal. Officials say the settlers agreed to sell most of the structures in which they grew plants on their farms.

5. American special representative James Wolfensohn collected about fourteen million dollars to buy the greenhouses for the Palestinians. He is the former president of the World Bank.

Ⅲ. Listen to the third and forth part of the news, and fill in the following table.

About what is happening after the withdrawal	
Who opposes the withdrawal	Their reasons and the protested way...
Benjamin Netanyahu	Resigned in protest as finance minister.
Opponents	The land is part of what they call Greater Israel. They say God promised it to the Jews.
Yet sixty percent of the people in Israel support the withdrawal. After the withdrawal...	
Who will govern Gaza	The Palestinian National Authority led by Mahmoud Abbas.
Who will keep order	A special force trained by Egypt.
The biggest change is	The end to the travel restrictions in occupied Gaza.
What is controlled by Israel	The border, coast and air space.
PM Ariel Sharon	Announced the withdrawal plan in December 2003.
The reason for the withdrawal according to Ariel Sharon	It would strengthen Israeli security, ease the responsibilities of the Israeli Defense Forces and reduce tensions with the Palestinians.
The real peace negotiations according to Israelis is	When Palestinian officials disarm groups like Hamas and Islamic Jihad.

Ⅳ. Listen to the last part of the news, and translate it into Chinese, then repeat it in English.

Palestinians hope for an independent nation with Jerusalem as the capital. Yet many see the Gaza withdrawal only as a way for Israel to increase control of the West Bank. The West Bank has two hundred forty thousand Israeli settlers and more than two million Arabs.

巴勒斯坦人盼望建立一个以耶路撒冷为其首都的独立国家。许多人认为加沙撤军只是以色列人为了加强对西岸控制的一个途径而已。西岸现有 24 万以色列移居者和超过 200 万的阿拉伯人。

Four small settlements in the West Bank are to be removed under the withdrawal plan. Prime Minister Sharon says the major ones will stay. But he suggested in comments reported Friday that more settlers could leave in the future.

按照撤退计划，西岸的四个定居点都将拆除。总理沙龙表示大型的定居点将保留下来。但他在星期五的报告中表示，未来将会有更多的犹太移居者离开。

In Gaza City on Friday, Palestinian officials held a big celebration of the withdrawal just days away.

星期五，加沙地区的巴勒斯坦官员将会为几天前进行的撤退举行一次大型庆祝活动。

Part Four Translation of the Text

Israel Withdrawing from Gaza after 38 Years
38 年之后以色列从加沙撤退

Gaza is a small area on the Mediterranean coast. It is long but narrow. Israel captured the Gaza Strip from Egypt in the nineteen sixty-seven war. It also captured the West Bank from Jordan. The war lasted six days. It began when Arab countries attacked Israel.

加沙是地处地中海海岸上的一个“小区”，长而狭窄。以色列在 1967 年的战争中从埃及手里夺得了加沙地带，同时也从约旦那里夺得了西岸。战争持续了 6 天。这场战争因阿拉伯国家攻击以色列而起。

More than one million Palestinians live in Gaza. So do around eight thousand five hundred Jewish settlers. Next week, the Israeli government wants them to leave their twenty-one settlements.

超过一百万巴勒斯坦人住在加沙。当中大约有 8 500 名犹太移居者。下星期，以色列政府要求犹太移居者离开他们的 21 个定居点。

Thousands of Israeli troops and police will help the settlers move out. After Wednesday, the troops will use force to remove any who stay. Soldiers will destroy all of the houses. The Palestinians want to build their own.

数以万计的以色列军队和警察将帮助犹太移居者搬走。星期三以后，军队将动用武力赶走任何留下的人。士兵会毁坏所有房子。巴勒斯坦人需重建自己的家园。

However, on Friday, an Israeli economic cooperation group announced a deal. Officials say the settlers agreed to sell most of the structures in which they grew plants on their farms. American special representative James Wolfensohn collected about fourteen million dollars to buy the greenhouses for the Palestinians. He is the former president of the World Bank.

然而，以色列经济合作小组星期五宣布了一单交易。官员说，犹太移居者同意出售大部分他们农场里用来培育植物的建筑物。美国特派专员詹姆斯·沃尔芬森为巴勒斯坦人募集到约 1 400 万美元买下这些温室。詹姆斯·沃尔芬森是世界银行的前总裁。

Conservative and religious political parties in Israel oppose the withdrawal from Gaza. Opponents say Israel will not be any safer from attacks. Earlier this month, Benjamin Netanyahu resigned as finance minister in protest. Opponents say the land is part of what they call Greater Israel. They say God promised it to the Jews. Yet public opinion research shows that sixty percent of the people in Israel support the withdrawal.

以色列的保守党和宗教政党反对从加沙撤退。反对者表示，以色列如果遭到攻击，将可能处于危险境地。本月初，本雅明·内塔尼亚胡为表示抗议而辞去财务大臣的职务。反对派更表示这块土地是“大以色列”国土的一部分。他们说是上帝将之赠送给犹太人的。而民意调查显示，百分之六十的以色列人支持撤退。

Under the plan, the Palestinian National Authority led by Mahmoud Abbas will govern the territory. A special force trained by Egypt is to keep order. Officials say the biggest change will be the end to the travel restrictions in occupied Gaza. But Israel will continue to control the border, coast and air space.

按照计划，由马哈茂德·阿巴斯领导的巴勒斯坦民族权力机构管辖这片领地。埃及训练的一支特种部队会负责维护秩序。官方表示最大的变化是结束了被占领的加沙的通行限制。但以色列将继续控制其边界、沿海和领空。

Prime Minister Ariel Sharon announced the withdrawal plan in December of two thousand three. He said it would strengthen Israeli security, ease the responsibilities of the Israeli Defense Forces and reduce tensions with the Palestinians. But Israelis says real peace negotiations can begin only when Palestinian officials disarm groups like Hamas and Islamic Jihad.

总理阿里埃勒·沙龙于2003年12月宣布此项撤退计划。他认为，这将加强以色列的安全，减轻以色列防御部队的责任，并且缓解与巴勒斯坦人之间的紧张气氛。但以色列人表示，真正的和平谈判只有当巴勒斯坦官方解除哈马斯和伊斯兰教杰哈德圣战等组织的武装时才能开始。

Palestinians hope for an independent nation with Jerusalem as the capital. Yet many see the Gaza withdrawal only as a way for Israel to increase control of the West Bank. The West Bank has two hundred forty thousand Israeli settlers and more than two million Arabs.

巴勒斯坦人盼望建立一个以耶路撒冷为其首都的独立国家。而许多人认为加沙撤军只是以色列人为了加强对西岸控制的一个途径而已。西岸现有24万以色列移居者和超过200万的阿拉伯人。

Four small settlements in the West Bank are to be removed under the withdrawal plan. Prime Minister Sharon says the major ones will stay. But he suggested in comments reported Friday that more settlers could leave in the future.

按照撤退计划，西岸的四个定居点都将拆除。总理沙龙表示大型的定居点将保留下来。但他在星期五的报告中表示，未来将会有更多的犹太移居者离开。

In Gaza City on Friday, Palestinian officials held a big celebration of the withdrawal just days away.

星期五，加沙地区的巴勒斯坦官员将为几天前进行的撤退举行一次大型庆祝活动。

Lesson 19　After Three Years, Iraq Still a Major Issue in American Politics

March 17, 2006

Part One　Background Information

战争与石油

"在我看来，美国入侵伊拉克的做法不符合联合国宪章，它是非法的。"

——联合国前任秘书长安南

2010年9月1日，美国终于决定正式从伊拉克撤军。现在来回顾这场战争对认识美国政府的本质应是正逢其时。实际上，布什当时是靠"宣传机器"来骗取人民对战争的支持。美国媒体不断按照政府的口径宣称伊拉克拥有大规模杀伤性武器，但即使到现在，美国人也没有找到所谓的大规模杀伤性武器，而美国政府依然"死磕"说这场战争是必要的，它将给伊拉克人民带来民主。美国政府耗费大约200亿美元①和牺牲数千美国士兵的生命进行的这场战争，难道真的是那么在乎伊拉克人民能否享有民主吗？"据英国《星期日独立报》报道，伊拉克议会未来几天将审议一份有争议的法案，伊拉克庞大的石油宝库届时将向西方石油公司敞开大门。自伊拉克石油工业1972年国有化以来，外国石油利益集团将第一次迎来在伊拉克的大规模开采行动。消息说，伊拉克副总理兼石油委员会主席巴勒姆·萨利赫预计将于1月7日公开这部法案。这部法案将赋予英国石油公司、壳牌石油和美国埃克森石油公司30年的原油开采权。据国际能源问题专家格雷格·穆蒂特透露，美国政府雇用的一家美国咨询公司协助起草了这部法案"。② 因此说"美国侵略伊拉克就是一场石油战争"，这一点也不为过。

如果认为以上提到的法案因得不到证实而不可信的话，我们再来看看以下这段文章：

"在过去十来年里，世界石油基本上在25美元/桶上下波动，趋于一个相对稳定的状态。美国入侵伊拉克之后，世界的石油价格才出现了这么大的波动。"

"炒作房地产可以挣钱，炒作股票可以挣钱，同样，炒作石油也是可以挣钱的。从目前来看，通过一个石油期货价格的炒作，且其主动权始终在美国人手里，所以他说涨，石油价格就涨，他说跌，石油价格就跌。请问世界上其他的国家，美国在这个过程中挣钱不挣钱？也就是说，无论石油是涨还是跌，由于控制涨跌的权利在美国，所以什么时候都是美国人在挣钱。"③

国外网友更是直截了当地挑明了布什为伊拉克石油而不惜牺牲数千美国士兵生命的观点：

---

① http://wzb.chd.edu.cn/Article/ShowArticle.asp ArticleID = 36

② 佚名. 美国侵略伊拉克就是一场石油战争. http://wx.longcity.net/go.asp id = 39292, 2007-01-11

③ 佚名. 石油涨价中哪些问题值得思考. bbs.people.com.cn/bbs/ReadFile whichfile = 5385&typeid = 40-22k

It's clear that the US-led invasion had little to do with national security or the events of Sept. 11... At the State Department, planning was also underway. Under the auspices of the "Future of Iraq Project", an "Oil and Energy Working Group" was established. The full membership of the group—described by the *Financial Times* as "Iraqi oil experts, international consultants" and State Department staffers—remains classified, but among them, according to Antonia Juhasz's "The Bush Agenda", was Ibrahim Bahr al-Uloum, who would serve in Iyad Allawi's cabinet during the period of the Iraqi Governing Council, and later as Iraq's oil minister in 2005. The group concluded that Iraq's oil "should be opened to international oil companies as quickly as possible after the war"①.

美国不顾国际关系的基本准则对伊拉克发动的这场战争，受到全世界大多数国家的反对。首先是法国、德国与俄罗斯联手在联合国安理会成功挫败了美英利用联合国使其对伊动武合法化的图谋。法国总统希拉克更是尖锐地指出，如果美国在伊拉克问题上得手，世界将成为单极世界。美国总统布什冒天下之大不韪，以数千美国士兵的生命为代价，一意孤行地进行了这次"十字军东征"，它获得的并不仅仅是政治利益——通过推翻萨达姆政权来实现对伊拉克的控制，进而达到改造整个伊斯兰世界的目的，而是早已预谋了其后所产生的巨大经济利益——让美英石油公司获得在伊拉克的石油开采权。

Part Two Exercises

Ⅰ. Listen to the first part of the news, and fill in the blanks with the words you hear.

1. Three years ago, on March nineteenth, President Bush ordered ______________________.

2. One goal was ______________________.

3. The other was to prevent Iraqi leader Saddam Hussein ______________________.

4. The United States believed ______________________.

5. The coalition forces ____________ and the Iraqi government was ____________.

6. ____________ were never found.

7. More than ____________ have died in Iraq in the past three years.

8. The Bush administration says at least ____________ have also died. Some reports say many more have been killed.

Ⅱ. Listen to the second part of the news, and answer the following questions.

1. What is the goal of American military operation today?

① Joshua Holland. Bush's Petro-Cartel Almost Has Iraq's Oil Posted. http://www.alternet.org/waroniraq/43045/October 16, 2006

2. What are the characteristics of a democracy in Iraq according to Bush?

3. Is Iraq a secure country?

4. What does this news think will help solve the secure problems in Iraq?

Ⅲ. Listen to the third part of the news, and write it down by memory.

Shiite 什叶派教徒 Kurdish 摩尔德人

Ⅳ. Listen to the fourth part of the news, and translate it into Chinese.

Ⅴ. Listen to the last part of the news, and repeat the whole paragraph with the "key words or phrases" given below.

1. CH – 47 Chinook helicopter Operation Swarmer near Samarra
2. most important issue
3. Mister Bush's presidency
4. the public's concerns about Iraq questions about the president's leadership
5. the American congressional elections in November
6. opposition Democratic Party

Part Three Keys to the Exercises

Ⅰ. Listen to the first part of the news, fill in the blanks with the words you hear.

1. Three years ago, on March nineteenth, President Bush ordered <u>American-led coalition</u>

forces to invade Iraq.

2. One goal was to free the Iraqi people.

3. The other was to prevent Iraqi leader Saddam Hussein from using weapons of great destruction.

4. The United States believed Iraq had such weapons.

5. The coalition forces gained a quick military victory and the Iraqi government was ousted.

6. But weapons of great destruction were never found.

7. More than two thousand three hundred American troops have died in Iraq in the past three years.

8. The Bush administration says at least thirty thousand Iraqis have also died. Some reports say many more have been killed.

Ⅱ. Listen to the second part of the news, and answer the following questions.

1. What is the goal of American military operation today?

President Bush says the goal of the military operation is to protect American security by turning Iraq into a democracy.

2. What are the characteristics of a democracy in Iraq according to Bush?

He adds that Iraq has gone from dictatorship to freedom, to self-rule, to a constitution, and to national elections.

3. Is Iraq a secure country?

No, but gaining a secure peace in Iraq has been difficult. Deaths and injuries to American troops continue. So do attacks against Iraqi civilians and violence among religious extremists.

4. What does this news think will help solve the secure problems in Iraq?

1) The United States has been training the Iraqi military and police so that they could accept more responsibility for security operations.

2) But some experts say training alone is not enough to provide security. They say Iraq needs a government that is both effective and permanent.

Ⅲ. Listen to the third part of the news, and write it down by memory.

Shiite and Kurdish coalitions won the most seats in parliament in the Iraqi elections last December. But the coalitions lack the clear majority needed to govern. The United States ambassador in Iraq has proposed creation of a national unity government that would include Sunni representatives. But this proposal has been met with resistance.

Ⅳ. Listen to the fourth part of the news, and translate it into Chinese.

President Bush has spoken around the country to increase support for his policy in Iraq. Last month, Mister Bush said his administration is fixing what has not worked. He said the administration would take necessary steps to make Iraq able to defend itself, and serve as a strong ally in the war on terror.

布什总统在美国各地进行巡回演讲，以增加民众对他在伊拉克政策上的支持。在上个月，布什表示政府正在修正无效政策，并将采取必要措施以确保伊拉克能自我防卫，使其成为反恐战争中的一个有力同盟。

But recent public opinion studies suggest that American support for the effort in Iraq is decreasing. Several opinion studies show that most Americans now oppose the war in Iraq. They do not believe the war effort was worth the cost. And, they fear Iraq may be close to civil war.

然而最近的民意调查显示，美国民众对政府在伊拉克行动上的支持正逐渐减少。几次民意调查都显示，目前多数美国民众反对伊拉克战争。他们认为战争所付出的代价是不值得的，他们对伊拉克可能爆发内战感到担忧。

V. Listen to the last part of the news, and repeat it with the "key words or phrases" given below.

1. Iraqi and US soldiers exit a CH－47 Chinook helicopter in support of Operation Swarmer, near Samarra.

2. Experts say Iraq is still the most important issue in American politics today.

3. This could affect the final three years of Mister Bush's presidency.

4. Political experts say the public's concerns about Iraq have raised questions about the president's leadership.

5. The president's Republican Party hopes the situation in Iraq will become more secure before the American congressional elections in November.

6. Experts say they expect the opposition Democratic Party to gain seats in the elections, at least in part, because of public dissatisfaction about the situation in Iraq.

Part Four　Translation of the Text

After Three Years, Iraq Still a Major Issue in American Politics

伊战3年后，伊拉克依然是美国政治要处理的主要问题

Three years ago, on March nineteenth, President Bush ordered American-led coalition forces to invade Iraq. One goal was to free the Iraqi people. The other was to prevent Iraqi leader Saddam Hussein from using weapons of great destruction. The United States believed Iraq had such weapons.

3年前的3月19日，布什总统命令美国为首的联军入侵伊拉克。目的是解放伊拉克人民，同时也为阻止伊拉克领导人萨达姆使用大规模杀伤性武器。美国一直认为伊拉克拥有这种武器。

The coalition forces gained a quick military victory and the Iraqi government was ousted. But weapons of great destruction were never found.

联军在伊拉克迅速获得了军事胜利，伊拉克政府被推翻。然而根本没有发现什么大规模杀伤性武器。

More than two thousand three hundred American troops have died in Iraq in the past three years. The Bush administration says at least thirty thousand Iraqis have also died. Some reports say many more have been killed.

在过去的3年中，超过2 300名美军在伊拉克阵亡。布什政府指出，迄今为止，至少有3万伊拉克人丧生，有些报道则声称丧生的人数远不止这个数目。

Today, President Bush says the goal of the military operation is to protect American security by turning Iraq into a democracy. He adds that Iraq has gone from dictatorship to freedom, to self-rule, to a constitution, and to national elections.

如今，布什总统表示，军事行动的目的是将伊拉克转变成一个民主国家，以保障美国的安全。他补充道，伊拉克从原先的独裁政府已变成一个自由、自治、宪制及举行国家大选的国家。

But gaining a secure peace in Iraq has been difficult. Deaths and injuries to American troops continue. So do attacks against Iraqi civilians and violence among religious extremists.

然而，要确保伊拉克拥有一个稳定的和平是艰难的。美军的伤亡在延续，针对伊拉克平民的袭击及宗教极端分子的暴行也在延续。

The United States has been training the Iraqi military and police so that they could accept more responsibility for security operations. But some experts say training alone is not enough to provide security. They say Iraq needs a government that is both effective and permanent.

美国一直在训练伊拉克军队和警察，以便他们在维持安全行动时能承担更多的责任。然而一些专家指出，单单训练是不能够提供安全保障的，伊拉克需要的是更有效率和更持久稳定的政府。

Shiite and Kurdish coalitions won the most seats in parliament in the Iraqi elections last December. But the coalitions lack the clear majority needed to govern. The United States ambassador in Iraq has proposed creation of a national unity government that would include Sunni representatives. But this proposal has been met with resistance.

在12月的伊拉克大选中，什叶派教徒和库尔德人的联盟赢得了议会的大部分席位，但缺少执政所需要的多数席位。美国驻伊拉克大使提议成立一个包括逊尼派教徒在内的全国联合政府，不过这提议遭遇抵制。

President Bush has spoken around the country to increase support for his policy in Iraq. Last month, Mister Bush said his administration is fixing what has not worked. He said the administration would take necessary steps to make Iraq able to defend itself, and serve as a strong ally in the war on terror.

布什总统在美国各地进行巡回演讲，以增加民众对他在伊拉克政策上的支持。在上个月，布什表示政府正在修正无效政策，并将采取必要措施以确保伊拉克能自我防卫，使其成为反恐战争中的一个有力同盟。

But recent public opinion studies suggest that American support for the effort in Iraq is decreasing. Several opinion studies show that most Americans now oppose the war in Iraq. They do not believe the war effort was worth the cost. And, they fear Iraq may be close to civil war.

然而最近的民意调查显示，美国民众对政府在伊拉克行动的支持正逐渐减少。几次民意调查都显示，目前多数美国民众反对伊拉克战争。他们认为战争所付出的代价是不值得的，他们对伊拉克可能爆发内战感到担忧。

Iraqi and US soldiers exit a CH－47 Chinook helicopter in support of Operation Swarmer, near Samarra.

伊拉克和美军撤出了一架 CH－47 型号的运输直升机，以支援在萨马拉附近进行的“蜂群行动”。

Experts say Iraq is still the most important issue in American politics today. This could affect the final three years of Mister Bush's presidency. Political experts say the public's concerns about Iraq have raised questions about the president's leadership. The president's Republican Party hopes the situation in Iraq will become more secure before the American congressional elections in November.

专家表示，目前伊拉克依然是美国最大的政治问题，并可能影响布什最后 3 年的任期。政治家指出，对伊拉克的关注已引起民众对总统领导能力的质疑。总统的共和党派希望伊拉克的局势能在 11 月的美国国会选举到来前更加稳定。

Experts say they expect the opposition Democratic Party to gain seats in the elections, at least in part, because of public dissatisfaction about the situation in Iraq.

专家表示，由于公众对伊拉克局势的不满，他们预料反对派的民主党至少可在部分选举中得到更多的席位。

(IN THE NEWS in VOA *Special English* was written by Shelley Gollust. I'm Steve Ember.)

Lesson 20 Palestinians Are Described as "Simply in Shock" after Hamas Wins Elections

By Nancy Steinbach

January 27, 2006

Part One Background Information

萨达姆在2006年的最后两天被送上了绞架，可以说是美国总统这一年中最称心的事了。以西方的民主理念来改造世界，摧毁与美国政府作对的"恐怖主义"集团正是美国领导人为之"呕心沥血"的事业。阿富汗正在走向"民主社会"，伊拉克也将走向"民主"，而巴勒斯坦通过选举"走向"哈马斯，却让西方始料未及。

2006年，巴勒斯坦伊斯兰抵抗组织哈马斯走上合法执政的前台，这对美国和以色列来说犹如遭受了一记"闷棍"。自2001年以来布什和沙龙相互唱和，蛮横地指责阿拉法特不是谈判对手，是恐怖分子，必欲去之而后快。阿拉法特含恨而去，正好给美国在巴勒斯坦推行大中东民主计划提供了完美的战线和演练机会。美国在这之前期望什么结果，我们不得而知，但哈马斯等成为巴勒斯坦的执政集团，是与美国所想背道而驰的。因为该集团是美国早已界定为不折不扣的"恐怖分子"的"正宗样板"，怎么能够期待它带领巴勒斯坦人民走向美国式的民主呢？然而，民主无戏言，严格按照美国的民主步骤，由巴勒斯坦选民理性选出的哈马斯政权既合法又光明，巴勒斯坦解放组织主流派法塔赫不得不沦为在野。这一切说明，中东形势发展由不得美国一手遮天了，也许这就是大中东民主计划在伊斯兰世界不可避免地沦为悖论并略显尴尬。

当然，人们期待着哈马斯会改变（当年的法塔赫也曾经被美国和以色列界定为"恐怖分子"）。哈马斯虽然誓言将继续从事抵抗以色列的活动，但其发言人表示，将寻求在巴勒斯坦控制区进行改革。具体的改革怎样进行，人们将拭目以待。不过与阿拉法特和阿巴斯等人比较起来，美以与哈马斯打交道时，如果再始终贯彻其强硬态度，其结果将是不言而喻的。

Part Two Exercises

I. Listen to the first part of the news, and fill in the blanks with the words you hear.

On Thursday the Islamic group Hamas won ____________ in the Palestinian parliament. Hamas the ruling Fatah party.

__________ is enough for Hamas to ____________ in the Palestinian Legislative Council. Fatah won ____________. Prime Minister Ahmed Qurei and his government

____________. On Friday Mahmoud Abbas, the Palestinian president, said he will ask Hamas to ____________.

Ⅱ. Listen to the second part of the news, and answer the following questions.

1. What is Hamas' determination? What is its strategy?

2. Why do Israel, the US and the European Union dislike Hamas?

3. What does Iran think of Hamas?

4. Why does Italian Prime Minister Silvio Berlusconi think the election result is not good for the creation of a Palestinian state?

Ⅲ. Listen to the third part of the news, and translate it into Chinese, then repeat it in English.

Ⅳ. Listen to the last two parts of news, and write them down with the words given below.

1. Oslo Peace Agreement Palestinian Authority
2. Hamas Israel
3. Palestinian Authority Israeli government
4. Israeli-Palestinian conflict
5. Hamas Palestinian Authority
6. Israel

7. Israel　Palestinians
8. Israelies　Gaza Strip
9. Hamas　Israeli withdrawal
10. Palestinians　Fatah
11. Palestinian　Khalil Assali

Part Three　Keys to the Exercises

Ⅰ. Listen to the first part of the news, and fill in the blanks with the words you hear.

On Thursday the Islamic group Hamas won seventy-six of the one hundred thirty-two seats in the Palestinian parliament. Hamas defeated the ruling Fatah party.

The majority is enough for Hamas to rule by itself in the Palestinian Legislative Council. Fatah won forty-three seats. Prime Minister Ahmed Qurei and his government resigned. On Friday Mahmoud Abbas, the Palestinian president, said he will ask Hamas to form the next government.

Ⅱ. Listen to the second part of the news, and answer the following questions.

1. What is Hamas' determination? What is its strategy?

The group is sworn to the destruction of Israel and has refused to disarm (to fight with armed forces).

2. Why do Israel, the US and the European Union dislike Hamas?

Because Hamas has carried out many attacks against Israelis. Israel, the United States and the European Union say they will not work with a government led by Hamas. They call it a terrorist organization.

3. What does Iran think of Hamas?

In Iran, the Foreign Ministry says the election will strengthen resistance against Israel.

4. Why does Italian Prime Minister Silvio Berlusconi think the election result is not good for the creation of a Palestinian state?

Italian Prime Minister Silvio Berlusconi says the results will only make the creation of a Palestinian state more difficult. Because Israel, the United States and the European Union say they will not work with a government led by Hamas. (So negotiations between Israel and Palestine will be difficult to continue.)

Ⅲ. Listen to the third part of the news, and translate it into Chinese, then repeat it in English.

European Union foreign ministers will meet Monday to discuss the situation. EU officials say they cannot give money to a government that carries on an armed fight with Israel.

欧盟的外交部长们将在星期一会面讨论此局势。欧盟的官员说，他们不能把钱给予一个坚持以武力对抗以色列的政府。

The international group that wrote the so-called road map to peace will also meet Monday. The members are the United Nations, the United States, Russia and the European Union.

起草那个所谓的和平路线图的国际组织也会在星期一会面。它的成员是联合国、美国、俄罗斯和欧盟。

Even as many world leaders expressed displeasure at the results, they praised the exercise in democracy. President Bush said the voting was a reminder that democracy "can open up the world's eyes to reality by listening to people".

尽管许多国家领导人表示对结果不满意，但他们对此次民主实践表示赞许。布什总统说，这次选举提醒人们注意，民主"可以通过听取人民的意见，让世界睁开眼睛看到现实"。

Mister Bush described the Hamas victory as a "wake-up call" to the leadership in the Palestinian territories. In his words, the people are demanding honest government. The people want services. But he added that he did not see how a group that supports the destruction of a country can be a partner in peace.

布什形容哈马斯的胜利是"唤醒"巴勒斯坦领地领导层的一个"声音"。用他的话说，人民要求一个有诚信的政府。人民需要的是服务。但他补充道，他不明白一个支持毁灭另一个国家的组织如何能够成为和平的伙伴。

Ⅳ. Listen to the last two parts of news, and write them down with the key words given below.

1. The nineteen ninety-three Oslo Peace Agreements created the Palestinian Authority to administer the territories.

2. Hamas does not recognize Israel.

3. Yet the Palestinian Authority must deal with the Israeli government in areas like water and power supplies.

4. The agreements also say that the Israeli-Palestinian conflict must be settled peacefully.

5. The question is how might Hamas change now that it will control the Palestinian Authority.

6. Israel will hold national elections at the end of March.

7. Some people think Israel is more likely now to take more steps on its own to separate itself from the Palestinians.

8. Some Israelis say their government never should have given up the Gaza Strip.

9. They say Hamas used the Israeli withdrawal last year for political gain.

10. Yet many Palestinians say they never expected Hamas to do so well, or Fatah to do so poorly.

11. Palestinian reporter Khalil Assali says: "People are simply in shock."

Part Four　Translation of the Text

Palestinians Are Described as "Simply in Shock" after Hamas Wins Elections

哈马斯赢得大选后，媒体报道巴勒斯坦人"简直是惊呆了"

Ⅰ. Listen to the first part of the news, and fill in the blanks with the words you hear.

On Thursday, the Islamic group Hamas won seventy-six of the one hundred thirty-two seats in the Palestinian parliament. Hamas defeated the ruling Fatah party.

星期四，伊斯兰组织哈马斯赢得了132个巴勒斯坦议会中的76个席位。哈马斯击败了执政党法塔赫。

The majority is enough for Hamas to rule by itself in the Palestinian Legislative Council. Fatah won forty-three seats. Prime Minister Ahmed Qurei and his government resigned. On Friday Mahmoud Abbas, the Palestinian president, said he will ask Hamas to form the next government.

过半数的选票足够让哈马斯独立领导巴勒斯坦的立法会。法塔赫赢得43个席位。巴勒斯坦总理库赖和他的政府辞职。巴勒斯坦总统阿巴斯星期五说，他要求哈马斯组建下一届政府。

The group is sworn to the destruction of Israel and has refused to disarm. Hamas has carried out many attacks against Israelis. Israel, the United States and the European Union say they will not work with a government led by Hamas. They call it a terrorist organization.

哈马斯组织发誓要消灭以色列，并拒绝解除武装。哈马斯对以色列人展开过多次袭击。以色列、美国和欧盟说，他们不会与哈马斯领导的政府合作。他们称它为恐怖主义组织。

In Iran, the Foreign Ministry says the election will strengthen resistance against Israel. But Italian Prime Minister Silvio Berlusconi says the results will only make the creation of a Palestinian state more difficult.

伊朗外交部长说，此次选举将会强化对以色列的抵抗行为。意大利总理贝卢斯科尼说，这个结果只会让巴勒斯坦建国更加艰难。

European Union foreign ministers will meet Monday to discuss the situation. EU officials say they cannot give money to a government that carries on an armed fight with Israel.

欧盟的外交部长们将会在星期一会面讨论此局势。欧盟的官员说，他们不能把钱给予一个坚持以武力对抗以色列的政府。

The international group that wrote the so-called road map to peace will also meet Monday. The members are the United Nations, the United States, Russia and the European Union.

起草那个所谓的和平路线图的国际组织也会在星期一会面。它的成员是联合国、美国、俄罗斯和欧盟。

Even as many world leaders expressed displeasure at the results, they praised the exercise in democracy. President Bush said the voting was a reminder that democracy "can open up the world's eyes to reality by listening to people".

尽管许多国家领导人表示对结果不满意，但他们对此次民主实践表示赞许。布什总统说，这次选举提醒人们注意，民主“可以通过听取人民的意见，让世界睁开眼睛看到现实”。

Mister Bush described the Hamas victory as a "wake-up call" to the leadership in the Palestinian territories. In his words, The people are demanding honest government. The people want services. But he added that he did not see how a group that supports the destruction of a country can be a partner in peace.

布什形容哈马斯的胜利是“唤醒”巴勒斯坦领地领导层的一个“声音”。用他的话说，人民要求一个有诚信的政府。人民需要的是服务。但他补充道，他不明白一个支持毁灭另一个国家的组织如何能够成为和平的伙伴。

The nineteen ninety-three Oslo Peace Agreements created the Palestinian Authority to administer the territories. Hamas does not recognize Israel. Yet the Palestinian Authority must deal with the Israeli government in areas like water and power supplies. The agreements also say that the Israeli-Palestinian conflict must be settled peacefully.

1993 年，因《奥斯陆和平条约》产生的巴勒斯坦权力机构管理着这块领地。哈马斯不承认以色列国。然而，巴勒斯坦权力机构必须与以色列政府交涉水电供应问题。这个协议还要求必须和平解决巴以冲突。

The question is how might Hamas change now that it will control the Palestinian Authority.

现在的问题是哈马斯控制巴勒斯坦权力机构，它将做何等的改变呢。

Israel will hold national elections at the end of March. Some people think Israel is more likely now to take more steps on its own to separate itself from the Palestinians. Some Israelis say their government never should have given up the Gaza Strip. They say Hamas used the Israeli withdrawal last year for political gain.

以色列会在三月底举行全国大选。有人认为，以色列现在可能会采取更多的措施以摆脱巴勒斯坦人。一些以色列人说，他们的政府决不会放弃加沙地带。他们认为，哈马斯利用以色列去年的撤军，在政治上占到了优势。

Yet many Palestinians say they never expected Hamas to do so well, or Fatah to do so poorly. Palestinian reporter Khalil Assali says："People are simply in shock."

然而许多巴勒斯坦人说，他们从来没有想到哈马斯表现如此突出，而法塔赫会如此糟糕。巴勒斯坦记者阿沙利说：“坦率地讲，人们感到震撼。”

Lesson 21　Tenth Anniversary of Ethnic Killings in Rwanda

By Cynthia Kirk

April 10, 2004

Part One　Background Information

种族是人类冲突的根源么

这是一个带给人类巨大悲痛的时期，1994年4月到7月，非洲小国卢旺达发生了持续三个月之久的种族灭绝大屠杀，80万人在大屠杀中丧生，100多万人流离失所。引发此次丧心病狂大屠杀的导火索是一起空难事件。1994年4月6日，一架载着卢旺达总统哈比亚利马纳（胡图族人）和布隆迪总统的座机被两枚火箭弹击落，机上人员全部遇难。几个小时后，种族屠杀开始了。

卢旺达大屠杀是长期种族矛盾引致的恶果。16世纪，图西人建立了封建王国，第一次世界大战后由比利时委任统治。第二次世界大战后改由比利时"托管"。托管期间，占人口14%的图西人统治占人口85%的胡图人。1962年7月1日卢旺达宣告独立，成立共和国。1973年7月5日，国民警卫军部长哈比亚利马纳发动军事政变，成立第二共和国。胡图人逐渐在反抗图西人统治的过程中占了上风，成立胡图人政府。1959年、1963年、1967年和1973年先后发生4次大规模种族流血冲突，一批又一批的图西人被迫逃往邻国。截至1990年10月，卢旺达流亡国外的难民多达50万人，其中绝大多数是图西人。其后，这种情况开始发生逆转，侨居乌干达的图西族难民组成卢旺达爱国阵线（简称"爱阵"）与胡图族政府军对抗，内战爆发。为了解决种族矛盾，1991年6月卢旺达开始实行多党制，在政府中引入不同党派势力。1993年8月4日，卢政府和"爱阵"在坦桑尼亚阿鲁沙签署和平协定，决定结束内战，但和平出人意料地短暂。第二年的4月6日，胡图族总统哈比亚利马纳因飞机遭袭身亡而导致种族大屠杀之后，图西族的"爱阵"取得军事胜利，夺取了政权。

1994年11月，联合国安理会设立了联合国卢旺达战犯法庭，审判犯有大屠杀罪的嫌疑犯。卢旺达大屠杀留下了深刻教训，引发了人们对安理会作用、联合国维和行动的有效性以及国际社会在预防此类屠杀事件中的责任等问题的沉重思索。2004年3月26日，联合国前任秘书长安南在纽约联合国总部举行的"卢旺达大屠杀10周年纪念会"上发表讲话，呼吁国际社会采取行动，防止卢旺达大屠杀事件重演。如今的卢旺达已是一个充满和平的国家，但为防止悲剧重演，卢旺达全国在每年的4月举办各种纪念活动，旨在追思过去、警示未来。非洲联盟也决定设置"和平与安全理事会"，以便在成员国发生武装政变、践踏民主的情况下可以武力干预，也可在成员国之间发生交战时及时派出维和部队①。

① 佚名. 卢旺达大屠杀十年祭. http://news.163.com/special/t/tusha040407.html

Part Two　Exercises

Ⅰ. Listen to the first part of the news, and complete the following sentences.

Wednesday was the tenth anniversary of the start of ________________ in Rwanda. Thousands of people attended a ________________ in the capital, Kigali (基加利). They gathered there ________________ and ________________ for the central African nation.

The leaders of ________________ attended the ceremony. Belgian Prime Minister Guy Verhofstadt was the ________________ to attend. Rwanda ________________ Western countries for ________________.

During the ceremony, Rwandan President Paul Kagame led Rwandans in ________________ for the victims. Earlier, he ________________ at the new Kigali National Memorial Center.

Ⅱ. Listen to the second part of the news, and complete the followning sentences.

1. On April seventh, nineteen-ninety-four, a plane...

2. Both leaders... Rwanda's President Juvenal Habyarimana...

3. Following the crash... in the Hatu... minority Tutsi...

4. An estimated eight-hundred-thousand... Tutsi and moderate Hutus...

5. The killings ended... Mister Kagame's Tutsi-led...

6. ... Hutus... Democratic Republic of Congo.

Ⅲ. Listen to the third part of the news, and translate it into Chinese, then repeat it in English.

From "In a speech..." to "... in Kigali (基加利)".

Ⅳ. Listen to the fourth part of the news about the situation in Rwanda paragraph by paragraph, then write it down.

From "Rwanda is one..." to the end.

Part Three Keys to the Exercises

Ⅰ. Listen to the first part of the news, and complete the following sentences.

Wednesday was the tenth anniversary of the start of widespread ethnic killings in Rwanda. Thousands of people attended a national burial ceremony in the capital, Kigali (基加利). They gathered there to honor the victims and to show support for the central African nation.

The leaders of South Africa, Kenya, Uganda and Ethiopia attended the ceremony. Belgian Prime Minister Guy Verhofstadt was the only Western leader to attend. Rwanda criticized Western countries for not sending high-level officials.

During the ceremony, Rwandan President Paul Kagame led Rwandans in observing three minutes of silence for the victims. Earlier, he lit a flame at the new Kigali National Memorial Center.

Ⅱ. Listen to the second part of the news, and complete the following sentences.

1. The killings in Rwanda began on April seventh, nineteen ninety-four, after a plane carrying the presidents of Rwanda and Burundi was shot down over Kigali.

2. Both leaders died in the crash. Rwanda's President Juvenal Habyarimana was an ethnic Hutu.

3. Following the crash, extremists in the Hutu government began a plan to kill all of the country's minority Tutsi population and politically moderate Hutus.

4. An estimated eight-hundred-thousand Tutsis and moderate Hutus were killed in three months of violence.

5. The killings ended when Mister Kagame's Tutsi-led rebel army ousted the extremist Hutu government and seized control of the capital.

6. More than two-million Hutus later fled to nearby Democratic Republic of Congo.

Ⅲ. Listen to the third part of the news, and translate it into Chinese, then repeat it in English.

In a speech during the ceremony in Kigali, President Kagame said Rwanda takes the most blame for the mass killings. But he criticized the international community for failing to intervene to stop the killings. He also repeated accusations that French officials helped train and arm the Hutu government soldiers and militants who carried out the killings.

卡加梅总统在基加利的葬礼仪式上指出，卢旺达在大屠杀事件中应承担绝大部分责任。他批评国际社会未能介入并阻止屠杀事件。他也重申了对法国官员的谴责，说他们为执行屠杀的胡图族政府军人及好战分子提供训练和武器装备。

France has denied the accusations. It later withdrew its deputy foreign minister from the ceremony in Kigali.

法国否认了有关指责，之后召回了出席基加利葬礼仪式的外交部副部长。

Ⅳ. Listen to the fourth part of the news about the situation in Rwanda paragraph by paragraph, then write it down.

Rwanda is one of the world's poorest countries. Many Rwandans are still suffering as a result of the violence ten years ago. Many women were infected with the disease AIDS during widespread sexual attacks. And thousands of children lost their parents in the mass killings or from AIDS.

Human rights officials say the situation in Rwanda now is calm and the government has control in the country. The International Criminal Tribunal for Rwanda is trialing some of those accused of planning and carrying out the killings. But tensions continue between the Hutus and Tutsis. And human rights groups say there are still very serious problems with the justice system because of the failure of Rwandan courts.

Former President Bill Clinton and United Nations Secretary General Kofi Annan have apologized for failing to intervene in Rwanda. During a ceremony in Geneva, Switzerland this week, Mister Annan proposed a five-point action plan designed to prevent future ethnic killings.

Part Four Translation of the Text

Tenth Anniversary of Ethnic Killings in Rwanda
卢旺达大屠杀十周年纪念日

Wednesday was the tenth anniversary of the start of widespread ethnic killings in Rwanda. Thousands of people attended a national burial ceremony in the capital, Kigali. They gathered there to honor the victims and to show support for the central African nation.

周三是卢旺达大规模种族屠杀的十周年纪念日。数千人出席了在首都基加利举行的国家葬礼仪式。人们齐聚缅怀受害者，以示对这个中非国家的支持。

The leaders of South Africa, Kenya, Uganda and Ethiopia attended the ceremony. Belgian Prime Minister Guy Verhofstadt was the only Western leader to attend. Rwanda criticized Western countries for not sending high-level officials.

出席该仪式的有南非、肯尼亚、乌干达及埃塞俄比亚的领导人。比利时总理居伊·费尔霍夫施塔特是唯一出席的西方国家领导人。卢旺达批评西方国家没有派遣高层官员出席该仪式。

During the ceremony, Rwandan President Paul Kagame led Rwandans in observing three minutes of silence for the victims. Earlier, he lit a flame at the new Kigali National Memorial Center.

卢旺达总统保罗·卡加梅在仪式中带领卢旺达人民对受害者进行3分钟默哀。之前，他在新的基加利国家纪念馆中心主持了点火仪式。

The killings in Rwanda began on April seventh, nineteen ninety-four, after a plane carrying the presidents of Rwanda and Burundi was shot down over Kigali. Both leaders died in the crash. Rwanda's President Juvenal Habyarimana was an ethnic Hutu.

卢旺达大屠杀始于1994年4月7日，当时卢旺达和布隆迪总统乘坐的飞机在基加利上空遭袭坠毁，两位总统丧生。卢旺达总统朱韦纳尔·哈比亚利马纳是胡图族人。

Following the crash, extremists in the Hutu government began a plan to kill all of the country's minority Tutsi population and politically moderate Hutus. An estimated eight-hundred-thousand Tutsis and moderate Hutus were killed in three months of violence.

坠机事件发生后，胡图族政府内部的激进分子开始执行屠杀该国少数民族图西人及胡图族政治温和派人士的计划。在为期3个月的暴乱中，估计有80万名图西人及胡图族温和派人士被杀。

The killings ended when Mister Kagame's Tutsi-led rebel army ousted the extremist Hutu government and seized control of the capital. More than two-million Hutus later fled to nearby Democratic Republic of Congo. In a speech during the ceremony in Kigali, President Kagame said Rwanda takes the most blame for the mass killings. But he criticized the international community for failing to intervene to stop the killings. He also repeated accusations that French officials helped train and arm the Hutu government soldiers and militants who carried out the killings.

在由卡加梅领导的图西族武装反抗军推翻激进的胡图族政府并占领首都后，大屠杀才结束。有两百多万名胡图人之后逃难至邻近的刚果民主共和国。卡加梅总统在基加利的葬礼仪式上指出，卢旺达在大屠杀事件中应承担绝大部分责任。他批评国际社会未能介入并阻止屠杀事件。他也重申了对法国官员的谴责，说他们为执行屠杀的胡图族政府军人及好战分子提供训练和武器装备。

France has denied the accusations. It later withdrew its deputy foreign minister from the ceremony in Kigali.

法国否认了有关指控，之后召回了出席基加利葬礼仪式的外交部副部长。

Rwanda is one of the world's poorest countries. Many Rwandans are still suffering as a result of the violence ten years ago. Many women were infected with the disease AIDS during widespread sexual attacks. And thousands of children lost their parents in the mass killings or from AIDS.

卢旺达是世界上最贫穷的国家之一。目前尚有许多卢旺达人承受着十年前暴乱种下的苦果，当时许多女性在普遍的性侵犯中染上了艾滋病，成千上万名孩童则因大屠杀事件或艾滋病的肆虐而失去了父母。

Human rights officials say the situation in Rwanda now is calm and the government has control in the country. The International Criminal Tribunal for Rwanda is trying some of those accused of planning and carrying out the killings. But tensions continue between the Hutus and Tutsis. And human rights groups say there are still very serious problems with the justice system because of the failure of Rwandan courts.

人权组织官员表示，目前卢旺达国内情况稳定，由政府掌控着国家。卢旺达国际刑事法庭对被指控策划及执行大屠杀的一些罪犯进行了审讯。然而目前胡图人和图西人之间的紧张关系依然持续。人权组织指出，卢旺达法庭的无能凸显了卢旺达的司法制度存在着非常严重的问题。

Former President Bill Clinton and United Nations Secretary General Kofi Annan have apologized for failing to intervene in Rwanda. During a ceremony in Geneva, Switzerland this week, Mister Annan proposed a five-point action plan designed to prevent future ethnic killings.

美国前总统克林顿及联合国秘书长安南对未能阻止卢旺达大屠杀一事致歉。安南于本周在瑞士日内瓦举行的一个仪式上提议了一个为防止未来发生种族屠杀而设计的五点行动计划。

(IN THE NEWS, in VOA *Special English*, was written by Cynthia Kirk. This is Steve Ember.)

Lesson 22　North Korean Nuclear Deal Called into Question

By Nancy Steinbach

September 23, 2005

Part One　Background Information

朝核问题因何而起

这个世界可真够让美国总统操心的了，美国政府一边投入近400亿美元用于反导系统的研发和试验，并且在未来几年内仍将每年投入90亿至100亿美元以加强美国反导系统对俄罗斯核导弹的拦截能力①，一边还得严密监视朝鲜核试验动向，尽其一切努力迫使朝鲜放弃核计划。然而，尽管朝鲜在2005年底之前参加了五轮朝核问题的“六方会议”，并在第四轮会谈中承诺，“放弃一切核武器及现有核计划，早日重返《不扩散核武器条约》，并回到国际原子能机构保障监督”②，但2006年7月5日，朝鲜再次试射了多枚导弹。7月15日，联合国安理会以15个成员国一致赞成的方式通过决议，对朝鲜实施有限制裁，并要求平壤中断弹道导弹计划。同年10月3日，安理会警告朝鲜如果无视国际社会劝阻坚持核试验，安理会将采取进一步行动。但国际社会的压力最终未能阻止朝鲜进行核试验的步伐。北京时间10月9日上午，朝鲜宣布成功进行了地下核试验③。

20世纪90年代初，美国开始怀疑朝鲜正在秘密研制核武器，并以朝鲜已签署《不扩散核武器条约》为名，要求进入朝鲜核查。1993年前后，美国政府甚至制订了一项对朝核设施进行外科手术式打击的计划，但由于韩国坚决反对而未能实施。1994年6月，美国前总统卡特赴朝同当时的朝领导人金日成会晤，朝核问题暂告缓解。不料这年7月8日金日成突然去世，计划中的朝韩峰会告吹。但这年的10月，美国以负责筹款，为朝鲜建设两座采用轻水反应堆的电站以及电站运转前，美国将向朝提供用作燃料的重油为承诺，劝服朝鲜在日内瓦框架协议上签了字，答应放弃其核计划，就这样化解了第一次朝核危机。

如果所有人都能按协议办事，世界上的冲突就会减少很多。朝美框架协议并没有得到执行，第二次朝核危机出现在2002年。10月3日，朝方代表在与美国为追究朝鲜“违约”而派出的特使凯利的会谈中，明确承认朝鲜业已恢复核计划，并称如果美国答应双方签订和平条约等4项条件，朝鲜就准备放弃核计划。为了表示美方的“愤怒”，美国决定对朝鲜实行不谈判，不作交易的基本政策，以强硬态度迫使朝鲜放弃核计划。2002年11月14日，美国主导的朝鲜半岛能源开发组织决定自12月起中断向朝提供重油。朝鲜方面

---

① 成戈. 俄部署核弹道打击系统 美反导系统紧盯俄核导弹. 环球时报，2005－12－28

② 田辉. 从核反应堆到核试验　朝鲜核计划走过半世纪. http：//mil. eastday. com/m/20061010/u1a2367684. html，2006－10－10

③ 朝核问题新动态综述：各方纷纷为危机化解努力. 央视国际，http：//www. cctv. com/news/world/20030113/100161. shtml，2003－01－13

也采取了一系列的行动。12 月 12 日，朝鲜宣布由于美方中断供油，朝鲜决定解除对核计划的冻结，重新启动用于电力生产的核设施。12 月 22 日，朝鲜宣布撕掉核封条，拆除国际原子能机构监视设备，随后驱逐其监控人员。美国原计划 2003 年完工的电站工程在该年仅仅完成约 24%。①

此后，美国与联合国安理会即使是软硬兼施，也无法阻止朝鲜核计划的实施。在 2003 年 4 月 23 日至 25 日举行的中、朝、美三方北京会谈中，朝鲜代表以非正式的方式，但用非常明确的语言告诉美国代表凯利：朝鲜已经制造出若干枚原子弹，并于 5 月 22 日宣布退出 1992 年它与韩国签署的《朝鲜半岛无核化宣言》。同年 8 月 27 日至 29 日，经中方多轮外交斡旋，由中美朝韩日俄参加的六方会谈在北京举行，朝方表示愿意考虑美方提出的书面安全保障，但要求美国放弃敌视朝鲜的政策之后再进行实质性弃核。布什政府反复强调无意侵犯朝鲜，无意改变朝鲜现行制度，希望通过和平谈判解决朝核问题。六方会谈没有耽搁朝鲜核计划开发的脚步，2005 年 5 月，朝鲜宣布从核反应堆内取出 8 000 根废燃料棒，并以美国对朝鲜进行核打击为由，重新启动了冻结的 5 兆瓦核反应堆，并恢复了 5 万千瓦和 20 万千瓦核反应堆的建设工作②。

第五轮六方会谈于 2005 年 11 月 9 日至 11 日在北京举行。12 月 6 日，朝鲜威胁称，如果美国不取消对朝鲜的经济制裁，朝鲜将不会重返六方会谈。但 2006 年 12 月 18 日六方会谈还是复会了，看来朝核问题的拉锯战不会在短期内结束。

Part Two　Exercises

Ⅰ. Listen to the first part of the negotiation news, and write down the main idea of the news in the following order.

1. The agreement:

1) when, who, where, about what

2) What is the condition North Korea asked for the agreement?

2. The time of the negotiation, and the countries attended:

3. The goal of the agreement:

①② 朝核问题新动态综述：各方纷纷为危机化解努力. http://www.cctv.com/news/world/20030113/100161.shtml, 2003-01-13

Ⅱ. Listen and repeat the second part of the news, and complete the following sentences.

1. One day later, on Tuesday, North Korea announced that it will not end its nuclear arms program ______.

2. The Bush administration ______.

3. The American State Department reacted by saying that ______.

4. Japan called North Korea's ______.

5. China said it expects all the nations involved ______.

6. South Korea said it would support North Korea's desire ______ ______. One is that the country must first ______. The other is that it must ______.

Ⅲ. Listen to the third part of the news, and translate it into Chinese.

Ⅳ. Listen to the fourth part of the news, and repeat it sentence by sentence, then write it down by memory.

Part Three　Keys to the Exercises

Ⅰ. Listen to the first part of the negotiation news, and write down the main idea of the news in the following order.

1. 1) On Monday, six nations signed an agreement in Beijing that would end North Korea's nuclear arms program.

2) But North Korea almost immediately demanded a civilian nuclear power station before

it would destroy its nuclear weapons.

2. The agreement was reached after two years of negotiations among North Korea, the United States, China, Japan, Russia and South Korea.

3. 1) The agreement says North Korea will end its nuclear arms program in exchange for economic aid and security guarantees.

2) Nuclear Non-Proliferation Treaty… North Korea agreed to return to the Nuclear Non-Proliferation Treaty and again permit international inspectors to make sure its nuclear arms program has ended.

3) North Korea also received recognition of its desire to keep a civilian nuclear program for electric power production.

4) This will involve building what is called a light-water reactor.

5) And the agreement says the nations will discuss building light-water reactors at the right time. But it does not say when that will be.

Ⅱ. Listen and repeat the second part of the news, and complete the following sentences.

1. One day later, on Tuesday, North Korea announced that it will not end its nuclear arms program until it gets light-water reactors from the United States.

2. The Bush administration has rejected this kind of negotiating.

3. The American State Department reacted by saying that North Korea should carefully think about the agreement that it signed.

4. Japan called North Korea's demand unacceptable.

5. China said it expects all the nations involved to carry out their responsibilities in a serious way.

6. South Korea said it would support North Korea's desire for peaceful nuclear energy on two conditions. One is that the country must first rejoin the non-proliferation treaty. The other is that it must bring back United Nations inspectors.

Ⅲ. Listen to the third part of the news, and translate it into Chinese.

American diplomats have praised the agreement because it shows that the five countries other than North Korea can agree on a plan. They say the importance of the agreement includes promises by North and South Korea to improve ties. It also includes promises from Japan and the United States to move closer to normal relations with North Korea. And they say it shows the great influence of China as North Korea's main ally. China also supplies most of North Korea's food and fuel.

美国外交人员就朝鲜以外五国能够达成协议感到满意。他们认为，协议的重要性在于朝鲜、韩国都承诺改善关系，也包括日、美两国承诺将逐步实现与朝鲜的关系正常化。同时，他们表示，协议亦反映了中国作为朝鲜主要盟友所发挥的重大影响力。中国为朝鲜提供了大量食物和燃料。

Ⅳ. Listen to the fourth part of the news, repeat it sentence by sentence, then write it down by memory.

Yet experts also criticized the agreement because it does not go into detail or provide time limits. One expert said North Korea apparently thinks the right time to discuss the civilian power question is before it takes any steps to end its nuclear arms program. The United States says the right time is after North Korea ends its nuclear arms program or takes the first steps toward disarming.

Some experts say the North Korean demand is a sign that its government is not serious about ending its nuclear arms program. However, representatives of the six nations are to meet again in November to continue discussions.

Part Four　Translation of the Text

North Korean Nuclear Deal Called into Question
朝鲜核能协议产生分歧

On Monday, six nations signed an agreement in Beijing that would end North Korea's nuclear arms program. But North Korea almost immediately demanded a civilian nuclear power station before it would destroy its nuclear weapons.

本周一，六国于北京签订了朝鲜结束核武计划的协议，但朝鲜旋即提出要求，在销毁核武器前建设一个民用核电站。

The agreement was reached after two years of negotiations among North Korea, the United States, China, Japan, Russia and South Korea. The agreement says North Korea will end its nuclear arms program in exchange for economic aid and security guarantees.

协议由朝鲜、美国、中国、日本、俄罗斯和韩国六国经过两年多的谈判后达成。协议声明朝鲜将结束核武计划，以换取经济援助和国家安全保证。

North Korea agreed to return to the Nuclear Non-Proliferation Treaty and again permit international inspectors to make sure its nuclear arms program has ended. North Korea also received recognition of its desire to keep a civilian nuclear program for electric power production.

朝鲜同意重返《不扩散核武器条约》，并重新接受国际检查员的视察，以确认其一切核武器计划已终止。朝鲜要求建立电厂而保留民用核能工程的愿望亦得到认可。

This will involve building what is called a light-water reactor. And the agreement says the nations will discuss building light-water reactors at the right time. But it does not say when that will be.

它涉及建立所谓的轻水式核反应堆。以上协议提到，与会国将在适当时间讨论兴建轻水式核反应堆的问题，但没有明确具体时间。

One day later, on Tuesday, North Korea announced that it will not end its nuclear arms program until it gets light-water reactors from the United States. The Bush administration has rejected this kind of negotiating.

一天后，即星期二，朝鲜宣布在没有从美方得到轻水式反应堆之前，不会结束核武计划。布什政府拒绝这等谈判要求。

The American State Department reacted by saying that North Korea should carefully think about the agreement that it signed. Japan called North Korea's demand unacceptable.

美国国务院回应说，朝鲜应审慎考虑自己签署的协议。日本称难以接受朝鲜的要求。

China said it expects all the nations involved to carry out their responsibilities in a serious way. South Korea said it would support North Korea's desire for peaceful nuclear energy on two conditions. One is that the country must first rejoin the non-proliferation treaty. The other is that it must bring back United Nations inspectors.

中国表示希望与会各国严肃地履行各自的责任。韩国表示在两种情况下会支持朝鲜和平使用核能的愿望。首先朝鲜必须重新加入《核不扩散条约》，其次朝鲜要重新接受联合国的监察员的检查。

American diplomats have praised the agreement because it shows that the five countries other than North Korea can agree on a plan. They say the importance of the agreement includes promises by North and South Korea to improve ties. It also includes promises from Japan and the United States to move closer to normal relations with North Korea. And they say it shows the great influence of China as North Korea's main ally. China also supplies most of North Korea's food and fuel.

美国外交人员就朝鲜以外五国能够达成协议感到满意。他们认为，协议的重要性在于朝鲜、韩国都承诺改善关系，也包括日、美两国承诺将逐步实现与朝鲜的关系正常化。同时，他们表示，协议亦反映了中国作为朝鲜主要盟友所发挥的重大影响力。中国为朝鲜提供了大量食物和燃料。

Yet experts also criticized the agreement because it does not go into detail or provide time limits. One expert said North Korea apparently thinks the right time to discuss the civilian power question is before it takes any steps to end its nuclear arms program. The United States says the right time is after North Korea ends its nuclear arms program or takes the first steps toward disarming.

但有专家批评协议不够详细，也没提出时限。有个专家说，朝鲜显然认为讨论民用核能问题的最佳时间是在采取任何措施终止其核武计划之前。而美国则认为最佳时机是朝鲜终止核武器项目之后，或者先进一步解除武装之后。

Some experts say the North Korean demand is a sign that its government is not serious about ending its nuclear arms program. However, representatives of the six nations are to meet again in November to continue discussions.

一些专家表示，朝鲜的要求反映出当局并无诚意终止核武计划。不过六国代表仍将在 11 月重开会议，继续讨论此事。

（In THE NEWS IN VOA *Special English* was written by Nancy Steinbach. Our reports are on the Web at voaspecialenglish. com. I'm Steve Ember. ）

Lesson 23 Iran Rejects Appeal to Stop Enriching Uranium

By Jerilyn Watson

April 15, 2006

Part One Background Information

伊朗人为什么仇恨美国

人们常说，国与国之间没有永远的朋友，只有永远的利益。美伊之间也曾有过“蜜月”，之后的分手并成仇敌无不体现了国与国之间的利益冲突。

伊朗人对美国的仇恨种子是在巴列维国王执政（1941—1979 年）时期种下的。在巴列维国王之前，由于英苏两国军队从 1909 年至 1921 年分占伊朗南北达 12 年之久，“二战”后，英国通过“英伊石油公司”将伊朗石油收益的绝大部分分据为已有。“以 1950 年为例，英伊石油公司的纯利润接近 2 亿英镑，而伊朗政府仅获得 1 600 万英镑。伊朗从该公司购买石油，甚至比从苏联进口还贵”①。而苏联干脆在北部的阿塞拜疆和库尔德人聚居区培植亲苏势力，意欲在伊朗建立国中之国。为了与英苏抗衡，巴列维国王选择与美国作为盟友。而美国在中东民族主义此起彼伏的浪潮中再也无法实施直接的军事干预，只能转而寻找地区代理人作为其外交政策的主攻对象，以防伊朗落入苏联之手。

伊朗石油国有化期间，美伊关系进入“蜜月“期。率先提出政治改革和对英伊石油公司在伊朗的资产实行国有化的民族阵线领导人摩萨台于 1951 年 4 月被任命为首相。在摩萨台的推动下，巴列维于 5 月 2 日签署了石油工业国有化法案，这样就对英伊石油公司实施国有化有了法律依据。为了抵制伊朗的石油国有化，英国人关闭了阿巴丹炼油厂，要求任何国家或公司不要购买伊朗石油，伊朗因此被排挤出世界石油市场，引发伊朗政府的财政危机。这时，美国政府出面了，杜鲁门总统向英国人施压，要求他们与伊朗谈判，谋求达成一个解决危机的协议。同时，美国政府根据这一年新通过的《共同安全法》，允诺向伊朗每年提供 2 300 万美元的军事援助和一定数量的经济援助；批准进出口银行给予伊朗 2 500 万美元的贷款（后来没有实施）；支持伊朗向世界银行申请 100 万美元的贷款②。有了美国政府的支持，伊朗军队在 9 月 27 日占领了英伊石油公司的炼油厂，迫使英国职员撤离伊朗。

此后，在一般伊朗人的心目中，美国是一个没有太多私利，反对欧洲殖民主义统治，帮助伊朗制衡英苏、实现其国家独立的伟大国家。然而，在 1953 年摩萨台政府试图推进一场激进的、与巴列维的亲美倾向背道而驰的、并将威胁到王室利益的民族主义改革之时，美国政府便决定除掉摩萨台，由中情局中东行动处处长克米特·罗斯福亲自策划，让

① 余火. 黑色记录：美国 1953 年颠覆伊朗政府回顾. 环球时报，2006 - 03 - 21

② 佚名. 美国和英伊冲突. http：//www. 21voc. com/book. php action = view&fid = 1074&aid = 100001902&page = 32

大量亲国王的民众包围了伊朗国会大厦，砸毁了亲人民党的报社。同时美国军队的坦克占领了伊朗国家电台，并向全国宣布巴列维国王撤销摩萨台职务的消息。当天晚上，摩萨台就被关进了大狱。为回报美国的恩情，巴列维把伊朗40%的石油开采权让给了美国财团[①]。由此，巴列维国王出卖国家利益的卑劣行为及其对美国政府的过度依赖激起了伊朗民众日益高涨的反美情绪。1963年1月，巴列维国王按照美国推动第三世界国家社会与经济变革的思想，开始了土地改革的“白色革命”，加速了整个社会的世俗化和西方化，再加上巴列维国王的高压统治引起了伊朗社会最为强大、最有组织性的伊斯兰什叶派上层的极度不满，终于引发了1978年反对国王统治的群众运动。次年，伊朗宗教领袖霍梅尼正式接管政权。霍梅尼领导的伊斯兰革命最为响亮的口号是“不要东方，不要西方，只要伊斯兰”。1980年，美国宣布与伊朗断交，并正式对其实行经济制裁，美国与伊朗的关系全面恶化。

在对待伊朗核开发的态度方面，美国其实没有什么准则，20世纪50年代美国政府与巴列维国王交好时，极力支持伊朗核能开发活动。1980年与伊朗断交后，即开始指责伊朗以“和平利用核能”为掩护秘密发展核武器，并对其采取“遏制”政策。2006年，新当选的伊朗总统穆罕默德·艾哈迈迪·内贾德26日誓言继续推进伊朗和平利用核能的计划，并表示伊朗不非常需要改善与美国的关系。

Part Two　Exercises

Ⅰ. Listen to the first part of the news, and complete the following sentences.

1. Iran has rejected an appeal from the head of the International Atomic Energy Agency ____________________.

2. __________ chief Mohamed ElBaradei met Thursday in Tehran with Iranian officials.

3. Mohamed ElBaradei __________ in Tehran, Iran Thursday.

4. Mister ElBaradei said Iran repeated its promise to answer questions about ____________________.

5. He also said he could not confirm Iran's claim that it has enriched uranium to ____________________.

6. Mister ElBaradei said the __________.

7. And he said there is enough time __________.

Ⅱ. Listen to the second part of the news, and answer the following questions.

1. Why do you think the International Atomic Energy Agency want Iran to suspend its uranium activity?

① 余火. 黑色记录：美国1953年颠覆伊朗政府回顾. 环球时报，2006－03－21

2. What's Iran's reaction to the IAEA's appeal?

3. What do Iranians do to the one thousand megawatt nuclear reactor（核反应堆）?

4. How many centrifuge devices（离心分离装置）are they going to increase?

Ⅲ. Listen to the third part of the news about the US' reaction to Iran's uranium activity, and translate it into Chinese.

Ⅳ. Listen to and repeat the last part of the news, and write it down.

Part Three Keys to the Exercises

Ⅰ. Listen to the first part of the news, and complete the following sentences.

1. Iran has rejected an appeal from the head of the International Atomic Energy Agency <u>to</u>

suspend its uranium enrichment activities.

2. United Nations nuclear agency chief Mohamed ElBaradei met Thursday in Tehran with Iranian officials.

3. Mohamed ElBaradei holds press conference in Tehran, Iran Thursday.

4. Mister ElBaradei said Iran repeated its promise to answer questions about issues involving its nuclear program.

5. He also said he could not confirm Iran's claim that it has enriched uranium to a level used in nuclear power centers.

6. Mister ElBaradei said the only way to solve the issue is through negotiation.

7. And he said there is enough time to negotiate a settlement.

Ⅱ. Listen to the second part of the news, and answer the following questions.

1. Why do you think the International Atomic Energy Agency want Iran to suspend its uranium activity?

1) Because earlier this week, Iran announced that it now can enrich uranium to the level used in nuclear power centers.

2) That would raise the possibility of making nuclear weapons.

2. What's Iran's reaction to the IAEA's appeal?

1) Iranian President Mahmoud Ahmadinejad said that international pressure would not influence his nation.

2) Mister Ahmadinejad said that from now on, the world would have to deal with Iran as a nuclear power.

3. What do Iranians do to the one thousand megawatt nuclear reactor（核反应堆）?

Iranian officials say they plan to make fuel for a one thousand megawatt nuclear reactor（核反应堆）.

4. How many centrifuge devices are they going to increase?

2, 836. The officials say they plan to greatly increase the centrifuge devices（离心分离机装置）needed for the process. They said they plan to expand the program to make three thousand centrifuges by the end of the year. They said they are currently using one hundred sixty-four centrifuges.

Ⅲ. Listen to the third part of the news about the US' reaction to Iran's uranium activity, and translate it into Chinese.

Iranian officials have said their nuclear activities are peaceful. But the United States and European nations believe the Iranians are operating a secret nuclear weapons program.

伊朗的官员说他们的核生产用于和平事业。但美国和欧洲国家认为伊朗人正在进行一个秘密的核武器项目。

In Washington, Secretary of State Condoleezza Rice criticized Iran. Miz Rice said the nation could face increasing international punishment if it does not stop its nuclear work.

在华盛顿，国务卿赖斯对伊朗提出批评。赖斯说，如果伊朗不停止核生产，它可能会面临更多的国际性制裁。

A high level State Department official, Nicholas Burns, spoke to a VOA reporter. Mister Burns said a large international coalition, including the United States, Russia, China and Europe, does not want Iran to develop nuclear weapons. He said these countries believe Iran has not told the truth about its secret nuclear weapons research program.

国务院高级官员尼古拉思·伯恩斯对美国之音记者说，包括美国、俄罗斯、中国和欧洲在内的大部分国际社会都不愿意看到伊朗发展核武器。他说这些国家相信伊朗没有如实说出有关它秘密研制核武器的计划。

Ⅳ. Listen to and repeat the last part of the news, and write it down.

Russia says it will hold more talks next week on the situation. Representatives from the United States, the European Union and China are to attend the meeting Tuesday in Moscow. On Friday, a Chinese diplomat began a visit to Iran and Russia to discuss the issue.

The United Nations Security Council meets later this month to consider punishing Iran for its nuclear program. The Council had told Iran to stop all uranium enrichment activities before the end of this month. The Council will wait to hear from Mister ElBaradei before deciding on its next step. Mister ElBaradei reports to the Security Council on April twenty-eighth.

Part Four　Translation of the Text

Iran Rejects Appeal to Stop Enriching Uranium

伊朗拒绝停止铀浓缩活动的要求

Iran has rejected an appeal from the head of the International Atomic Energy Agency to suspend its uranium enrichment activities.

伊朗拒绝了国际原子能机构领导人呼吁它停止铀浓缩活动的要求。

United Nations nuclear agency chief Mohamed ElBaradei met Thursday in Tehran with Iranian officials.

联合国核能机构的主任穆罕默德·巴拉迪星期四在德黑兰会见伊朗官员。

Mister ElBaradei said Iran repeated its promise to answer questions about issues involving its nuclear program. He also said he could not confirm Iran's claim that it has enriched uranium to a level used in nuclear power centers. Mister ElBaradei said the only way to solve the issue is through negotiation. And he said there is enough time to negotiate a settlement.

巴拉迪先生说，伊朗再三承诺将回答有关核计划的问题。同时他说无法证实伊朗声称的铀浓缩水平已经达到核电厂要求。巴拉迪先生说解决问题的唯一方法是谈判，而且他说有充足的时间可以谈判解决。

Earlier this week, Iran announced that it now can enrich uranium to the level used in nuclear power centers. That would raise the possibility of making nuclear weapons.

本星期初，伊朗宣布它现在的铀浓缩已达应用于核电厂的水平。这会增加制造核武器的可能性。

Iranian President Mahmoud Ahmadinejad said that international pressure would not influence his nation. Mister Ahmadinejad said that from now on, the world would have to deal with Iran as a nuclear power.

伊朗总统穆罕默德·艾哈迈迪·内贾德说，国际的压力不会影响他的国家。他还说，从现在开始，世界将不得不正视伊朗这个核大国的现实。

Iranian officials say they plan to make fuel for a one thousand megawatt nuclear reactor. The officials say they plan to greatly increase the centrifuge devices needed for the process. They said they plan to expand the program to make three thousand centrifuges by the end of the year. They said they are currently using one hundred sixty-four centrifuges.

伊朗的官员说他们计划为一个百万千瓦级核反应堆准备原料。官方说他们计划为此目的大幅地增加离心分离机装置，到年底将此工程扩张到3 000个离心分离机，而现在正在使用的离心分离机仅164个。

Iranian officials have said their nuclear activities are peaceful. But the United States and European nations believe the Iranians are operating a secret nuclear weapons program.

伊朗的官员说，他们的核生产用于和平事业。但美国和欧洲的国家认为伊朗人正在进行一个秘密的核武器项目。

In Washington, Secretary of State Condoleezza Rice criticized Iran. Miz Rice said the nation could face increasing international punishment if it does not stop its nuclear work.

在华盛顿，国务卿赖斯对伊朗提出批评。赖斯说，如果伊朗不停止核生产，它可能会面临更多的国际性制裁。

A high level State Department official, Nicholas Burns, spoke to a VOA reporter. Mister Burns said a large international coalition, including the United States, Russia, China and Europe, does not want Iran to develop nuclear weapons. He said these countries believe Iran has not told the truth about its secret nuclear weapons research program.

国务院高级官员尼古拉思·伯恩斯对美国之音记者说，包括美国、俄罗斯、中国和欧洲在内的大部分国际社会都不愿意看到伊朗发展核武器。他说这些国家相信伊朗没有如实说出有关它秘密研制核武器的计划。

Russia says it will hold more talks next week on the situation. Representatives from the United States, the European Union and China are to attend the meeting Tuesday in Moscow. On Friday, a Chinese diplomat began a visit to Iran and Russia to discuss the issue.

俄罗斯说，它下个星期将会议召开会谈讨论此事。来自美国、欧盟和中国的代表将参加星期二在莫斯科的会议。星期五，一位中国外交官开始访问伊朗和俄罗斯以讨论此问题。

The United Nations Security Council meets later this month to consider punishing Iran for its nuclear program. The Council had told Iran to stop all uranium enrichment activities before the end of this month. The Council will wait to hear from Mister ElBaradei before deciding on its next step. Mister ElBaradei reports to the Security Council on April twenty-eighth.

联合国安理会这个月下旬将会考虑因伊朗核计划而如何制裁伊朗。安理会已告诫伊朗在本月底之前停止所有的铀浓缩活动。安理会等听过巴拉迪先生的报告之后再决定下一步骤。巴拉迪先生会在 4 月 28 日向安理会做报告。

Lesson 24 Putin Calls for Changes in Russia's Political Changes

By Cynthia Kirk
September 18, 2004

Part One Background Information

普京为何进行政治改革

普京的总统任期将于2008年春结束，他已表示不会修改宪法参加第三次竞选。美国《商业周刊》2005年2月28日发表的“解读普京”说，“这个俄罗斯总统看上去就像是苏联时期的独裁者转世：他限制媒体，废除地区选举，还插手邻国大选。在其他时候，他则表现得像一个敢作敢为的市场改革者”。人们对他褒贬、爱恨不一，尤其体现在对他的政治改革措施上。

与戈尔巴乔夫、叶利钦的权威型政府比较起来，普京政府更充满了“强有力的政府执政理念和行为”。正如普京说过的：俄罗斯当局是按照本国民族众多、土地辽阔的特点来发展民主的。但除此以外，俄罗斯特定的历史条件还催生出一批经济寡头的怪胎。20世纪90年代初，在国家政局剧烈动荡和经济秩序极度混乱时期，俄政府开始廉价拍卖国有资产，即所谓私有化。一些人利用种种非法手段，乘机将能源、原材料和金融等领域的大批国有企业和资产占为己有，成为一夜暴富的寡头，而广大民众却被推向贫困的边缘。这些一夜之间暴富的新权贵凭着手中几亿、几十亿美元的个人财产创造了足以左右俄罗斯发展的“影子政治”和“影子经济”，实现了他们将资本权力化的目标，他们在政治上左右政局，政府要员成了他们手中的玩偶，国家法令成了他们赚钱的工具；他们在经济上呼风唤雨，公共财富和资源成了他们巧取豪夺、任意瓜分的对象；与此同时，他们还垄断了舆论工具，大众媒体成为他们试图瓜分公共权力的喉舌，民意被他们引导和操控。[①] 普京正是在与这些寡头较量的过程中，重整了国家纲纪。从拘留“大桥媒体集团公司”总裁、传媒大亨古辛斯基和伏尔加汽车营销公司总裁、多家媒体公司的控股人及联邦安全会议副秘书和国家杜马议员的别列佐夫斯基，到2003年逮捕俄罗斯首富霍多尔科夫斯基，普京为俄罗斯政坛清除了富翁干预政治和“曲线”参政的“左派”势力，为2003年12月的杜马大选完成了具有决定性意义的权力洗牌，使三权分立式的民主模式在俄罗斯不复存在，换句话说，他同时为自己的第二任参选铺平了道路。2004年9月13日，普京提出了俄罗斯10多年来最具震撼力的政治改革方案，应该说是他整顿俄罗斯政坛、强化中央权力的一个延续。此方案包括各联邦主体的高层官员将由总统提名、经地方议会选举产生，同时取消地方长官由当地选民直接选举的办法；国家杜马实行比例选举制，议员完全由政党产生，同

① 龚泽宣. 俄罗斯民主化时代的政治腐败——再论“民主不是万应灵丹”. 东南亚研究，2006（1）

时取消各地区的“直举”①。这一政治改革方案将各地方联邦主体变成了单一制国家下的行政单位，彻底改变了俄罗斯自苏联解体以来按照西方民主模式构建的政治制度。

多家媒体均批评普京以反恐战争的名义扩大个人集权，但事实上，对普京而言，此次集权措施对于增加普京手中个人权力的实际意义不大，因为他已宣布将不会修改宪法以谋求再次连任或延长总统任期。而此次地方政府领导人产生和联邦议会下院国家杜马组成的改变，将有利于俄罗斯建立纵向权力体系，扩大全国性政党的规模②。可见，普京此举在于强化国家政权，实行“可控民主”，以维护国家统一，实现政治与经济的“强国”目标。

Part Two Exercises

Ⅰ. Listen to the first part of the news, and write it down in the following order.

1. The political changes: Russian President Vladimir Putin. . .

2. The measures. . .

3. The reasons for the proposals. . .

1）

2）

4. “Terrorists' attacks” in Russia:

1）in the southern town of Beslan:

Half:

2）near an underground train station in Moscow:

100:

3）A Chechen rebel leader, Shamil Basayev:

4）independence for Chechnya

①② 王正泉. 普京政改举措符合俄罗斯客观需要. http: //www. qianlong. com/2006 - 10 - 09

Ⅱ. Listen to and repeat the second part of the news, then complete the following sentences.

1. In Moscow, President Putin said Friday that Russia ______________________.

2. He said ______________________ Russian and international law.

3. Mister Putin announced the ______________________ Monday.

4. He said Russia needs a ______________________ that is able not only to deal with attacks but also to work to prevent them.

5. He said the new agency should have the power ______________________ and, if necessary, in other countries.

Ⅲ. Listen to the third part of the news, and translate it into Chinese, then repeat it in English.

the Duma 杜马

Ⅳ. Listen to the last part of the news, and write it down paragraph by paragraph.

Part Three　Keys to the Exercises

Ⅰ. Listen to the first part of the news, and write it down in the following order.

1. The political changes: Russian President Vladimir Putin...

This week, Russian President Vladimir Putin announced a plan for changes in the political system in Russia.

2. The measures...

The measures would increase the powers of the central government.

3. The reasons for the proposals...

1) Mister Putin said the proposals are needed to improve security.

2) He said those responsible for terrorist acts seek to ruin Russia.

4. "Terrorists' attacks" in Russia:

1) Beslan: Earlier this month, more than three hundred people were killed at Middle School Number One in the southern town of Beslan. Half were children.

2) near an underground train station in Moscow: The hostage crisis followed bombings on two Russian airplanes and near an underground train station in Moscow. One-hundred people were killed in those attacks.

3) A Chechen rebel leader, Shamil Basayev:

A Chechen rebel leader, Shamil Basayev, reportedly claimed responsibility for all the attacks in a letter Friday on a Web site.

4) The letter threatened more violence and urged Russia to recognize independence for Chechnya.

Ⅱ. Listen to and repeat the second part of the news, then complete the following sentences.

1. In Moscow, President Putin said Friday that Russia is preparing what he called pre-emptive action against terrorists.

2. He said it would follow Russian and international law.

3. Mister Putin announced the proposed changes Monday.

4. He said Russia needs a single anti-terrorism agency that is able not only to deal with attacks but also to work to prevent them.

5. He said the new agency should have the power to destroy criminals in their hideouts and, if necessary, in other countries.

Ⅲ. Listen to the third part of the news, and translate it into Chines, then repeat it in English.

Mister Putin also called for changes in the rules for electing parliament. His plan would end local elections that now fill half of the four hundred fifty seats in the lower house, the Duma. Instead, all members would be elected from party lists chosen by Russia's main national parties. The changes must be approved by the Duma, which is controlled by supporters of Mister Putin.

普京总统同时要求对选举议会的规则进行改革。他计划终止地方选举，现今的地方选举将填补杜马（下议院）450 个议会席位中的一半议员。取而代之的是，所有议员都将从俄罗斯主要党派的名单中选出。这些改革必须由杜马（下议院）批准，杜马由普京总统的支持者掌控。

Also, the Russian leader called for local governors to be nominated by the president and approved by local parliaments. In recent years, the eighty-nine governors have been elected directly by the people.

同时，俄罗斯总统呼吁由总统提名地方官员人选，然后由地方议会批准。近年来，89 名地方官员是由人民直接选举出来的。

Ⅳ. Listen to the last part of the news, and write it down paragraph by paragraph.

Critics say the changes would violate Russia's Constitution. Some say they do not believe the moves will really help fight terrorism. They say the government is using the recent attacks as a chance to expand its power. Mister Putin faces little organized opposition.

For ten years, Russian troops have attempted to crush the independence movement for Chechnya and its mostly Muslim population. Russian officials say there is evidence that international terrorists are involved.

The United States says it supports a political solution to the Chechen conflict. It also says it supports Russia in its struggle against terrorism. But American officials say they are concerned that the changes will harm democracy in Russia.

Part Four　Translation of the Text

Putin Calls for Changes in Russia's Political Changes
普京要求俄罗斯进行政治体制改革

This week, Russian President Vladimir Putin announced a plan for changes in the political system in Russia. The measures would increase the powers of the central government. Mister Putin said the proposals are needed to improve security. He said those responsible for terrorist acts seek to ruin Russia.

本周，俄罗斯总统普京宣布了一项政治体制的改革计划。其措施将加强中央政府的权力。普京先生说，这个提案为改善国家安全状况之所需，并对恐怖主义分子企图摧毁俄罗斯的行为负责。

Earlier this month, more than three hundred people were killed at Middle School Number One in the southern town of Beslan. Half were children. The hostage crisis followed bombings on two Russian airplanes and near an underground train station in Moscow. One hundred people were killed in those attacks.

这个月月初，在别斯兰南部小镇的第一中学有300多人被杀害，其中一半是儿童。这次人质危机事件是在两架俄罗斯飞机被炸和莫斯科地铁附近的爆炸事件后发生的，100人在这几次袭击事件中丧生。

A Chechen rebel leader, Shamil Basayev, reportedly claimed responsibility for all the attacks in a letter Friday on a Web site. The letter threatened more violence and urged Russia to recognize independence for Chechnya. In Moscow, President Putin said Friday that Russia is preparing what he called pre-emptive action against terrorists. He said it would follow Russian and international law.

一名车臣叛军领袖巴萨耶夫星期五在网络上的一信件里宣称对所有袭击负责。这封信恐吓说将有更多的暴力事件发生，并威胁俄罗斯承认车臣独立。星期五，普京总统在莫斯科说，俄罗斯准备采用所谓“先发制人”的措施来对付恐怖主义分子。他表示俄政府会遵守俄罗斯法律及国际法。

Mister Putin announced the proposed changes Monday. He said Russia needs a single anti-terrorism agency that is able not only to deal with attacks but also to work to prevent them. He said the new agency should have the power to destroy criminals in their hideouts and, if necessary, in other countries.

星期一普京总统宣布了改革的提案。他说俄罗斯需要一个独立的反恐机构，不仅能够对付袭击，同时也能防止袭击事件的发生。他表示，如果有必要，新机构应有权利将犯罪分子消灭在潜伏场所与他国。

Mister Putin also called for changes in the rules for electing parliament. His plan would end local elections that now fill half of the four hundred fifty seats in the lower house, the Duma. Instead, all members would be elected from party lists chosen by Russia's main national parties. The changes must be approved by the Duma, which is controlled by supporters of Mister Putin.

普京总统同时要求对选举议会的规则进行改革。他计划终止地方选举，现今的地方选举将填补杜马（下议院）450个议会席位中的一半议员。取而代之的是，所有议员都将从俄罗斯主要党派的名单中选出。这些改革必须由杜马（下议院）批准，杜马由普京总统的支持者掌控。

Also, the Russian leader called for local governors to be nominated by the president and approved by local parliaments. In recent years, the eighty-nine governors have been elected directly by the people.

同时，俄罗斯总统呼吁由总统提名地方官员人选，然后由地方议会批准。近年来，89名地方官员是由人民直接选举出来的。

Critics say the changes would violate Russia's Constitution. Some say they do not believe the moves will really help fight terrorism. They say the government is using the recent attacks as a chance to expand its power. Mister Putin faces little organized opposition.

评论家说这些改革将会违反俄罗斯的宪法。有些人表示他们不认为这些举措真正有助于打击恐怖主义。他们说政府正是利用目前的恐怖袭击来扩展其势力。普京先生面临一小部分有组织的反对派。

For ten years, Russian troops have attempted to crush the independence movement for Chechnya and its mostly Muslim population. Russian officials say there is evidence that international terrorists are involved.

10 年来，俄罗斯军队试图镇压车臣的独立运动及大部分的穆斯林人民。俄罗斯官员说，有证据证明国际恐怖主义分子涉足其中。

The United States says it supports a political solution to the Chechen conflict. It also says it supports Russia in its struggle against terrorism. But American officials say they are concerned that the changes will harm democracy in Russia.

美国表示支持用政治途径解决车臣冲突。它也表示支持俄罗斯对恐怖主义进行的斗争。不过，美国官员说他们担心改革将会给俄罗斯的民主带来损害。

Lesson 25 Germany Awaits a New Leader, and a New Day

By Jerilyn Watson

October 15, 2005

Part One Background Information

德国女总理

德国实行联邦制，国家政体为议会共和制。联邦总统是国家元首，由联邦大会选举产生，任期5年，可以连任一次。总统有权向联邦议院提议总理人选，经议会选举后任命。议会由联邦议院和联邦参议院组成，德意志联邦议院由人民每4年选举一次。联邦议院的任务是立法，选举联邦总理和监督政府。联邦议院的议员是全民的代表，并不完全代表议员所在政党的利益。联邦参议院是16个联邦州的代表机构，参与联邦的立法与行政，其议员由各州政府成员或其全权代表组成，每州有3—6个席位①。

联邦德国的多党制呈现“二元体制”与“三党鼎足”之势，基民盟、基社盟和社民党是议会主要政党，其中，基民盟（基督教民主联盟）长期处于执政地位。该民盟连任25年的主席赫尔穆特·科尔（1973—1998）担任联邦总理长达16年，阿登纳任联邦总理达13年之久。然而，在巴伐利亚州，由“二战”中反法西斯统治的基督徒组成的基社盟（基督教社会联盟）则连续一党执政整整45年。科尔执政的16年间，实现了德国统一，实现了采用欧元，将欧洲统一大大向前推进了一步。但他在任期内造就了约400万失业大军，1998年9月因爆出政治献金丑闻而被社民党在全国大选中拉下马②。

由于社会福利措施周全，企业渐渐失去奖勤罚懒的机制，使得失业者既没有生活压力，也没有再就业的动力，许多失业者宁愿领取失业保险金或社会救济金，也不愿接受低工资的工作，德国因此获得了“欧洲经济病人”的称号。社民党领导人施罗德上任后力排众议，准备对制约该国经济发展的高福利制度进行大刀阔斧的改革。但受到来自各方面的抵制和反对，最让施罗德寒心的是，最大的阻力竟来自社会民主党内部，社民党的伙伴和德国最有影响的工会组织也进行了坚决的抵制。虽然改革方案勉强通过，但施罗德政府推行的税收、社会保险金方面的新政策触动了中产阶级的利益。2005年，德国经济增长率只有1%，在欧盟25国当中表现最差，其失业率也攀升至“二战”以来的新高，达到12.6%，致使德国社民党在2005年的大选中丧失了多数议席，失去了组阁的领导权。害怕变化的德国民众虽然无法彻底接受施罗德的改革方案，却无力抵制基民盟历史上第一位女主席默克尔提出的改革政策。默克尔在2000年成功当选为基民盟主席，2005年她带领基民盟赢得了多个州选举的胜利，迫使施罗德总理宣布提前大选，最后赢得了德国下议院614

---

① 佚名. 德国概况. http://www-user. tu-chemnitz. de/~yuhao/new_ page_ 2-9. htm

② 佚名. 德国将迎来历史上首位女总理 经济界没有掌声. Finance. ICXO. Com, 2005-10-11

个席位中397的多数票，成为德国“二战”后第八位总理，也是第一位来自东德地区的总理①。

德国经济要走出低谷，就必须大刀阔斧地改革。从莱比锡大学物理学毕业，在原东德科学院物理化学研究中心从事科研工作的默克尔从政后，经常被人们称作“德国的撒切尔”和“德国铁娘子”。就任后，默克尔确定了她的执政目标：在十年内使德国重新回到欧洲经济增长率前三位行列中，在她的五年任期内大幅降低高达11%的失业率。在签署联合政府协议时，她称：“我们的目标是创造更多的就业机会。在四年内，人们应该能够说他们比过去生活得更好。”

Part Two Exercises

Ⅰ. Listen to the first part of the news, and fill in the blanks with the words you hear.

The major political parties in Germany are working to ____________________. When they finish, Parliament is expected to elect Angela Merkel ____________________. She is a ____________________ who would be the first woman to lead Germany. Angela Merkel would also be ____________________.

Her party, the Christian Democratic Union, ____________________ last month for the Bundestag（德国联邦议院）, the German parliament. But it did not ____________________. The Christian Democrats and the Social Democratic Party of Chancellor Gerhard Schroeder agreed Monday to ____________________.

Ⅱ. Listen to the second part of the news, and answer the following questions.

1. What is the problem the new chancellor will face?

2. How is the the German economy?

3. How many years has Mister Schroeder been a chancellor untit 2005?

4. Tell which party leads which ministry.

---

① 佚名. 默克尔正式当选德首位女总理 重振经济为首要任务. http://cn.news.yahoo.com/05-11-22/1063/2g6xl.html

5. What is the influence of the coalition government on Angela Merkel?

6. What's the difference between Angela Merkel and unions?

7. What's the difference between Miz Merkel and Mester Schroeder on their attitudes toward the US?

8. Why does Miz Merkel want to improve relations with the US?

Ⅲ. Listen to and repeat the third part of the news, and translate it into Chinese.

Ⅳ. Listen to and repeat the fourth part of the news, and write it down.

Begin from "She became active...".

Part Three　Keys to the Exercises

Ⅰ. Listen to the first part of the news, fill in the blanks with the words you hear.

The major political parties in Germany are working to complete negotiations for a new government. When they finish, Parliament is expected to elect Angela Merkel as the new chancellor. She is a conservative who would be the first woman to lead Germany. Angela Merkel would also be the first leader from the former East Germany.

Her party, the Christian Democratic Union, narrowly won elections last month for the Bundestag（德国联邦议院）, the German parliament. But it did not receive enough votes for a majority. The Christian Democrats and the Social Democratic Party of Chancellor Gerhard Schroeder agreed Monday to form a coalition.

Ⅱ. Listen to the second part of the news, and answer the following questions.

1. What is the problem the new chancellor will face?

The next chancellor will face a national unemployment rate of more than eleven percent.

2. How is the German economy?

The German economy is the largest in Europe. But economic growth has slowed.

3. How many years has Mister Schroeder been a chancellor until 2005?

Seven years. Mister Schroeder said this week that he would not take part in the new government. He has been chancellor since nineteen ninety-eight.

4. Tell which party leads which ministry.

Under the coalition agreement, the ministries led by Social Democrats would include the Foreign Ministry. Miz Merkel's party and the allied Christian Social Union would get leadership of the defense and economy ministries, among others.

5. What is the influence of the coalition government on Angela Merkel?

Political experts say sharing power with her opponents almost surely will limit the ability of Angela Merkel to make changes.

6. What's the difference between Angela Merkel and unions?

For example, she wants to ease laws that protect jobs and help keep labor costs high in Germany. But unions support the protections.

7. What's the difference between Miz Merkel and Mester Schroeder on their attitudes toward the US?

Miz Merkel also says she wants to improve relations with the United States. Mister Schroeder refused to support American plans for the invasion of Iraq in two thousand and three. However, Germans do not expect Miz Merkel to want to send troops to Iraq, either.

8. Why does Miz Merkel want to improve relations with the US?

Germany does wants a permanent seat on the United Nations Security Council. The United

States has not shown support for that idea.

Ⅲ. Listen to and repeat the third part of the news, and translate it into Chinese.

Angela Merkel is fifty-one years old. She was born Angela Kasner in Hamburg, West Germany. Her father was a Lutheran clergyman. He was sent to lead a small church in East Germany while Angela was a baby. So she grew up under Communist rule.

安格拉·默克尔今年 51 岁。她出生在西德汉堡的安格拉卡斯勒。她的父亲是路德教会的一个牧师。当安格拉还是一个婴儿的时候，她父亲被派去东德的一个小教堂任职。她在共产主义的统治下成长。

There, she received a doctoral degree in physics at the University of Leipzig in nineteen eighty-six. Later she did research in East Berlin. She is married to a chemistry professor, Joachim Sauer. They have no children.

她于 1986 年在莱比锡大学获得物理博士学位，后来在东德柏林做研究。她嫁给了一个名叫绍尔的化学教授，他们没有孩子。

Ⅳ. Listen to and repeat the fourth part of the news, and write it down.

She became active in the democracy movement in East Germany in nineteen eighty-nine. She joined the Christian Democratic Union about the time East and West Germany re-united in nineteen ninety. Voters elected her to Parliament the following year.

She soon became minister for women and young people, in the cabinet of Chancellor Helmut Kohl. Angela Merkel has chaired the Christian Democratic Union since two thousand. She has led its delegation in Parliament since two thousand two. Her forceful personality often leads to comparisons with the former British prime minister Margaret Thatcher.

Part Four Translation of the Text

Germany Awaits a New Leader, and a New Day

德国等待着新一任领导人和新一天的到来

The major political parties in Germany are working to complete negotiations for a new government. When they finish, Parliament is expected to elect Angela Merkel as the new chancellor. She is a conservative who would be the first woman to lead Germany. Angela Merkel would also be the first leader from the former East Germany.

德国的主要政党正在努力为新一届政府达成协议。之后，人们期望议会选出安格拉·默克尔为德国新任总理。她是一位保守党员，将成为德国首位女总理。安格拉·默克尔也是第一个来自前东德的领导人。

Her party, the Christian Democratic Union, narrowly won elections last month for the Bundestag, the German parliament. But it did not receive enough votes for a majority. The

Christian Democrats and the Social Democratic Party of Chancellor Gerhard Schroeder agreed Monday to form a coalition.

她所在政党——基督教民主联盟在上个月举行的德国联邦议会大选中险胜，但是没能得到多数选票。基民盟和格哈德·施罗德领导的社民党同意在周一组成联合政府。

The next chancellor will face a national unemployment rate of more than eleven percent. The German economy is the largest in Europe. But economic growth has slowed.

新一任总理将要面对全国超过11%的失业率。虽然德国经济在欧洲是最强的，但其经济增长已经减慢。

Mister Schroeder said this week that he would not take part in the new government. He has been chancellor since nineteen ninety-eight. Under the coalition agreement, the ministries led by Social Democrats would include the Foreign Ministry. Miz Merkel's party and the allied Christian Social Union would get leadership of the defense and economy ministries, among others.

施罗德本周说他将不加入新政府。他自1998年始任德国总理。根据联合协议，社民党领导的部门包括外交部，而默克尔政党及基督教社会联盟获得国防部、经济部等其他部的领导权。

Political experts say sharing power with her opponents almost surely will limit the ability of Angela Merkel to make changes. For example, she wants to ease laws that protect jobs and help keep labor costs high in Germany. But unions support the protections.

政治学家说，与对手分享权力，安格拉·默克尔的改革能力毫无疑问会受到限制。例如，她要放宽德国工作保障法，并保持劳动力的高成本。但联合政府支持保护企业。

Miz Merkel also says she wants to improve relations with the United States. Mister Schroeder refused to support American plans for the invasion of Iraq in two thousand three. However, Germans do not expect Miz Merkel to want to send troops to Iraq either.

默克尔说她要改善美德关系。在2003年，施罗德拒绝支持美国入侵伊拉克的计划。然而，德国人民亦不希望默克尔派军队去援助伊拉克。

Germany does wants a permanent seat on the United Nations Security Council. The United States has not shown support for that idea.

德国想在联合国安理会获得常任理事国的席位，美国没有表示支持。

Angela Merkel is fifty-one years old. She was born Angela Kasner in Hamburg, West Germany. Her father was a Lutheran clergyman. He was sent to lead a small church in East Germany while Angela was a baby. So she grew up under Communist rule.

安格拉·默克尔今年51岁。她出生在西德汉堡的安格拉卡斯勒。她的父亲是路德教会的一个牧师。当安格拉还是一个婴儿的时候，她父亲被派去东德的一个小教堂任职。她在共产主义的统治下成长。

There, she received a doctoral degree in physics at the University of Leipzig in nineteen eighty-six. Later she did research in East Berlin. She is married to a chemistry professor, Joachim Sauer. They have no children.

她于1986年在莱比锡大学获得物理博士学位，后来在东德柏林做研究。她嫁给了一个名叫绍尔的化学教授，他们没有孩子。

She became active in the democracy movement in East Germany in nineteen eighty-nine. She joined the Christian Democratic Union about the time East and West Germany re-united in nineteen ninety. Voters elected her to Parliament the following year.

在 1989 年东德的民主运动中，她是个活跃分子。1990 年东西两德统一的时候，她参加了基民盟，第二年就被选进议会。

She soon became minister for women and young people, in the cabinet of Chancellor Helmut Kohl. Angela Merkel has chaired the Christian Democratic Union since two thousand. She has led its delegation in Parliament since two thousand two. Her forceful personality often leads to comparisons with the former British prime minister Margaret Thatcher.

她很快就在科尔内阁出任妇女与青年部部长。2000 年安格拉 · 默克尔成为基民盟的主席。自 2002 年起，她成为议会中基民盟代表团的领导。她强有力的个性常常使得人们将她比作英国前任首相玛格利特 · 撒切尔。

第三部分　政治、法律、科学报道、文化等新闻

Lesson 26　International Criminal Court

By Caty Weaver

April 13, 2002

Part One　Background Information

人类丧失理性的时候谁来管

亚里士多德说，人是理性的动物。可是，谁能说清楚，为什么会发生卢旺达种族大屠杀，为什么被认为是“理性”的德国人会丧尽天良地虐待犹太人，并且企图灭绝犹太人？笔者不揣浅陋，认为没有惩罚制度，是人失去理性的原因之一。

在过去的20世纪里，人类的某些角落经受了一轮又一轮的“危害人类罪”、“战争罪”和“灭绝人类罪”。“二战”中，数以百万的犹太人死于希特勒的集中营；二十世纪七十年代，柬埔寨估计有200万人被红色高棉杀害。继1993年前南斯拉夫爆发种族清洗后，1994年卢旺达也发生了惨无人道的种族大屠杀，“短短百日之内，近百万无辜者被残酷杀害，200多万难民逃亡国外，另有200多万人流离失所”①。

正如中国的俗话所说，天网恢恢，疏而不漏。国际刑事法院就是这样一个“网”，它是人类理性的象征，代表着人类正义向失去人性的人拔出了惩罚的剑。1948年12月9日，联合国大会第260号决议中说：“有史以来，灭绝种族行为殃祸人类至为惨烈；深信欲免人类再遭此类狞恶之浩劫，国际合作实所必需。”为此，联合国通过了《防止及惩治灭绝种族罪公约》。公约第一条将灭绝种族定性为“国际法上的一种罪行”，第六条则规定，凡被诉犯灭绝种族罪者，“应交由行为发生地国家的主管法院或……（具有）管辖权的国际刑事法庭审理”。在该决议中，大会还请国际法委员会“研究宜否及可否设立一个国际司法机构以审判被控犯灭绝种族罪的人……”② 这便是国际刑事法院成立的萌芽。1998年7月17日，《国际刑事法院规约》在罗马通过，于2002年7月1日生效，国际刑事法院正式成立。

国际刑事法院，主要指由国家选举出来的若干个独立的法官组成的、审判特定的国际

---

① 李新烽．“非洲人的命不值钱”卢旺达大屠杀谁之过．环球时报，2004-04-09

② 李宇先．国际刑事法院概述．http：//www. un. org/chinese. law. /icc/overview. htm

罪行并对罪犯处以法定刑罚的国际刑事审判机构。它既包括永久性国际刑事裁判机构，还包括为特定目的而设立的临时或特设性质的国际刑事审判机构，如欧洲国际军事法庭和远东国际军事法庭，以及由联合国安理会设立的前南问题国际法庭和卢旺达问题国际法庭。国际刑事法院在理论上可以管辖各种国际罪行，以及可以对一切国籍的罪犯行使管辖权，在法律适用上，国际刑事法院必须适用各缔约国普遍接受的国际法，不像在它之前的几个特别法庭，可以灵活地适用国际法①。

自2002年国际刑事法院正式运转以来，收到了几百件关于国际犯罪案件的受理申请，但该法院一直都没有正式受理。它所受理的第一起案件是应乌干达总统穆塞韦尼的请求，对乌干达反政府武装“圣灵抵抗军”的罪行进行调查。但直到2005年7月，国际刑事法院才发出了首批逮捕令，通缉五名被指控犯下严重侵犯人权罪行的乌干达“圣灵抵抗军”领导人。与此同时，国际刑事法院还在调查刚果民主共和国、苏丹达尔富尔等案件。

值得注意的是，按照《国际法院规约》于1946年4月在荷兰海牙成立的国际法院与国际刑事法院有很大的区别，国际法院是处理国际争端的世界性机构，它没有刑事管辖权，因此无法审判个人。但它是联合国的主要司法机关，是联合国的下属机构，因而联合国各会员国都是《国际法院规约》的参加者。而国际刑事法院的主要目标之一，是保护世界各地个人的人权和基本自由，确保那些煽动种族灭绝行动，发动族裔清洗运动，在武装冲突中杀害、强奸和残暴伤害平民，或者用儿童进行令人发指的医学实验的人得到应有的惩罚。中国和美国都不是该法院的成员国。

Part Two　Exercises

Ⅰ. Listen to the first part of news, and complete the sentences with the words you hear.

1. ____________________ International Criminal Court was established this week.
2. The governments of sixty-six countries have ____________________.
3. However, the governments of ____________________ have not approved the treaty.
4. The United States ____________________.

Ⅱ. Listen to the second part of the news, and answer the following questions.

1. What is the role of the International Criminal Court (ICC)?

2. What are serious crimes against human rights according to the ICC?

① 王能干. 论国际刑事法院作用的有限性. http://www.hicourt.gov.cn/theory/artilce_list.aspid=1828&l_class=3

3. Will the court try suspects all over the world?

4. Will all historical suspects against human rights be tried by the ICC?

5. Before the ICC, were there any international courts? Will they combine together?

6. Where is the new ICC based? When will it begin operations?

7. Where do the judges of the ICC come from? How long can they serve the ICC for each term?

Ⅲ. Listen to the third and forth part of the news, and translate it into Chinese with the outline given below.

1. The three ways to bring case to the ICC:

1) A nation that has approved the treaty can...

2) The United Nations Security Council can...

3) And, an International Criminal Court lawyer can...

4) The court will be able...

2. ... the United Nations

3. ... the costs of the court.

4. A ceremony...

Ⅳ. Listen and repeat the last part of the news, and write it down by memory.

Begin from " UN Secretary General Kofi Annan... ".

Ⅴ. Tell the difference between the ICC and the Internation Court.

Part Three Keys to the Exercises

Ⅰ. Listen to the first part of news, and complete the sentences with the words you hear.

1. The world's first permanent International Criminal Court was established this week.

2. The governments of sixty-six countries have approved the treaty establishing the court.

3. However, the governments of China, Russia and the United States have not approved the treaty.

4. The United States strongly opposes the court.

Ⅱ. Listen to the second part of the news, and answer the following questions.

1. What is the role of the International Criminal Court (ICC)?

The International Criminal Court will charge and try individuals for very serious human rights violations.

2. What are serious crimes against human rights according to the ICC?

These include crimes against humanity, war crimes and genocide (种族灭绝).

3. Will the court try suspects all over the world?

No, the court will try suspects only if their own governments are unwilling or unable to do so.

4. Will all historical suspects against human rights be tried by the ICC?

No, the treaty is to go into effect July first. The International Criminal Court will be able to try crimes that are carried out after that date.

5. Before the ICC, were there any international courts? Will they combine together?

Yes, there are two existing United Nations courts for Bosnia and Rwanda. No, they will continue to try war crimes suspects, independent of the new court.

6. Where is the new ICC based? When will it begin operations?

The new International Criminal Court will be based in The Hague, the Netherlands. It is expected to begin operations next year.

7. Where do the judges of the ICC come from? How long can they serve the ICC for each term?

The nations that approved the treaty will elect eighteen judges to nine-year terms early next year.

Ⅲ. Listen to the third and forth part of the news, and translate it into Chinese with the outline given below.

1. Cases can be brought to the International Criminal Court in three ways.

1) A nation that has approved the treaty can request that the court investigate a situation.

2) The United Nations Security Council can also request such action.

3) And, an International Criminal Court lawyer can start an investigation based on reports from victims and other people.

The court will be able to investigate and try suspects from nations that are not part of the treaty if the nations permit it.

有三种方法在国际刑事法院立案:

1) 参加此条约的国家可以请求法院对某个案情进行调查;

2) 联合国安理会也可以提出此请求;

3) 国际刑事法院的律师可以根据受害人和其他人的举报进行调查。

如果嫌疑犯所属国家允许，法院可以调查并审判来自非条约国家的嫌疑犯。

2. The International Criminal Court will not be part of the United Nations.

国际刑事法院不属于联合国。

3. The countries that are part of the treaty will pay the costs of the court.

由条约国支付法庭的费用。

4. A ceremony launching the International Criminal Court was held at UN headquarters in New York City Thursday.

星期四，联合国总部在纽约举行了庆祝国际刑事法院成立的典礼。

Ⅳ. Listen to and repeat the last part of the news, and write it down by memory.

UN Secretary General Kofi Annan sent a message praising the court. He said countries with good judicial systems that carry out the rule of law do not need to fear the court.

Most democratic nations and human rights groups welcomed the action.

European nations praised the creation of the court as the most important action against war criminals this century. They urged the United States, China and Russia to approve the treaty. The United States signed the International Criminal Court Treaty in Two-Thousand during the administration of former President Bill Clinton. But Mister Clinton did not seek legislative approval of the treaty.

However, the administration of President Bush strongly opposes the court. It says the court could lead to unfair legal action against American officials and soldiers in other countries. The administration says it is considering cancelling the United States signing of the treaty.

Part Four Translation of the Text

International Criminal Court

国际刑事法院

The world's first permanent International Criminal Court was established this week. The governments of sixty-six countries have approved the treaty establishing the court. However, the governments of China, Russia and the United States have not approved the treaty. The United States strongly opposes the court.

世界上第一个永久性的国际刑事法庭于本周成立。66 个国家政府已经批准建立该法院的条约。然而，中国、俄罗斯和美国政府不同意该条约。美国强烈反对成立该法院。

The International Criminal Court will charge and try individuals for very serious human rights violations. These include crimes against humanity, war crimes and genocide. The court will try suspects only if their own governments are unwilling or unable to do so. The treaty is to go into effect July first. The International Criminal Court will be able to try crimes that are carried out after that date.

国际刑事法院将对严重侵犯人权的个人行为提出指控并进行审判。这些行为包括反人性罪、战争罪和种族灭绝罪。该法院只有在嫌疑犯所属政府不愿意或无能力对嫌疑犯进行审讯时，才会参与此事。该条约于 7 月 1 日生效。国际刑事法庭院有权审判在这个日期之后所犯下的罪行。

The two existing United Nations courts for Bosnia and Rwanda will continue to try war crimes suspects, independent of the new court.

现有的两个联合国法院是波斯尼亚法院和卢旺达法院，它们将会继续审判战争嫌疑犯而独立于新法院。

The new International Criminal Court will be based in The Hague, the Netherlands. It is expected to begin operations next year. The nations that approved the treaty will elect eighteen judges to nine-year terms early next year.

新的国际刑事法院总部设在荷兰的海牙，预计于明年开始运行。同意参加该条约的国家将在明年初选举 18 个法官，他们的任期为九年。

Cases can be brought to the International Criminal Court in three ways. A nation that has approved the treaty can request that the court investigate a situation. The United Nations Security Council can also request such action. And, an International Criminal Court lawyer can start an investigation based on reports from victims and other people. The court will be able to investigate and try suspects from nations that are not part of the treaty if the nations permit it.

有三种方法在国际刑事法庭立案：参加此条约的国家可以请求法院对某个案情进行调查；联合国安理会也可以提出此请求；国际刑事法院的律师可以根据受害人和其他人的举报进行调查。如果嫌疑犯所属国家允许，法院可以调查并审判来自非条约国家的嫌疑犯。

The International Criminal Court will not be part of the United Nations. The countries that are part of the treaty will pay the costs of the court.

国际刑事法院不属于联合国。由条约国支付法院的费用。

A ceremony launching the International Criminal Court was held at UN headquarters in New York City Thursday. UN Secretary General Kofi Annan sent a message praising the court. He said countries with good judicial systems that carry out the rule of law do not need to fear the court.

星期四，联合国总部在纽约举行了庆祝国际刑事法院成立的典礼。联合国秘书长安南发来贺信，对该法院的建立表示赞许。他说，有良好司法系统实行法制的国家是不需要害怕国际刑事法院的。

Most democratic nations and human rights groups welcomed the action. European nations praised the creation of the court as the most important action against war criminals this century. They urged the United States, China and Russia to approve the treaty. The United States signed the International Criminal Court Treaty in Two-Thousand during the administration of former President Bill Clinton. But Mister Clinton did not seek legislative approval of the treaty.

大多数的民主国家和人权组织对国际刑事法院表示欢迎。欧洲国家称赞该法院的成立是本世纪反战争罪最重要的一个举措，并敦促美国、中国和俄罗斯加入该条约。美国前任总统克林顿政府在2000年曾经签署了国际刑事法院条约，但是克林顿先生并没有寻求立法机构的批准。

However, the administration of President Bush strongly opposes the court. It says the court could lead to unfair legal action against American officials and soldiers in other countries. The administration says it is considering cancelling the United States signing of the treaty.

然而布什政府强烈反对该法院。它认为该法院可能导致美国官员和士兵在他国受到不公平的法律制裁。布什政府说正在考虑取消美国签署的条约。

(This VOA *Special English* program IN THE NEWS was written by Caty Weaver. This is Steve Ember.)

Lesson 27 Powerful US Lawmaker Accused of Election Law Violation in Texas

By Nancy Steinbach

October, 2005

Part One Background Information

美国总统选举与政治献金问题

在美国，参加总统选举是个拿红包的“天赐良机”。小布什在大选中得到竞选资金近7亿美元，而克里的竞选资金总额也不少于4亿美元①。这些钱来自哪里？根据初步统计，有150家以上的公司、工会组织和民间基金会向民主党和共和党捐款1亿多美元。这种政治献金并不包括为政治家和会议代表举行的音乐会、晚宴、午餐会等社交活动所花费的钱。美国著名金融大亨乔治·索罗斯和保险公司执行官彼得·刘易斯分别捐款1 270万和1 400万美元。其他的大财团比如普华永道、安永和德勤三大会计师事务所、摩根士丹利、美林、瑞银华宝、高盛等都对小布什一掷千金，当然还有以做假账而臭名昭著的美国安然公司。而时代华纳、维亚康母这两大传媒集团、美国多家著名的律师行也排在克里的捐款名单上。通用汽车、通用电气、花旗集团、IBM、美国国际集团在内的一些大公司，给民主党的政治献金是3 950万美元，给小布什的政治献金是6 400万美元②。

腐败是什么？“它是指利用公共资源谋取局部或个人利益的行为”③。2000年总统大选期间，德州有一家名为“德州人支持公共正义协会”的俱乐部，共有成员212名，专门为小布什竞选筹集资金。据统计，他们每人为小布什筹得的款项都在10万美元左右。小布什上台后，共有43位谋得要职。其中，出任内阁部长的就有两名——劳工部长赵小兰、国土安全办公室主任里奇；另有19名成员出任驻法国、荷兰、新西兰、挪威、葡萄牙、西班牙和瑞士等国的大使④。这样看来，美国人在总统竞选中是可以公开搞腐败了。

但并不是完全如此，美国的政治献金有“硬钱”和“软钱”之分。“硬钱”指符合联邦选举委员会（FEC）限额规定的募捐（每人在一次选举中为一个候选人捐款不超过2 000美元，为某一政党捐的用于选举的款项不能多于2万美元）。问题出在“软钱”上，“软钱”的募捐没有上限，只要是政党用来支付其活动和议题广告费用就行。“软钱”也要公开，但不受FEC的监管，所以，各类利益团体通过五花八门的途径将“硬钱”变通为“软钱”。比如，将企业的捐款转移到个人名下或某个组织名下。本课所涉内容即是一个实例，很不幸的是被发现了。

---

①② 盛立中. 金钱铺路的美国总统选举. http://www.globalview.cn/ReadNews.asp NewsID=2121

③ 佚名. 腐败的定义. zh.wikipedia.org/wiki/

④ 盛立中. 金钱铺路的美国总统选举. http://www.globalview.cn/ReadNews.asp NewsID=2121

Part Two　Exercises

Ⅰ. Listen to the first part of the news, and answer the following questions.

1. Who charged Whom?

2. What's the result of the charge?

3. What's the reason for the charge?

4. What is the election law about?

Ⅱ. Listen to the second part of the news, and complete the sentences that explain how Tom DeLay pass money to the campaigns in the state.

1. First, he set up a ________________.
2. Second, the group illegally ________________.
3. How much money he sent ________________.
4. Others who receive illegally the same amount of money were ________________.
5. The motives for this wrongdoing in Texas ________________.
6. The result of the election violation: ________________.
7. Another result of the election violation: ________________.

Ⅲ. Listen to the third and fourth part of the news sentence by sentence, and translate them into Chinese, then repeat them in English.

1. Mister DeLay ________________.
2. He could ________________.
3. A judge set ________________.
4. Two other men ________________.
5. Mister DeLay says ________________.
6. He says ________________.
7. He says Travis County District Attorney Ronnie Earle in Austin, the state capital, ________________.
8. Mister Earle is a Democrat ________________.

9. Republicans in Congress have chosen Missouri Representative Roy Blunt ______________________________.

10. But a Republican spokesman said Mister DeLay ______________________.

Ⅳ. Listen and repeat the last part of the news, and write it down with the words given below.

1. Tom DeLay...
2. ... Capitol Hill...
3. ... House...
4. Republicans...
5. The House Ethics Committee...
6. ... Democrats... ammunition（军火、弹药）...
7. ... Senate majority leader, Bill Frist...
8. ... company...

Part Three Keys to the Exercises

Ⅰ. Listen to the first part of the news, and answer the following questions.

1. Who charged whom?

A grand jury in Texas brought a charge against the Republican leader of the United States House of Representatives.

2. What's the result of the charge?

Texas Representative Tom DeLay has temporarily surrendered his position as majority leader, as required by rules, but he keeps his seat in Congress.

3. What's the reason for the charge?

He is charged with a violation of Texas election law.

4. What is the election law about?

It bans using money from businesses to support the election or defeat of political candidates.

Ⅱ. Listen to the second part of the news, and complete the sentences that explain how Tom DeLay pass money to the campaigns in the state.

1. First, he set up a political action committee he helped set up in Texas.

The case involves a political action committee he helped set up in Texas.

2. Second, the group illegally passed money from companies to campaigns in the state through the Republican National Committee.

The charge says the group illegally passed money from companies to campaigns in the state through the Republican National Committee.

3. How much money he sent one hundred ninety thousand dollars to the committee in

Washington.

In two thousand two, the Texas group sent one hundred ninety thousand dollars to the committee in Washington.

4. Others who receive illegally the same amount of money were seven Teaxas candidates.

The charge says the national committee also got a list of seven Texas candidates to receive, in total, that same amount.

5. The motives for this wrongdoing in Texas was part of an effort to help Republicans win control of the Texas House of Representatives.

The charge says the money was part of an effort to help Republicans win control of the Texas House of Representatives.

6. The result of the election violation: for the first time in one hundred thirty years.

They did win in two thousand two, for the first time in one hundred thirty years.

7. Another result of the election violation: the House of Representatives in Washington received five more Republicans from Texas.

Texas lawmakers drew a new map of voting areas. As a result, the House of Representatives in Washington received five more Republicans from Texas.

Ⅲ. Listen to the third and fourth part of the news, and translate them into Chinese, then repeat them in English.

Mister DeLay is accused of criminal conspiracy. He could face up to two years in prison if found guilty. A judge set a court appearance for October twenty-first. Two other men also face charges.

迪雷先生被指控犯有阴谋罪，如果罪名成立，他将会面临最高两年的监禁。法官将于10月21开庭，还有另外2个人也将面临指控。

Mister DeLay says he is innocent. He says he had nothing to do with the day-to-day operation of the Texas committee. He says Travis County District Attorney Ronnie Earle in Austin, the state capital, charged him for political reasons.

迪雷先生辩称他是清白的，他说他与德克萨斯州的日常工作没有丝毫关系。他称奥斯汀州特拉维斯郡的罗尼·厄尔检察官指控他，是出于政治上的原因。

Mister Earle is a Democrat who notes that he has also brought charges against Democrats in the past.

厄尔先生是民主党人，他提到自己过去也曾经指控过民主党人。

Republicans in Congress have chosen Missouri Representative Roy Blunt to act as majority leader temporarily. But a Republican spokesman said Mister DeLay will remain what he called a "very powerful adviser" to the party leadership.

国会里的共和党人选择了密苏里代表罗伊临时担任多数党领导人，但是共和党的发言人称迪雷先生仍然是党的领导层中“强有力的顾问”。

Ⅳ. Listen and repeat the last part of the news, and write it down with the words given below.

1. Tom DeLay...

Tom DeLay has often been called the most powerful Republican in Congress.

2. ... Capitol Hill...

He is known on Capitol Hill as "The Hammer" for his ability to pass legislation and enforce policies.

3. ... House...

All four hundred thirty-five members of the House are elected every two years.

4. Republicans...

Republicans have a twenty-nine-seat majority. The next election is in November of two thousand six.

5. The House Ethics Committee...

The House Ethics Committee criticized Mister DeLay three times last year for violations of House rules.

6. ... Democrats... ammunition（军火、弹药）...

Political experts say the situation now gives Democrats more ammunition to charge wrongdoing and poor leadership by Republicans.

7. ... Senate majority leader, Bill Frist...

Adding to the problems is a federal investigation of the Senate majority leader, Bill Frist.

8. ... company...

It involves the sale of his stock in a company started by his family. Senator Frist says he did nothing wrong.

Part Four Translation of the Text

Powerful US Lawmaker Accused of Election Law Violation in Texas

美国权威立法者在德克萨斯州被指控违反选举法

On Wednesday, a grand jury in Texas brought a charge against the Republican leader of the United States House of Representatives.

星期三，德克萨斯州的一个陪审团对美国众议院共和党领导提出指控。

Texas Representative Tom DeLay has temporarily surrendered his position as majority leader, as required by rules. But he keeps his seat in Congress. He is charged with a violation of Texas election law. It bans using money from businesses to support the election or defeat of political candidates.

按照规定，德克萨斯州的众议员汤姆·迪雷已被暂时停止其多数党领导职务，但仍然保留他在国会的席位。他被控告违反了德克萨斯州的选举法。该法禁止利用企业捐款进行选举或用于击败政治候选人。

The case involves a political action committee he helped set up in Texas. The charge says the group illegally passed money from companies to campaigns in the state through the Republican National Committee.

这宗案件涉及他在德克萨斯州协助设立的一个政治活动委员会。该指控提到，这个组织通过共和党全国委员会把公司资金非法转移到州竞选活动中。

In two thousand two, the Texas group sent one hundred ninety thousand dollars to the committee in Washington. The charge says the national committee also got a list of seven Texas candidates to receive, in total, that same amount.

2002 年，德克萨斯州组织给华盛顿的委员会送去 190 000 美元。指控还提到，国家委员会也拿到一张七个德克萨斯州候选人收受了同样总额的名单。

The charge says the money was part of an effort to help Republicans win control of the Texas House of Representatives. They did win in two thousand two, for the first time in one hundred thirty years.

这项指控还提到，这些钱是用于帮助共和党赢取德克斯萨州众议院控制权计划的一部分。他们在 2002 年确实赢得了选举，这是他们 130 年来头一次获得成功。

Later, Texas lawmakers drew a new map of voting areas. As a result, the House of Representatives in Washington received five more Republicans from Texas.

之后，德克萨斯州的立法者绘制了一张新的投票区域图。结果，华盛顿众议院多接收了五个德克萨斯州的共和党人。

Mister DeLay is accused of criminal conspiracy. He could face up to two years in prison if found guilty. A judge set a court appearance for October twenty-first. Two other men also face charges.

迪雷先生被指控犯有阴谋罪，如果罪名成立，他将会面临最高两年的监禁。法官将于 10 月 21 开庭，还有另外两个人也将面临指控。

Mister DeLay says he is innocent. He says he had nothing to do with the day-to-day operation of the Texas committee. He says Travis County District Attorney Ronnie Earle in Austin, the state capital, charged him for political reasons.

迪雷先生辩称他是清白的，他说他与德克萨斯州的日常工作没有丝毫关系。他称奥斯订州特拉维斯郡的罗尼·厄尔检察官指控他，是出于政治上的原因。

Mister Earle is a Democrat who notes that he has also brought charges against Democrats in the past.

厄尔先生是民主党人，他提到自己过去也曾经指控过民主党人。

Republicans in Congress have chosen Missouri Representative Roy Blunt to act as majority leader temporarily. But a Republican spokesman said Mister DeLay will remain what he called a "very powerful adviser" to the party leadership.

国会里的共和党人选择了密苏里代表罗伊临时担任多数党领导人，但是共和党的发言人称迪雷先生仍然是党的领导层中“强有力的顾问”。

Tom DeLay has often been called the most powerful Republican in Congress. He is known on Capitol Hill as “The Hammer” for his ability to pass legislation and enforce policies.

汤姆·迪雷常常被称为国会中最强势的共和党人，他因为具有通过立法和贯彻政策的能力而在国会山以“铁锤”闻名。

All four hundred thirty-five members of the House are elected every two years. Republicans have a twenty-nine-seat majority. The next election is in November of two thousand six.

435 个议员每两年选举一次。共和党人占 29 个席位的多数，下一次选举将在 2006 年 11 月举行。

The House Ethics Committee criticized Mister DeLay three times last year for violations of House rules. Political experts say the situation now gives Democrats more ammunition to charge wrongdoing and poor leadership by Republicans.

议院职业规范委员会指责迪雷先生去年三次违反议院条例。政治学家指出，这种情况为民主党人指证共和党人不道德行为和领导能力低下提供了口实。

Adding to the problems is a federal investigation of the Senate majority leader, Bill Frist. It involves the sale of his stock in a company started by his family. Senator Frist says he did nothing wrong.

联邦政府对参议院多数党领导人比尔·弗瑞斯特的调查可谓是雪上加霜。此案涉及他出售其家族公司的股票。弗瑞斯特参议员称他没有做错任何事。

（IN THE NEWS in VOA *Special English* was written by Nancy Steinbach. I'm Steve Ernber.）

Lesson 28 United States Releases Yearly Report on Human Rights around the World

By Nancy Steinbach
March 11, 2006

Part One Background Information

人权报告是外交的一张牌?

提起美国的年度人权报告，很多人就会生气，因为“美国人关心人权是假，扰乱主权是真”，“美国在报告中对中国进行了多方面的攻击。攻击中国的政治制度，攻击中国的国家安全部门，攻击中国对于所谓持不同政见者的处理，攻击中国的法轮功政策，攻击中国的新闻政策，攻击中国的少数民族政策，攻击中国的所谓非司法行为，攻击中国随意逮捕、刑讯及处罚犯罪嫌疑人”[①]。另有学者对美国人权外交的目的给予了抨击：“美国要用‘民主’、‘人权’等手段，把资本主义市场经济，加上西方模式的多党制、议会民主的社会制度推广到全世界，对社会主义国家演变其基本制度，对广大发展中国家加强控制，从而保持美国霸主地位和控制能力，使下一个世纪变成‘美国的世纪’。”[②] 对于美国把国际人权活动纳入干涉、支配他国内政轨道的“人权外交”策略，我们确实应该明察秋毫，但另一方面，对于“人权”，我们应该以崇敬的心态来看待国人的“人权意识”。

人权（天赋人权或自然权利），按照自然法，是属于所有人并且是不可剥夺的权利[③]。“人权的本质特征是自由和平等，其实质内容和目标是人的生存与发展。没有自由、平等作保证，人就不能作为人来生存和发展，也就谈不上人权。自由、平等的目的是使人摆脱一切压迫、剥削和歧视，获得有尊严的生存和全面自由的发展。”[④]

西方传统人权概念主要体现为早期资产阶级启蒙学者提出的“天赋人权”学说。在这种学说中，个人始终处于中心地位，是自私自利的权利主体，任何社会秩序都是以个人的契约自由为基础的，法律的目的是保护和扩大个人自由，对政府权力的限制也是为了确保个人的自由权利不受侵犯。为了确保个人的中心地位，自然法赋予个人以不可转让、不可剥夺的自然权利。[⑤]

值得欣慰的是，目前全世界人民都遵从的人权概念来自于1948年12月10日由联合国第三届大会在巴黎通过的《世界人权宣言》。它第一次提出了人权的基本内容和人类共同的奋斗目标。首先，它确定了不同种族、肤色、性别、语言、财产、宗教、政治或其他

---

① 王巍. 美国借人权干涉主权. http: //www. jjxj. com. cn/news_ detail. jsp keyno =6044
② 刘奋之. 美国人权战略解析. www. people. com. cn 2001 - 11 - 12
③ http: //zh. wikipedia. org/wiki/
④ 汪进元. 什么是人权. 人民日报，2005 - 01 - 12
⑤ 中国人权研究会. 西方传统人权概念的基本内涵是什么. 人民日报，2005 - 01 - 28

见解、国籍与其他出身、身份的人“在尊严和权利上一律平等；人人都有资格享受本《世界人权宣言》所载的一切权利和自由”；其次，它将人权的范畴界定为“公民权利和政治权利以及经济、社会和文化权利两大类”。“其中，公民权利和政治权利包括：生命权、人身权、不受奴役和酷刑权、人格权、法律面前人人平等权、无罪推定权、财产权、婚姻家庭权、思想良心和宗教自由权、参政权和选举权等”①；人的参政权意味着“人人有直接或通过自由选择的代表参与治理本国的权利”，“人民的意志是政府权力的基础，这一意志应以定期的和真正的选举予以表现”；《世界人权宣言》中还提到了人民的传播权即“人人有权享有主张和发表意见的自由；此项权利包括持有主张而不受干涉的自由和通过任何媒介，不论国界寻求、接受和传递消息和思想的自由”，这一条原则已成为世界各国人民争取新闻自由的圭臬。此外，经济、社会和文化权利包括“工作权、同工同酬权、休息和定期带薪休假权、组织和参加工会权、受教育权、社会保障和享受适当生活水准权、参加文化生活权等”②。

《世界人权宣言》是世界人权史上的一个重要里程碑，到目前为止，没有哪个政府或个人敢公开宣称与它为敌，它对人权所作的具体定义和描述为世界人权事业描绘了发展的蓝图。

Part Two　Exercises

Ⅰ. Listen to the first part of the news, and answer the following questions.

1. What did the the State Department released?

2. What is the yearly report for?

3. Why did the Congress need those reports?

4. How many countries are added to the report since the first one?

5. What are the criterion for the rights described in the report?

---

① 中国人权研究会.“世界人权宣言”是一个什么样的文件.人民日报，2005－03－02

② 世界人权宣言. http://www.un.org/chinese/work/rights/rights.htm

6. What are the rights included in the reports?

Ⅱ. The following table tells you what is listed as human conditions in the report. Listen and fill in the table with the information about the human conditions of the countries in the left column.

Human Rights Conditions	Names of the Countries
	North Korea, Burma, Iran, Zimbabwe, Cuba and Belarus
	Burma, North Korea, Iran and Syria
	Darfur area of Sudan, Nepal, Ivory Coast, Chechnya and elsewhere in Russia's Northern Caucasus area, and countries in central Africa
	Columbia
	Cambodia, Zimbabwe, Venezuela, Belarus and Russia
	Iraq, Afghanistan, Ukraine, Indonesia, Lebanon and Liberia
	Egypt, Ethiopia, Azerbaijan and Kazakhstan

Ⅲ. Listen to and repeat the last part of the news, and translate it into Chinese.

Ⅳ. Try to repeat the human rights and violation of those rights included in the human rights report.

Part Three Keys to the Exercises

Ⅰ. Listen to the first part of the news, and answer the following questions.

1. What did the the State Department released?

This week, the State Department released its "Country Reports on Human Rights Practices".

2. What is the yearly report for?

American officials use these yearly reports to develop policies, carry out diplomacy and decide about aid and other assistance.

3. Why did the Congress need those reports?

The first ones appeared in nineteen seventy-seven as required by Congress. They began with eighty-two countries which all received American aid.

4. How many countries have been added to the report since the first one?

196 - 82 = 114. Now, there are reports on one hundred ninety-six countries.

5. What are the criterion for the rights described in the report?

The reports are based on rights described in the United Nations Universal Declaration of Human Rights.

6. What are the rights included in the reports?

These include individual, civil, political and worker rights.

Others are freedom from torture or cruel punishment and from long terms in jail without charges.

They also include freedom from secret imprisonment and from other violations of the right to life, liberty and personal security.

Ⅱ. The following table tells you what is listed as human conditions in the report. Listen and fill in the table with the information about the human conditions of the countries in the left column.

Human Rights Conditions	Names of the Countries
Countries ruled by single persons or small groups	North Korea, Burma, Iran, Zimbabwe, Cuba and Belarus
Nations violate the rights of their own people	Burma, North Korea, Iran and Syria
Most serious violations during armed conflicts	Darfur area of Sudan, Nepal, Ivory Coast, Chechnya and elsewhere in Russia's Northern Caucasus area, and countries in central Africa
Human rights violation but fewer killings	Columbia

（续上表）

Used laws against the media and non-governmental organizations	Cambodia, Zimbabwe, Venezuela, Belarus and Russia
Nations that held democratic elections	Iraq, Afghanistan, Ukraine, Indonesia, Lebanon and Liberia
Nations where serious problems were reported in elections	Egypt, Ethiopia, Azerbaijan and Kazakhstan

Ⅲ. Listen to and repeat the last part of the news, and translate it into Chinese.

The report says many countries had mixed progress last year on democratic reform and human rights. For example, it notes that President Pervez Musharraf has stated his support for democratic change in Pakistan. But it says that country's human rights record continued to be poor.

报告认为有许多国家去年在民主改革和尊重人权方面取得了交叉式进步。例如，巴基斯坦的穆沙拉夫总统明确表示支持民主改革，但该国的人权状况还有待改善。

The Chinese government now reacts to American criticism with its own reports on the United States. China's report called American democracy "a game for the rich". It says the United States has a high murder rate, spies on its own people and violates the rights of prisoners in Iraq and Guantanamo Bay, Cuba.

目前中国政府也发布了有关美国人权的报告，以此回应美国的批评。中国的人权报告称美国的民主是“富人的游戏”。报告中说，美国谋杀案发生频率高，对本国人民实行秘密监视，在伊拉克和古巴关塔那摩监狱中侵犯犯人的人权等。

Part Four Translation of the Text

United States Releases Yearly Report on Human Rights around the World

美国颁布世界年度人权报告

This week, the State Department released its "Country Reports on Human Rights Practices". American officials use these yearly reports to develop policies, carry out diplomacy and decide about aid and other assistance.

本周，美国国务院发布了“各国人权记录”报告。美国官方根据此年度报告制定政策、发展外交关系，并由此决定援助计划与其他资助政策。

The first ones appeared in nineteen seventy-seven as required by Congress. They began with eighty-two countries which all received American aid. Now, there are reports on one hundred ninety-six countries.

1997 年出台的第一个人权报告是应国会的要求。最初是针对接受美国援助的 82 个国家，现在报告涉及 196 个国家。

The reports are based on rights described in the United Nations *Universal Declaration of Human Rights*. These include individual, civil, political and worker rights.

该报告以联合国《世界人权宣言》中提到的权利为基准，这些权利包括个人的、公民的、政治的权利及劳动者权利。

Others are freedom from torture or cruel punishment and from long terms in jail without charges. They also include freedom from secret imprisonment and from other violations of the right to life, liberty and personal security.

另外还包括不受虐待或者残酷惩罚以及在没有受到指控的情况下不被长期关押的自由。其中也包括不受秘密监禁的自由与生命、自由和个人安全等权利不受侵犯的自由等。

The new report says countries ruled by a single person or a small group are often the "most systematic human rights violators". Seven countries are listed as examples: North Korea, Burma, Iran, Zimbabwe, Cuba, China and Belarus.

今年的报告中提到，由单个人或者由小集团统治的国家通常是"最系统地侵犯人权的国家"。列入其中的有 7 个国家：朝鲜、缅甸、伊朗、津巴布韦、古巴，中国和白俄罗斯。

It says nations that violate the rights of their own people are likely to be threats to other nations as well. Here the examples given are Burma, North Korea, Iran and Syria.

报告中还提到，侵犯本国人权的国家很可能对其他国家构成威胁，如缅甸、朝鲜、伊朗和叙利亚。

Some of the most serious violations take place during armed conflicts. One example listed is the continued violence in the Darfur area of Sudan. Others are the conflicts in Nepal, Ivory Coast, Chechnya and elsewhere in Russia's Northern Caucasus area, and countries in central Africa.

在武装冲突期间常常发生最严重的侵犯人权的行为。苏丹达尔富尔地区连续发生的暴乱被列入其中。另外还有尼泊尔、象牙海岸、车臣和俄罗斯北部高加索地区和中非等地的冲突。

In Columbia, human rights violations continued but fewer killings and kidnappings were reported.

哥伦比亚发生的侵权行为仍然存在，但被报道的杀人和绑架事件有所减少。

The report also names countries that used laws against the media and non-governmental organizations last year. Examples listed are Cambodia, Zimbabwe, Venezuela, Belarus and Russia.

该报告中还点名报道了去年利用法律反对媒介和非政府组织的国家，列举的名单上有柬埔寨、津巴布韦、委内瑞拉、白俄罗斯和俄罗斯。

The State Department report praises nations that held democratic elections in two thousand five. The examples given are Iraq, Afghanistan, Ukraine, Indonesia, Lebanon and Liberia. Nations where serious problems were reported in elections included Egypt, Ethiopia, Azerbaijan and Kazakhstan.

美国国务院的报告对2005 年举行了民主选举的国家表示赞誉，其中有伊拉克、阿富汗、乌克兰、印度尼西亚、黎巴嫩和利比亚。报告中提到在选举中存在着严重问题的国家是埃及、埃塞俄比亚、阿塞拜疆和哈萨克斯坦。

The report says many countries had mixed progress last year on democratic reform and human rights. For example, it notes that President Pervez Musharraf has stated his support for democratic change in Pakistan. But it says that country's human rights record continued to be poor.

报告认为有许多国家去年在民主改革和尊重人权方面取得了交叉式进步。例如，巴基斯坦的穆沙拉夫总统明确表示支持民主改革，但该国的人权状况有待改善。

The Chinese government now reacts to American criticism with its own reports on the United States. China's report called American democracy "a game for the rich". It says the United States has a high murder rate, spies on its own people and violates the rights of prisoners in Iraq and Guantanamo Bay, Cuba.

目前中国政府也发布了有关美国人权的报告，以此回应美国的批评。中国的人权报告称美国的民主是"富人的游戏"。报告中说，美国谋杀案发生频率高，对本国人民实行秘密监视，在伊拉克和古巴关塔那摩监狱中侵犯犯人的人权等。

(IN THE NEWS in VOA *Special English* was written by Nancy Steinbach. I'm Steve Ember.)

附　录：

世界人权宣言①

1948年12月10日联合国大会通过并公布《世界人权宣言》，全文载列于后。经此历史之盛举后，大会促请所有会员国将宣言全文加以宣传，并"以学校及其他教育机构为主要对象，促使广为流传、展示、阅读及阐述，不因各国或各领土之政治地位之不同，而有所区别"。

序　言

鉴于对人类家庭所有成员固有尊严及其平等的和不移的权利的承认，乃是世界自由、正义与和平的基础，鉴于对人权的无视和蔑视已发展为野蛮暴行，这些暴行玷污了人类的良心，而一个人人享有言论和信仰自由并免予恐惧和匮乏的世界的来临，已被宣布为普通人民的最高愿望，鉴于为使人类不致迫不得已铤而走险对暴政和压迫进行反叛，有必要使人权受法治的保护，有必要促进各国间友好关系的发展，鉴于各联合国国家的人民已在联合国宪章中重申他们对基本人权、人格尊严和价值以及男女平等权利的信念，并决心促成较大自由中的社会进步和生活水平的改善，鉴于各会员国业已誓愿同联合国合作以促进对人权和基本自由的普遍尊重和遵行，鉴于对这些权利和自由的普遍了解对于这个誓愿的充分实现具有很大的重要性，因此现在，大会发布这一世界人权宣言，作为所有人民和所有国家努力遵行的共同标准，以期每一个人和社会机构经常铭念本宣言，努力通过教诲和教育促进对权利和自由的尊重，并通过国家的和国际的渐进措施，使这些权利和自由在各会员国本身人民及在其管辖领土下的人民中得到普遍和有效的承认和遵行。

① 中国人权研究学会. http: //www. humanrights-china. org/china/rqfg/R120011029133820. htm

第一条

人人生而自由，在尊严和权利上一律平等。他们富有理性和良心，并应以兄弟关系的精神相对待。

第二条

人人有资格享受本宣言所载的一切权利和自由，不分种族、肤色、性别、语言、宗教、政治或其他见解、国籍或社会出身、财产、出生或其他身份等任何区别。并且不得因一人所属的国家或领土的、政治的、行政的或者国际的地位之不同而有所区别，无论该领土是独立领土、托管领土、非自治领土或者处于其他任何主权受限制的情况之下。

第三条

人人有权享有生命、自由和人身安全。

第四条

不得使任何人为奴隶或被奴役；一切形式的奴隶制度和奴隶买卖，均应予以禁止。

第五条

对任何人不得加以酷刑，或施以残忍的、不人道的或侮辱性的待遇或刑罚。

第六条

人人在任何地方有权被承认在法律上的人格。

第七条

在法律前人人平等，并有权享受法律的平等保护，不受任何歧视。人人有权享受平等保护，以免受违反本宣言的任何歧视行为以及煽动这种歧视的任何行为之害。

第八条

任何人当宪法或法律所赋予他的基本权利遭受侵害时，有权由合格的国家法庭对这种侵害行为作有效的补救。

第九条

对任何人不得加以任意逮捕、拘禁或放逐。

第十条

人人完全平等地有权由一个独立而无偏倚的法庭进行公正和公开的审讯，以确定他的权利和义务，并判定他提出的任何刑事指控。

第十一条

（一）凡受刑事控告者，在未经获得辩护上所需的一切保证的公开审判而依法证实有罪以前，有权视为无罪。

（二）任何人的任何行为或不行为，在其发生时依国家法或国际法均不构成刑事罪者，不得被判为犯有刑事罪。刑罚不得重于犯罪时适用的法律规定。

第十二条

对任何人的私生活、家庭、住宅和通信不得任意干涉，对他的荣誉和名誉不得加以攻击。人人有权享受法律保护，以免受这种干涉或攻击。

第十三条

（一）人人在各国境内有权自由迁徙和居住。

（二）人人有权离开任何国家，包括其本国在内，并有权返回他的国家。

第十四条

（一）人人有权在其他国家寻求和享受庇护，以避免迫害。

（二）在真正由于非政治性的罪行或违背联合国的宗旨和原则的行为而被起诉的情况下，不得援用此种权利。

第十五条

（一）人人有权享有国籍。

（二）对任何人的国籍不得任意剥夺，亦不得否认其改变国籍的权利。

第十六条

（一）成年男女，不受种族、国籍或宗教的任何限制，有权婚嫁和成立家庭。他们在婚姻方面、在结婚期间和在解除婚约时，应享有平等的权利。

（二）只有经男女双方自由的和完全的同意，才能缔婚。

（三）家庭是天然的和基本的社会单元，应受社会和国家的保护。

第十七条

（一）人人有单独的财产所有权以及同他人合有财产的所有权。

（二）对任何人的财产不得任意剥夺。

第十八条

人人有思想、良心和宗教自由的权利；此项权利包括他的宗教或信仰的自由，以及单独或集体、公开或秘密地以教义、实践、礼拜和戒律表示他的宗教或信仰的自由。

第十九条

人人有权享有主张和发表意见的自由；此项权利包括持有主张而不受干涉的自由，通过任何媒介和不论国界寻求、接受和传递消息和思想的自由。

第二十条

（一）人人有权享有和平集会和结社的自由。

（二）不得迫使任何人隶属于某一团体。

第二十一条

（一）人人有直接或通过自由选择的代表参与治理本国的权利。

（二）人人有平等机会参加本国公务的权利。

（三）人民的意志是政府权力的基础，这一意志应以定期和真正的选举予以体现，而选举应依据普遍和平等的投票权，并以不记名投票或相当的自由投票程序进行。

第二十二条

每个人作为社会的一员，有权享受社会保障，并有权享有个人尊严和人格自由发展所必需的经济、社会和文化方面各种权利的实现，这种实现是通过国家努力和国际合作并依照各国的组织和资源情况来达成的。

第二十三条

（一）人人有权工作、自由选择职业、享受公正和合适的工作条件、享受免于失业的保障。

（二）人人有同工同酬的权利，不受任何歧视。

（三）每一个工作的人，有权享受公正和合适的报酬，保证使他本人和家属有一个符合人的尊严的生活条件，必要时辅以其他方式的社会保障。

（四）人人有为维护其利益而组织和参加工会的权利。

第二十四条

人人有享受休息和闲暇的权利，包括工作时间有合理限制和定期给薪休假的权利。

第二十五条

（一）人人有权享受为维持他本人和家属的健康和福利所需的生活水准，包括食物、衣着、住房、医疗和必要的社会服务；在遭受失业、疾病、残废、守寡、衰老或在其他不能控制的情况下丧失谋生能力时，有权享受保障。

（二）母亲和儿童有权享受特别照顾和协助。一切儿童，无论婚生或非婚生，都应享有同样的社会保护。

第二十六条

（一）人人都有受教育的权利，教育应当免费，至少在初级和基本阶段应如此。初级教育应属义务性质，技术和职业教育应普遍设立，高等教育应根据成绩而对一切人平等开放。

（二）教育的目的在于充分发展人的个性并加强对人权和基本自由的尊重。教育应促进各国、各种族或各宗教集团的了解、容忍和友谊，并应促进联合国维护和平的各项活动。

（三）父母对其子女所应接受的教育的种类，有优先选择的权利。

第二十七条

（一）人人有权自由参加社会的文化生活，享受艺术，并分享科学进步及其产生的福利。

（二）人人因他所发明或创作的任何科学、文学或艺术而带来的精神的和物质的利益，有享受保护的权利。

第二十八条

人人有权要求一种社会的和国际的秩序，在这种秩序中，本宣言所载的权利和自由能获得充分实现。

第二十九条

（一）人人对社会负有义务，因为只有在社会中他的个性才可得到自由和充分的发展。

（二）人人在行使他的权利和自由时，只受法律规定的限制，规定此种限制的唯一目的在于保证对旁人的权利和自由给予应有的承认和尊重，并在一个民主社会中应适应道德、公共秩序和普遍福利方面的正当需要。

（三）这些权利和自由的行使，在任何情况下均不得违背联合国的宗旨和原则。

第三十条

本宣言的任体条文，不得解释为默许任何国家、集团或个人有权进行任何旨在破坏本宣言所载的任何权利和自由的活动或行为。

Lesson 29　Corruption Digs Deepest in Countries in Conflict

By Brianna Blake
November 28, 2009

Part One　Background Information

腐败的方式[①]

世界各国都有不同程度的腐败问题，腐败形式各异。本课新闻认为贫穷与富裕都可能导致腐败，但监督、惩治不力才是腐败蔓延的根源。如利用职务之便捞取好处，管钱、管事、收费和专营性质的国家机关或公共事企业单位吃拿卡要、敲诈勒索等。除了个人腐败以外，还有行业、部门、机关的集体腐败，各行业行政主管部门为了本行业、本系统、本部门利益争着、抢着增设行业性管理、收费、罚款项目，以费代管，以罚代法，加重罚款，变相收费等，严重加大了企业、个体户和城乡部门的负担。司法和纪检、监察、审计、地方党政要员的违法违纪行为对腐败起到了推波助澜的作用。

腐败扭曲了人们的思想和价值观念，直接降低了政府在投资、公共服务等方面的经济和社会效益。腐败使行政成本增加，行政效益降低，国家的惠民政策特别是惠民资金在落实的过程中不断被蒸发。教育乱收费、卫生乱收费、药价居高不下，人民得的实惠严重缩水。更严重的是，腐败问题极大地削弱了政府的威信，影响人民对政府的信任和支持，严重制约了国民经济和社会各项事业的长足发展。有的地方投资环境很差，就是吏治方面扯皮推诿，吃拿卡要，办事效率低下，巧立名目胡乱收费，产权保护意识差等，导致投资者望而却步。

改革地方纪检委、检察院、法院、监察局、审计局、公安局由地方党委统一领导的方式、实行中央统一管理是扯破地方势力关系网，从根本上切除地方党政领导干扰执法问题的根本措施，而对公检法、监察、审计等机构不能进行公开的舆论监督就无法彻底铲除中国的腐败。

Part Two　Exercises

Ⅰ. Listen to the first part of the news, and fill in the blanks with the words you hear.

__________ International is out with its two thousand nine report on corruption around the world. The __________ organization has released its Corruption __________ each year since nineteen ninety-eight.

---

① http://theory.people.com.cn/GB/49154/49156/4198266.html

This year the country seen as least corrupt is ________. ________ shared first place last year with ________ and ________. This year ________ is ranked second, and ________ shares third place with ________.

At the ________ of the list, ranked last for the third year, is ________.

The ________ of the list is based on how corrupt a country's government is considered by a number of international organizations. These include the World Bank, the World ________ ________ and the ________ and ________ banks.

Ⅱ. Listen to the second part of the news, and answer the following questions.

1. What is the international organization's mission?

2. What kinds of countries are most affected by corruption?

3. What is the money source for corruptions in Afghanistan and Iraq?

4. Where did Iraq rank in the list of corruption last year? Where is Sudan ranked this year?

5. Where was Afghanistan ranked in the list of corruptions last year?

6. How does Transparency International define corruption? And what is the cause for people to support the Taliban?

Ⅲ. Listen to the third part of the news, and take it down, then repeat it.

From "The United States. . ." to ". . . investigation".

Ⅳ. Listen to the last part of the news, and translate it into Chinese.

Begin from "In this year...".

Part Three　Keys to the Exercises

Ⅰ. Listen to the first part of the news, and fill in the blanks with the words you hear.

Transparency International is out with its two thousand nine report on corruption around the world. The nongovernmental organization has released its Corruption Perceptions Index each year since nineteen ninety-eight.

This year the country seen as least corrupt is New Zealand. New Zealand shared first place last year with Denmark and Sweden. This year Denmark is ranked second, and Sweden shares third place with Singapore.

At the bottom of the list, ranked last for the third year, is Somalia.

The order of the list is based on how corrupt a country's government is considered by a number of international organizations. These include the World Bank, the World Economic Forum and the Asian and African development banks.

Ⅱ. Listen to the second part of the news, and answer the following questions.

1. What is the international organization's mission?

Transparency International, based in Berlin, ①works to fight corruption and increase public awareness. ②To report yearly on one hundred eighty countries about their corruption.

2. What kinds of countries are most affected by corruption?

The group says unstable countries damaged by war and ongoing conflict continue to be those most affected by corruption.

3. What is the money source for corruptions in Afghanistan and Iraq?

Two nations that receive billions of dollars in international aid.

4. Where did Iraq rank in the list of corruption last year? Where is Sudan ranked this year?

Iraq ranked the second from the bottom. Sudan rank the fourth from the bottom. (The Iraq moved up two places this year and is now ranked fourth from the bottom, along with Sudan.)

5. Where was Afghanistan ranked in the list of corruptions last year?

It was ranked the fifth from the bottom. (But Afghanistan fell three places to just above Somalia, meaning Afghanistan is seen as the second most corrupt country.)

6. How does Transparency International define corruption? And what is the cause for people

to support the Taliban?

It says people have to pay bribes to receive basic services. A lack of government enforcement against corruption is blamed for helping the Taliban gain supporters.

Ⅲ. Listen to the third part of the news, and take it down, then repeat it.

1. The United States has approved close to forty billion dollars in aid for Afghanistan over the past eight years of war.

2. President Obama is preparing to announce his new war plan on Tuesday.

3. The plan is expected to include thousands of additional American troops.

4. Afghan President Hamid Karzai began a second term last week after an election in which widespread cheating was found.

5. He is under increased international pressure to fight corruption.

6. Last week his government announced new efforts to investigate top officials.

7. A group of current and former cabinet ministers are reportedly under investigation.

Ⅳ. Listen to the last part of the news, and translate it into Chinese.

1. In this year's corruption report, the United States dropped one place, to nineteenth from eighteenth last year.

在今年的腐败年度报告中，美国从去年的18位下降了一位至19位。

2. Yet the score actually improved by two-tenths of a point.

实际上分数比去年增加了0.2分。

3. Transparency International says there are many concerns about supervision of the American financial industry.

国际透明组织称，有许多人对美国金融业的监督颇为关注。

4. Many of the countries at the bottom of the list are in sub-Saharan Africa.

在名单上排名最后的许多国家位于非洲撒哈拉沙漠以南。

5. Patrick Berg is a program coordinator for Transparency International.

帕特里克·贝尔格是国际透明组织的一名项目协调员。

6. Patrick Berg: "Where you find poverty, corruption usually hits people the hardest."

他说："哪里有贫困，那里的人们受腐败的伤害最深。

7. In some of the more affluent countries, corruption may be a major problem.

在某些较为富裕的国家，腐败能成为一个大问题。

8. But it does not keep people from getting health care or clean water to their houses.

但它还不至于妨碍人们获得医疗保障和家庭清洁用水。

9. But he says some countries—including Botswana, Mauritius and Cape Verde—have worked hard to improve their governance.

但他说有的国家，包括博茨瓦纳、毛里求斯、佛得角，都在努力改善政府管理。

10. As a result, they have improved their standing on the list.

因此其名字在名单上也有所上升。

Part Four Translation of the Text

Corruption Digs Deepest in Countries in Conflict
冲突中的国家腐败植根最深

Transparency International is out with its two thousand nine report on corruption around the world. The nongovernmental organization has released its Corruption Perceptions Index each year since nineteen ninety-eight.

国际透明组织公布了其2009年的全世界腐败情况的报告。该非政府组织自1998年以来每年公布其全球贪污调查指数（也译作：清廉指数）报告。

This year the country seen as least corrupt is New Zealand. New Zealand shared first place last year with Denmark and Sweden. This year Denmark is ranked second, and Sweden shares third place with Singapore.

今年新西兰被认为是腐败最少的国家。去年新西兰和丹麦、瑞典并列第一。今年丹麦排名第二，而瑞典和新加坡并列第三。

At the bottom of the list, ranked last for the third year, is Somalia.

索马里在名单上连续三年排名最后。

The order of the list is based on how corrupt a country's government is considered by a number of international organizations. These include the World Bank, the World Economic Forum and the Asian and African development banks.

名单的排名是根据数个国际组织对该国政府腐败程度的评价来定的。这些组织包括世界银行、世界经济论坛和亚非发展银行。

Transparency International, based in Berlin, works to fight corruption and increase public awareness. Its yearly report has grown to a list of one hundred eighty countries.

总部在柏林的国际透明组织旨在对抗腐败，唤起公众注意。其年度报告已经扩展至180个国家。

The group says unstable countries damaged by war and ongoing conflict continue to be those most affected by corruption. Those countries include Afghanistan and Iraq, two nations that receive billions of dollars in international aid.

该组织称，那些受战乱和持续冲突破坏的动乱国仍旧受腐败的严重影响。这些国家包括阿富汗和伊拉克，他们接受了数以十亿美元的国际援助。

Iraq moved up two places this year and is now ranked fourth from the bottom, along with Sudan. But Afghanistan fell three places to just above Somalia, meaning Afghanistan is seen as the second most corrupt country.

伊拉克今年上升了两位，和苏丹一起并列倒数第四。而阿富汗则下跌三位至索马里之前，这就意味着阿富汗被认为是世界第二腐败的国家。

Transparency International says people have to pay bribes to receive basic services. A lack of government enforcement against corruption is blamed for helping the Taliban gain supporters.

国际透明组织称，在这些国家，人们需要进行贿赂才能获得一些最基本的服务。人们指责政府缺乏打击腐败力度是塔利班获得支持者的部分原因。

The United States has approved close to forty billion dollars in aid for Afghanistan over the past eight years of war. President Obama is preparing to announce his new war plan on Tuesday. The plan is expected to include thousands of additional American troops.

在过去的8年间，美国批准给阿富汗的援助接近四百亿美元。奥巴马总统将在周二宣布其新作战计划。估计该计划将向阿富汗增兵数千。

Afghan President Hamid Karzai began a second term last week after an election in which widespread cheating was found. He is under increased international pressure to fight corruption.

阿富汗总统哈米德·卡尔扎伊在人们发现存在普遍欺骗行为的大选后，于上周开始连任。他面临越来越大的反腐国际压力。

Last week his government announced new efforts to investigate top officials. A group of current and former cabinet ministers are reportedly under investigation.

上周其政府宣布了调查高官的新举措。据报道，一些现任和前任内阁成员正接受调查。

In this year's corruption report, the United States dropped one place, to nineteenth from eighteenth last year. Yet the score actually improved by two-tenths of a point. Transparency International says there are many concerns about supervision of the American financial industry.

在今年的腐败年度报告中，美国从去年的18位下降一位至19位。实际上分数比去年增加了0.2分。国际透明组织称，有许多人对美国金融行业的监督颇为关注。

Many of the countries at the bottom of the list are in sub-Saharan Africa. Patrick Berg is a program coordinator for Transparency International.

在名单上排名最后的许多国家位于非洲撒哈拉沙漠以南。帕特里克·贝尔格是国际透明组织的一名项目协调员。

Patrick Berg: "Where you find poverty, corruption usually hits people the hardest. In some of the more affluent countries, corruption may be a major problem. But it does not keep people from getting health care or clean water to their houses."

他说："哪里有贫困，那里的人们受腐败的伤害最深。在某些较为富裕的国家，腐败能成为一个大问题，但它还不至于妨碍人们获得医疗保障和家庭清洁用水。"

But he says some countries—including Botswana, Mauritius and Cape Verde—have worked hard to improve their governance. As a result, they have improved their standing on the list.

但他说有的国家，包括博茨瓦纳、毛里求斯和佛得角，都在努力改善政府管理。因此其名字在名单上也有所上升。

(And that's IN THE NEWS in VOA *Special English*, written by Brianna Blake. I'm Steve Ember.)

Lesson 30 Investigative Reporting, Coverage of Katrina Earn Pulitzer Prizes for US Newspapers

By Nancy Steinbach

April 22, 2006

Part One Background Information

普利策奖与西方新闻价值观

普利策生前因经营《快邮报》和《纽约世界报》获得巨大成功而攒下了2.8亿美元的家产，他在遗嘱中将两百万美元捐赠给哥伦比亚大学，用以建立一所新闻学院。其中50万美元用于“设立鼓励公共服务、公共道德、美国文学、促进教育的奖项或奖学金”。此奖项便是普利策奖，该奖自1917年以来每年颁发一次，主要分为新闻奖和文化艺术奖。但普利策奖委员会在第一年之后便将奖项扩大到21个，在原来规定的四项新闻奖、四项文学戏剧奖和一项教育奖，以及四项旅行奖学金外，陆续增设了诗歌、音乐和摄影奖。其中，文学奖包含一本美国小说、一部在纽约上演的美国独创戏剧、一本有关美国历史的图书、一位美国人的传记和一本有关公共服务历史的图书。首届普利策摄影奖是1942年颁发的。此后，除1946年外，每年颁发一次。从1968年开始，摄影类增设了专题新闻摄影奖，获奖作品通常由一组照片组成。

普利策设立该项奖的初衷是：“我对新闻业的进步与提高深感兴趣，因为我一生从事这个行业，把它看作是一个崇高的职业，一个因其对人民心灵和道德产生影响的具有无与伦比重要性的职业。我希望能够协助吸引正直和能干的年轻人加入这个行列，同时也帮助那些业已从事这个行业的人们能够获得最高水准的道德和智力培训。”① 普利策生前在他所办的报纸中倾注了他的新闻理想，他提出了报纸的社会责任理念，揭露社会弊病成了他毕生的办报宗旨，但同时为了扩大发行量他不顾社会舆论的反对，大量刊登庸俗的社会新闻以增加报纸的趣味性和刺激性。

90多年来，作为美国新闻界最高荣誉的普利策奖忠实地贯彻着设奖人的精神，获得新闻奖的大部分新闻报道是“揭丑新闻”。据统计，“在1917—1990年的580个新闻奖中，约有40%属于此类新闻。在2006年评出的13项获奖作品（特稿写作奖未颁出）中，属于负面的有10项，占了总数的76.9%，属于正面的只有一项——《洛杉矶时报》因对沃尔玛的商业策略报道而获得解释性报道奖”；2006届获奖作品中负面报道的题材广泛，涉及职场安全、森林火灾、入学黑幕、越战丑闻、伊战报道、政府腐败等问题②。以上新闻奖

---

① Seymour Topping. 不受制约的新闻界普利策其人其奖. http://chinese.usembassy-china.org.cn/jl020301_pulitzer.html

② 李萌. 从普利策新闻奖透视美国新闻价值观. www.xinhuanet.com/2004-06-14

的评选标准实际上显示了美国社会的主流价值观，“即自由意志、社会责任感、民众知情权、信用、监督权、社会正义与同情心等”①。虽然美国新闻自由在实践中受各种因素干扰会偏离其原始轨道，但正是普利策这些怀有崇高新闻理想的前辈为美国新闻界促使社会改革、维护社会正义奠定了思想基础。

附　录：

普利策奖评奖项目②

新闻界奖		创作界奖
1. 普利策优异公众服务奖	2. 普利策普通新闻报道奖	1. 普利策小说奖
3. 普利策国内报道奖	4. 普利策国际报道奖	2. 普利策戏剧奖
5. 普利策调查性报道奖	6. 普利策释义性新闻奖	3. 普利策历史奖
7. 普利策专业性新闻奖	8. 普利策社论写作奖	4. 普利策传记奖
9. 普利策漫画创作奖（1922 年开始）	10. 普利策现场新闻摄影奖（1942 年开始，1968 年分为现场新闻和特写）	5. 普利策诗歌奖（1922 年开始）
11. 普利策特写摄影奖（1942 年开始，1968 年分为现场新闻和特写）	12. 普利策评论奖	6. 普利策非小说类作品奖（1962 年开始）
13. 普利策批评奖	14. 普利策特稿写作奖	7. 普利策音乐奖（1943 年开始）

Part Two　Exercises

Ⅰ. Listen to the first part of the news, and complete the sentences with the words you hear.

1. This week, Columbia University in New York ____________ this year of the Pulitzers.

2. The Pulitzer Prize ____________ for American newspapers.

3. *The Washington Post* ____________.

4. Susan Schmidt, James Grimaldi and Jeffrey Smith received the ____________.

5. They reported on ____________ Jack Abramoff.

6. David Finkel won the ____________ for stories on United States efforts to bring democracy to Yemen.

7. Dana Priest won the ____________. She reported on ____________ ____________.

---

① 李萌. 从普利策新闻奖透视美国新闻价值观. www. xinhuanet. com/2004 - 06 - 14

② http：//gb. chinabroadcast. cn/321/2004/04/07/242@121733. htm

8. And Robin Givhan received the criticism award for ______________________.

9. *The New York Times* won three Pulitzers. Nicholas Kristof received the commentary award for ____________ in Darfur, Sudan.

10. Joseph Kahn and Jim Yardley won the international reporting award for ________.

11. And James Risen and Eric Lichtblau received a ____________________.

12. They reported that the government in its war on terrorism ______________.

13. An award also went to the San Diego *Union-Tribune* and *Copley News Service*. Their stories ____.

Ⅱ. Listen to and complete the following sentences, then translate them into Chinese orally.

The Rocky Mountain News in Denver, Colorado, ______________. Jim Sheeler won the ______________________ for a story about a Marine who helps families of those killed in Iraq. And Todd Heisler won the ____________________ for pictures of the funerals of local Marines killed in Iraq. The Pulitzer for ______________ went to the *Dallas Morning News* for the effects of Hurricane Katrina in New Orleans. Reporting on Katrina earned ____________________ for the *Times-Picayune* in New Orleans and the *Sun Herald* in Biloxi, Mississippi. The *Times-Picayune* also won the Pulitzer for ____________________. And the Pulitzer for ______________ went to Rick Attig and Doug Bates of the Oregonian for describing conditions at a state mental hospital.

Ⅲ. Listen to and repeat the rest of the news, and write it down.

From "This was the..." to the end.

Part Three Keys to the Exercises

Ⅰ. Listen to the first part of the news, and complete the sentences with the words you hear.

1. This week, Columbia University in New York announced the winners this year of the Pulitzers.

2. The Pulitzer Prize in Journalism is the top honor for American newspapers.

3. *The Washington Post* won four awards.

4. Susan Schmidt, James Grimaldi and Jeffrey Smith received the investigative reporting award.

5. They reported on wrongdoing in Congress involving lobbyist Jack Abramoff.

6. David Finkel won the explanatory reporting prize for stories on United States efforts to bring democracy to Yemen.

7. Dana Priest won the beat reporting prize. She reported on secret prisons and other parts of the government's anti-terrorism campaign.

8. And Robin Givhan received the criticism award for turning commentary about fashion into critical observations of society.

9. *The New York Times* won three Pulitzers. Nicholas Kristof received the commentary award for writing about the violence in Darfur, Sudan.

10. Joseph Kahn and Jim Yardley won the international reporting award for stories about the changing legal system in China.

11. And James Risen and Eric Lichtblau received a national reporting award.

12. They reported that the government in its war on terrorism was listening to the calls of some Americans.

13. An award also went to the San Diego *Union-Tribune* and Copley News Service. Their stories led to prison for a dishonest congressman.

Ⅱ. Listen and complete the following sentences, then translate them into Chinese orally.

The Rocky Mountain News in Denver, Colorado, won two Pulitzers. Jim Sheeler won the feature writing award for a story about a Marine who helps families of those killed in Iraq. And Todd Heisler won the feature photography award for pictures of the funerals of local Marines killed in Iraq.

在科罗拉多的丹佛，《洛基山日报》获得两个普利策奖。吉姆·希勒获得特写报道奖，此报道是关于一个海军陆战队员帮助那些在伊拉克阵亡将士的家庭的故事。托德·海斯勒因拍摄了在伊拉克被杀的海军陆战队员的葬礼照片而获得特写摄影奖。

The Pulitzer for breaking news photography went to the *Dallas Morning News* for the effects of Hurricane Katrina in New Orleans.

普利策突发新闻摄影奖是由《达拉斯晨报》拍摄了发生在新奥尔良的卡特里娜飓风带来影响的照片而获得。

Reporting on Katrina earned public service awards for the *Times-Picayune* in New Orleans and the *Sun Herald* in Biloxi, Mississippi. The *Times-Picayune* also won the Pulitzer for breaking news reporting.

对卡特里娜飓风的报道也为新奥尔良的《时报—平民报》和密西西比州比洛克西的《太阳先驱报》赢得了公共服务奖。《时报—平民报》同时获得了突发新闻奖。

And the Pulitzer for editorial writing went to Rick Attig and Doug Bates of the Oregonian for describing conditions at a state mental hospital.

普利策社论写作奖杯奖被俄勒冈的里克·阿提格和多格·巴特斯获得，他们因反映了州立精神病院的情况而获此殊荣。

Ⅲ. Listen to and repeat the rest of the news, and write it down.

1. This was the ninetieth year of the Pulitzers. Newspaper publisher Joseph Pulitzer left money to Columbia University to establish them. There are also prizes in letters, drama and music. Winners receive a medal and most get ten thousand dollars.

2. The award ceremony is May twenty-second.

3. And Mike Luckovich of the Atlanta Journal-Constitution will take home his second Pulitzer for editorial cartooning.

4. The judging committee praised his drawings as powerful yet simple.

5. For example, one last year marked the deaths of two thousand American soldiers in Iraq.

6. Their names formed the word "WHY" followed by a question mark.

Part Four　Translation of the Text

Investigative Reporting, Coverage of Katrina Earn Pulitzer Prizes for US Newspapers

调查性报道，关于卡特里娜的报道赢得美国报纸普利策奖

This week, Columbia University in New York announced the winners this year of the Pulitzers. The Pulitzer Prize in Journalism is the top honor for American newspapers.

本周，在纽约的哥伦比亚大学宣布了本年度普利策奖获奖者的名单。普利策新闻奖是美国报纸的最高荣誉。

The Washington Post won four awards. Susan Schmidt, James Grimaldi and Jeffrey Smith received the investigative reporting award. They reported on wrongdoing in Congress involving lobbyist Jack Abramoff.

《华盛顿邮报》获得了四个奖项。苏珊·希米特、詹姆士·格瑞马迪和杰弗里·史密斯获得了调查报道奖，他们披露了涉及说客杰克·阿布拉莫夫的国会丑闻。

David Finkel won the explanatory reporting prize for stories on United States efforts to bring democracy to Yemen. Dana Priest won the beat reporting prize. She reported on secret prisons and other parts of the government's anti-terrorism campaign.

戴维·芬克尔获得了解释性报道奖，他报道了美国为使也门实行民主政治而作出的努力。达纳·普瑞斯特获得了独家报道奖。她报道了政府在反恐怖主义的运动中设置秘密监狱与其他行为。

And Robin Givhan received the criticism award for turning commentary about fashion into critical observations of society.

罗宾·吉万恩因将有关时尚的评论演绎成对社会的批评性观察而赢得批评报道奖。

The New York Times won three Pulitzers. Nicholas Kristof received the commentary award for writing about the violence in Darfur, Sudan. Joseph Kahn and Jim Yardley won the international reporting award for stories about the changing legal system in China.

纽约时报获得三个普利策奖。尼古拉斯·克里斯托夫写有关苏丹达尔富尔发生的暴乱而获得评论奖。约瑟夫·卡恩和吉姆·亚尔德利报道中国司法制度的改革情况而获得国际报道奖。

And James Risen and Eric Lichtblau received a national reporting award. They reported that the government in its war on terrorism was listening to the calls of some Americans. An award also went to the San Diego *Union-Tribune* and Copley News Service. Their stories led to prison for a dishonest congressman.

詹姆斯·瑞森、埃里克·里奇布劳获得了国内报道奖。他们对政府在恐怖主义战争中窃听美国人电话的事件进行了报道。圣地亚哥《联盟论坛报》和科普利报系也获得一个奖项，他们的报道使犯有欺诈行为的国会议员受到监禁。

The Rocky Mountain News in Denver, Colorado, won two Pulitzers. Jim Sheeler won the feature writing award for a story about a Marine who helps families of those killed in Iraq. And Todd Heisler won the feature photography award for pictures of the funerals of local Marines killed in Iraq.

在科罗拉多的丹佛，《洛基山日报》获得两个普利策奖。吉姆·希勒获得特写报道奖，此报道是关于一个海军陆战队员帮助那些在伊拉克阵亡将士的家庭的故事。托德·海斯勒因拍摄了在伊拉克被杀的海军陆战队员的葬礼照片而获得特写摄影奖。

The Pulitzer for breaking news photography went to the *Dallas Morning News* for the effects of Hurricane Katrina in New Orleans.

普利策突发新闻摄影奖是由《达拉斯晨报》拍摄了发生在新奥尔良的卡特里娜飓风带来的影响照片而获得。

Reporting on Katrina earned public service awards for the *Times-Picayune* in New Orleans and the *Sun Herald* in Biloxi, Mississippi. The *Times-Picayune* also won the Pulitzer for breaking news reporting.

对卡特里娜飓风的报道也为新奥尔良的《时报—平民报》和密西西比州比洛克西的《太阳先驱报》赢得了公共服务奖。《时报—平民报》同时获得了突发新闻报道奖。

And the Pulitzer for editorial writing went to Rick Attig and Doug Bates of the Oregonian for describing conditions at a state mental hospital.

普利策社论写作奖被俄勒冈的里克·阿提格和多格·巴特斯获得，他们因反映了州立精神病院的情况而获此殊荣。

This was the ninetieth year of the Pulitzers. Newspaper publisher Joseph Pulitzer left money to Columbia University to establish them. There are also prizes in letters, drama and music.

这是普利策奖实行颁奖的第九十年。普利策奖由报纸出版商约瑟夫·普利策遗赠给哥伦比亚大学资金而创立。它也有文学、戏剧和音乐方面的奖项。

Winners receive a medal and most get ten thousand dollars. The award ceremony is May twenty-second.

获奖者会接受一个奖牌，而且大部分人会得到一万美元的奖金。颁奖典礼在 5 月 22 日举行。

And Mike Luckovich of the Atlanta *Journal-Constitution* will take home his second Pulitzer for editorial cartooning. The judging committee praised his drawings as powerful yet simple.

亚特兰大《宪政报》的麦克·卢克维奇捧回了他的第二个普利策社论漫画奖。评审委员会称赞他的画简洁，但具有非凡的影响力。

For example, one last year marked the deaths of two thousand American soldiers in Iraq. Their names formed the word "WHY" followed by a question mark.

举例来说，去年的一幅画记录了在伊拉克死亡的两千个美国军人。他们的名字被写成了英文的"为什么"，后面是一个问号。

(IN THE NEWS in VOA *Special English* was written by Nancy Steinbach. I'm Steve Ember.)

Lesson 31 Exercise in Free Expression: How It Led to Deadly Costs

By Nancy Steinbach
February 11, 2006

Part One Background Information

新闻自由与民族关系

民族问题对于新闻媒体来说永远是个敏感的问题，处理不好，主编或值班编辑被解雇是小事，引发民族冲突则是大事。中国新闻界以往出现类似的事件往往是因为编辑的疏忽或对民族风俗不熟悉而造成的，但在西方国家，则是因为价值观之间的差异造成冲突所致。2005 年 9 月，丹麦最大的报纸《日兰德邮报》因发表了 12 幅关于伊斯兰教先知穆罕默德的漫画而引发了全世界穆斯林国家的谴责，该报主编被迫在网上公开道歉，但他的道歉引来了西方国家媒体的“声援”。2006 年 1 月和 2 月，挪威的一家报纸和法国《法兰西晚报》又刊登了有争议的漫画，法国《法兰西晚报》还配以社论《是的，我们有权丑化上帝》，社论认为：“伊斯兰教禁止其信徒体现先知穆罕默德形象，接下来要问的是，非穆斯林人难道都必须遵守这一教规吗?” 由此，一场西方媒体与穆斯林国家的对抗风波拉开了序幕。

为了捍卫伊斯兰教的尊严，2006 年 1 月 29 日，利比亚外交部决定关闭利比亚驻丹麦人民办事处（使馆），沙特阿拉伯召回了驻丹麦大使，埃及议会也通过了抵制丹麦商品的决议，加沙地区甚至还爆发了反对丹麦的游行示威，印度尼西亚则谴责丹麦媒体利用新闻自由侮辱宗教。

双方阵营的内部合作此时显得非常默契，以上国家的谴责和报复行为刺激了西方国家的“联合抵制”。德国、西班牙、瑞士、意大利、捷克、荷兰、匈牙利等近十个欧洲国家的大报纷纷以捍卫言论自由的名义同时刊登了这组漫画。法国《世界报》在社评中指出：“一幅丑化穆罕默德的画可能会令穆斯林人感到震惊，但一个民主国家不可能允许思想警察的存在，除非它想践踏人权。”[①] 尽管《法兰西晚报》宣布解除其出版经理勒福郎的职务，但法国一家周刊的主编菲力普瓦勒为抗议这一解职立即宣布将在本周版刊发该受争议的漫画。瓦勒说：“政教合一被废除整整一个世纪之后，一位出版经理因发表穆罕默德漫画被解职，这不是令人尴尬的事，而是完全不可以接受的事。我们生活在大思想家伏尔泰的国度而不是精神领袖霍梅尼的国度。” 接着，英国广播公司于 2006 年 2 月 10 日也播放了被指对先知穆罕默德不敬的漫画，声称是为了帮助观众了解故事带出的“强烈感受”；法国《世界报》更在同日以头版刊载该套漫画，并在社评中表示捍卫嘲讽各宗教的权利。

---

① 佚名. 穆罕默德漫画风波加剧 伊斯兰反欧潮一触即发. http://chinanews.com/ 2006 - 2 - 3

不知西方各国关于新闻自由的章程内是否有允许利用自己办的媒体嘲笑、作弄他人或讽刺他人宗教信仰的条款？假如有的话，设想一下，如果有人讽刺基督教或其他宗教的上帝，将会发生什么样的事？或者，打个简单的比方，有媒体嘲笑某个有暴力倾向儿子的父母（即使他的父母亲有缺点），这个儿子会怎样呢？对于穆斯林国家来说，这样的事很不幸地落在了他们的身上，他们已宣称“丹麦人、法国人、挪威人和德国人都将成为他们攻击的目标”；巴勒斯坦的两个激进组织甚至包围了欧盟驻加沙办事处；突尼斯、摩洛哥宣布禁止销售那天的《法兰西晚报》；巴基斯坦、伊拉克等国都出现了游行抗议活动，示威者还焚烧了丹麦和法国国旗①。可以想象，如果其他宗教教徒遇到自己的上帝被嘲弄时也采取同样激进措施的话，世界的民族矛盾必将会越来越激化。因为一个文明社会至少会遵循这样一个原则：我们应该尊重他人的宗教信仰。

Part Two　Exercises

Ⅰ. Listen to the first part of the news, and answer the questions according to the following outline.

1. Who evoked the conflict?

2. What is the conflict about?

1) The *Jyllands-Posten*（《日兰德邮报》）________________________.

2) Many Muslims say Islam ________________________.

3) Yet one cartoon, for example, ________________________.

3. What is the cause of the conflict?

4. Why did the *Jyllands-Posten* want to protest?

1) Another newspaper had reported ________________________.

2) Artists ________________________.

Ⅱ. Listen to the second part of the news, and say how the conflict goes on according to the following outline.

1. Muslim nations' protest:

1) In October, ambassadors from ten Muslim nations and the Palestinian representative in Denmark ________________________.

2) They urged him to ________________________.

2. Prime Minister Anders Fogh Rasmussen's reaction:

1) He has said ________________________.

2) But he has ________________________.

3. Danish Muslim groups' second step:

1) ________________________.

---

① 佚名．穆罕默德漫画风波加剧 伊斯兰反欧潮一触即发．http：//chinanews. com/ 2006－2－3

2) In December, ______________________________.

3) ______________ in Saudi Arabia in Islam's holiest city, Mecca.

4) Delegates from a Danish coalition of twenty-seven Muslim groups ______________.

5) The delegates also ______________________________.

6) A spokesman has said they ______________________________.

7) He says they were ______________________________.

4. European's reaction:

1) In January, Danish government lawyers ______________________.

2) A few days later, a publication in Norway ______________________.

5. Saudi Arabia's action: ______________________________.

6. *Jyllands-Posten's* reaction: A statement from the *Jyllands-Posten* ______________. Since then, ______________________________.

Ⅲ. Listen to the third part of the news, and translate it into Chinese orally.

Ⅳ. Listen to and repeat the last part of the news, then write it down.

Part Three Keys to the Exercises

Ⅰ. Listen to the first part of the news, and answer questions according to the following outline.

1. Who evoked the conflict?

The drawings that have led to increasing protests by Muslims in recent days first appeared in a Danish newspaper last September.

2. What is the conflict about?

1) The *Jyllands-Posten* (《日兰德邮报》) published twelve images of the Prophet Mohammed.

2) Many Muslims say Islam bars showing any images of the prophet.

3) Yet one cartoon, for example, showed Mohammed as a terrorist with a bomb on his head.

3. What's the cause of the conflict?

The newspaper says it published the cartoons as a form of political protest.

4. Why did the *Jyllands-Posten* want to protest?

1) Another newspaper had reported that a writer could not find anyone to draw pictures for a book about the prophet.

2) Artists reportedly were afraid to draw them.

Ⅱ. Listen to the second part of the news, and say how the conflict goes on according to the following outline.

1. Muslim nations' protest:

1) In October, ambassadors from ten Muslim nations and the Palestinian representative in Denmark wrote to the Danish prime minister.

2) They urged him to take action against those responsible for the drawings.

2. Prime Minister Anders Fogh Rasmussen's reaction:

1) He has said he is sorry the cartoons offended Muslims.

2) But he has refused to apologize for their being published.

3. Danish Muslim groups' second step:

1) Began legal action against the newspaper that published them.

2) In December, leaders from the Organization of the Islamic Conference condemned the cartoons.

3) They discussed them during their meeting in Saudi Arabia in Islam's holiest city, Mecca.

4) Delegates from a Danish coalition of twenty-seven Muslim groups had brought the cartoons to the Middle East in December to seek support.

5) The delegates also included some images that had not been published.

6) A spokesman has said they were not an attempt to mislead.

7) He says they were mailed to Danish Muslims who had criticized the published cartoons.

4. European's reaction:

1) In January, Danish government lawyers decided not to bring charges against the newspaper.

2) A few days later, a publication in Norway printed the cartoons to show support for the Danish paper and for freedom of the press.

5. Saudi Arabia's action: withdrew its ambassador from Denmark and began a boycott of Danish goods.

6. *Jyllands-Posten's* reaction: A statement from the *Jyllands-Posten* apologized for offending Muslims, but supported the decision to print the drawings. Since then, news media in other countries have also printed them.

Ⅲ. Listen to the third part of the news, and translate it into Chinese orally.

As protests spread to different countries, they turned violent and deadly. Danish and Norwegian embassies have been attacked.

随着抗议之声蔓延至不同的国家，抗议活动变得暴烈并引发伤亡，丹麦和挪威的大使馆受到袭击。

There has been much debate about the reasons behind the protests.

人们纷纷对抗议背后的原因进行争论。

Many people say the protests show the anger of Muslims at treatment by Westerners. They say the demonstrations also show anger at the occupation of Iraq and Afghanistan. But even some Muslims say the protests are being used in some cases to push for goals unrelated to defending Islam.

很多人认为，抗议表明穆斯林对西方人处理方式的愤怒。他们说，示威行动也表露了对侵占伊拉克和阿富汗的愤怒。但是，有些穆斯林人认为，在某些情况下抗议活动被利用于与保护伊斯兰教无关之目的。

Ⅳ. Listen and repeat the last part of the news, then write it down.

Denmark's prime minister says "religious extremists" have fueled the flames. In published comments this week Mister Rasmussen also criticized Syria and Iran. He says they have used the situation to gain support because they are both under international pressure.

He says Denmark is a liberal country, but its values must be honored. These include freedom of expression, equality for men and women and a separation of politics and religion.

Part Four　Translation of the Text

Exercise in Free Expression: How It Led to Deadly Costs
实施言论自由带来的致命代价

The drawings that have led to increasing protests by Muslims in recent days first appeared in a Danish newspaper last September.

最近导致穆斯林的抗议不断升级的画像子于年九月首先出现在丹麦的一份报纸上。

The Jyllands-Posten published twelve images of the Prophet Mohammed. Many Muslims say Islam bars showing any images of the prophet. Yet one cartoon, for example, showed Mohammed as a terrorist with a bomb on his head.

《日兰德邮报》刊登了12幅先知穆罕默德的图像，许多穆斯林说伊斯兰教禁止展示先知的任何图像。而其中一幅漫画将穆罕默德画成了一个头上扛着一枚炸弹的恐怖分子。

The newspaper says it published the cartoons as a form of political protest. Another newspaper had reported that a writer could not find anyone to draw pictures for a book about the prophet. Artists reportedly were afraid to draw them.

该报称，刊登该漫画是一种政治的抗议形式。据另一份报纸报道，有个作家找不到人为他的一本关于先知的书作画。据报道，这是因为画家们不敢画这样的画。

In October, ambassadors from ten Muslim nations and the Palestinian representative in Denmark wrote to the Danish prime minister. They urged him to take action against those responsible for the drawings.

去年十月，十个穆斯林国家的大使和驻丹麦的巴勒斯坦代表写信给丹麦首相，催促他对那些负责刊登漫画的人采取行动。

Prime Minister Anders Fogh Rasmussen has said he is sorry the cartoons offended Muslims. But he has refused to apologize for their being published.

首相安诺斯·福格·拉斯穆森说，他为这些漫画冒犯了穆斯林而感到抱歉，但他拒绝为出版这些漫画而道歉。

Danish Muslim groups began legal action against the newspaper that published them.

丹麦的穆斯林组织开始采取法律措施抗议刊登漫画的报纸。

In December, leaders from the Organization of the Islamic Conference condemned the cartoons. They discussed them during their meeting in Saudi Arabia in Islam's holiest city, Mecca.

去年12月，伊斯兰会议组织领导人强烈谴责刊登此组漫画。他们在沙特阿拉伯、伊斯兰教圣地麦加举行会议专门讨论此事。

Delegates from a Danish coalition of twenty-seven Muslim groups had brought the cartoons to the Middle East in December to seek support. The delegates also included some images that had not been published. A spokesman has said they were not an attempt to mislead. He says they were mailed to Danish Muslims who had criticized the published cartoons.

去年12月，来自丹麦27个穆斯林组织联盟的代表把此组漫画带到中东去寻求支持。这些代表所带的图像中还包括一些从未被出版的画像。发言人指出他们不是试图误导，而是将此邮寄给那些对刊登漫画提出批评的丹麦穆斯林人。

In January, Danish government lawyers decided not to bring charges against the newspaper. A few days later, a publication in Norway printed the cartoons to show support for the Danish paper and for freedom of the press. Saudi Arabia withdrew its ambassador from Denmark and began a boycott of Danish goods.

今年1月份，丹麦政府的律师决定不对报纸提出起诉。几天之后，挪威一家出版社刊印了那些漫画，以表示对丹麦报纸和出版自由的支持。沙特阿拉伯召回了驻丹麦的大使，并开始抵制丹麦货物。

A statement from the *Jyllands-Posten* apologized for offending Muslims, but supported the decision to print the drawings. Since then, news media in other countries have also printed them.

《日兰德邮报》发表声明，对触犯穆斯林表示道歉，但仍然支持刊印图像的决定。自此，其他国家的新闻媒体也开始刊印那些画像。

As protests spread to different countries, they turned violent and deadly. Danish and Norwegian embassies have been attacked.

随着抗议之声蔓延至不同的国家，抗议活动变得暴烈并引发伤亡，丹麦和挪威的大使馆受到袭击。

There has been much debate about the reasons behind the protests.

人们纷纷对抗议背后的原因进行争论。

Many people say the protests show the anger of Muslims at treatment by Westerners. They say the demonstrations also show anger at the occupation of Iraq and Afghanistan. But even some Muslims say the protests are being used in some cases to push for goals unrelated to defending Islam.

很多人认为，抗议表明穆斯林对西方处理方式的愤怒。他们说，示威行动也表露了对侵占伊拉克和阿富汗的愤怒。但是，有些穆斯林人认为，在某些情况下抗议活动被利用于与保护伊斯兰教无关之目的。

Denmark's prime minister says "religious extremists" have fueled the flames. In published comments this week Mister Rasmussen also criticized Syria and Iran. He says they have used the situation to gain support because they are both under international pressure.

丹麦首相指出，"宗教极端分子"是在火上浇油。拉斯穆森在本周发表的评论中批评了叙利亚和伊朗。他指出，两国利用这个形势去争取支持，原因是两国都受到很多国际上的压力。

He says Denmark is a liberal country, but its values must be honored. These include freedom of expression, equality for men and women and a separation of politics and religion.

首相称丹麦是一个自由主义国家，因而必须尊重其价值观，包括言论自由、男女平等及政教分离。

(IN THE NEWS in VOA *Special English* was written by Nancy Steinbach. I'm Steve Ember.)

Lesson 32 40th Anniversary of Martin Luther King Jr's Death

By Brianna Blake

April 4, 2008

Part One Background Information

美国近代民权运动简介[1]

美国民权运动可分为两个时期，前期美国民权运动（1886—1954 年）和近代美国民权运动（1955—1968 年）。从历史的角度来看，民权运动的迅速发展往往因为国家的某项政策或某个利益集团严重地伤害了某部分人群的公民权利。近代美国民权运动就是如此，非裔美国人长期以来受到主流社会的歧视和隔离，这起源于 1896 年美国联邦最高法院作出的“普莱西诉弗格森案”（Plessy V. Ferguson）判决，该判决确立对黑人采取“隔离但平等”的措施合法，从而导致南方出现种族隔离制度的法令，学校、工厂、医院及军队都采取种族隔离，由此导致一连串非裔美国人民权运动的正式出场。

1955 年，在实施种族隔离制的代表性城市阿拉巴马州蒙哥马利市，黑人罗莎·帕克斯夫人在公共汽车上拒绝让座给白人，被捕入狱。马丁·路德·金牧师带领该市黑人公民，以全面罢乘来反对公共汽车上的黑白种族隔离。经过一年的抗争，终于迫使蒙哥马利市的巴士取消了种族隔离措施。这次的罢乘公共汽车运动对全美各地的黑人起到了鼓舞作用，为以后的民权运动奠定了法律基础。马丁·路德·金也因此获得 1964 年诺贝尔和平奖。

1957 年，金牧师及其支持者组成南方基督教领袖会议，将运动深入南部的各个生活领域。1958 年，南方 21 个主要城市组织集会，发动黑人争取公民权利。1960 年 2 月 1 日，北卡罗来纳州格林斯伯勒城 4 个黑人大学生进入一餐馆，白人服务员命令他们走开，他们静坐不动。这一英勇行为立刻得到南部广大黑人学生响应，发展为大规模静坐运动，迫使近 200 个城市的餐馆取消种族隔离制。1961 年 5 月初，种族平等大会又开展自由乘客运动。不久，该运动得到许多白人的支持，逐渐发展为全国性运动，迫使南部诸州取消州际公共汽车乘坐上的种族隔离制。

1963 年 3 月，金牧师等人在南部种族隔离极其严重的伯明翰组织示威游行，要求取消全城隔离制。示威群众受到残酷镇压，但由于金牧师的坚持和美国联邦政府被迫进行干预，该城种族隔离制全部被取消。

伯明翰事件后，民权运动队伍迅速扩大。1963 年 8 月 28 日，民权运动组织 25 万人（其中 1/4 为白人）向华盛顿进军，要求就业，要求“立即自由”。另外，有些城市的黑人还开展以暴力对付暴力的斗争。1964 年迫使林登·约翰逊总统签署了《民权法》。但南部诸州仍采用各种手法阻止黑人选民登记。于是，金牧师等在种族主义非常猖獗的阿拉巴

---

① http://baike.baidu.com/view/190927.htm

马州塞尔马市进行黑人选民登记运动，并于1965年3月冒着被殴打、杀害的危险，由塞尔马向州首府蒙哥马利进军，最后参加人数达15万。在世界人民谴责面前，美国政府于同年8月要求国会通过了《选民登记法》。

上述两法未能完全取消南部种族隔离与歧视制度，而北部的种族歧视事实上还有加剧之势。1968年3月，金牧师组织了穷人运动，在途经田纳西州孟菲斯市时被种族主义分子枪杀。美国黑人领袖们前赴后继，后来分别又发起了民族自觉运动、黑人权力运动、黑豹党运动以及黑人群众自发的大规模城市骚动等。

美国黑人民权运动是现代非暴力运动的典型，在全世界被压迫阶级之中影响深远，它使人们看到可以通过合法的群众运动获得民主权利的可能，也使人看到世界必将走向民主与平等的趋势。

Part Two　Exercises

Ⅰ. Listen to the first part of the news, and fill in the blanks with the words you hear.

Forty years ago, African American ____________, the Reverend Doctor Martin Luther King, Junior, was shot and killed. He died on April fourth, nineteen sixty-eight in Memphis, Tennessee.

On Friday, in that city, ____________ and thousands of citizens came together. They honored Doctor King for leading ____________.

During the nineteen fifties and sixties, Doctor King had led a ____________. His work was aimed at ____________ against African Americans.

His efforts led to ____________ of nineteen sixty-four. That year, he won the Nobel Peace Prize.

Ⅱ. Listen to the second part of the news, and answer the following questions.

1. How did Doctor King fight for economic justice?

2. Did the sanitation workers（清扫垃圾的工人）enjoyed economic justice forty years ago?

3. What did Doctor King do before he was thirty-nine years old?

Ⅲ. Describe the situation in USA after Doctor King's murder with the key words given below.

incited

the race riots

burned
control the violence
arrested, killed, damaged or destroyed
race relations in the United States

Ⅳ. Listen to the forth part of the news, and translate it into Chinese, then repeat it in English.

Begin from "In the years since his death...".

Part Three Keys to the Exercises

Ⅰ. Listen to the first part of the news, and fill in the blanks with the words you hear.

Forty years ago, African American civil rights leader, the Reverend Doctor Martin Luther King Junior, was shot and killed. He died on April fourth, nineteen sixty-eight in Memphis, Tennessee.

On Friday, in that city, presidential candidates, civil rights leaders, labor activists and thousands of citizens came together. They honored Doctor King for leading the struggle for racial equality and economic justice.

During the nineteen fifties and sixties, Doctor King had led a campaign of non-violent protests. His work was aimed at ending racial separation and discrimination against African Americans.

His efforts led to passage of the Civil Rights Act of nineteen sixty-four. That year, he won the Nobel Peace Prize.

Ⅱ. Listen to the second part of the news, and answer the following questions.

1. How did Doctor King fight for economic justice?

Forty years ago, Doctor King was in Memphis to organize a strike for workers' rights.

2. Did the sanitation workers (清扫垃圾的工人) enjoyed economic justice forty years ago?

No, the sanitation workers in the city were protesting their low wages and poor working conditions.

3. What did Doctor King do before he was thirty-nine years old?

Led the nation's civil rights movement. (Doctor King was thirty-nine years old at the time, and had become the nation's chief civil rights leader.)

Ⅲ. Describe the situation in USA after Doctor King's murder with the key words given below.

His murder incited riots in more than one hundred American cities. The race riots lasted for days. Many African American neighborhoods burned. The government ordered about fifty thousand soldiers to help control the violence. An estimated twenty-one thousand people were arrested. Almost fifty people were killed. And millions of dollars in property was damaged or destroyed.

His murder also brought about a divisive and difficult period for race relations in the United States.

Ⅳ. Listen to the forth part of the news, and translate it into Chinese, then repeat it in English.

In the years since his death, Doctor King has often been called one of the most honored Americans in history. But for many, his work for racial equality remains unfinished.

金博士死后多年，仍常被称为历史上最受尊敬的美国人之一。但对于许多人来说，他为种族平等所做的奋斗仍未完成。

In the past forty years, African Americans have become successful in education, business, entertainment and politics. The rise of Democratic Party presidential candidate Barack Obama is a powerful sign of racial progress. If elected in November, Mister Obama would become America's first black president.

40 年来，非裔美国人在教育、商业、娱乐和政治方面都取得很大成就。民主党总统候选人巴拉克 · 奥巴马的成功就是种族进步的一个有利证明。如果能在 11 月当选，奥巴马先生将成为美国第一位黑人总统。

Yet experts say the black population as a whole has not reached equality with white people socially and economically. Black Americans experience greater rates of poverty and crime than whites.

然而专家称，黑人作为一个整体尚未在社会和经济方面达到与白人平等。美国黑人有着比白人更高的贫穷和犯罪率。

Civil rights leaders say that forty years after his death, many African Americans still seek Doctor King's dream of equality and opportunity.

人权运动领袖说，马丁 · 路德 · 金死后40 年，许多非裔美国人仍在追求金博士所梦想的平等和机会。

Martin Luther King Junior is best remembered for his nineteen sixty-three "I Have a Dream" speech. It brought together millions of people in the United States and around the world to work for racial justice.

马丁 · 路德 · 金最让人们怀念的就是他在 1963 年的演讲"我有一个梦想"。它让美国和世界无数人团结在一起为种族平等而奋斗。

Part Four　Translation of the Text

40th Anniversary of Martin Luther King Jr's Death
马丁·路德·金逝世四十周年纪念

Forty years ago, African American civil rights leader, the Reverend Doctor Martin Luther King Junior, was shot and killed. He died on April fourth, nineteen sixty-eight in Memphis, Tennessee.

40 年前，非裔美国人的民权运动领袖，神学博士马丁·路德·金被枪杀身亡。他在 1968 年 4 月 4 日死于田纳西州的孟菲斯市。

On Friday, in that city, presidential candidates, civil rights leaders, labor activists and thousands of citizens came together. They honored Doctor King for leading the struggle for racial equality and economic justice.

周五，总统候选人、民权运动领袖、工会积极分子以及数以千计的民众聚集在那个城市。他们缅怀金博士，纪念他为争取种族平等和经济公平而领导的斗争。

During the nineteen fifties and sixties, Doctor King had led a campaign of non-violent protests. His work was aimed at ending racial separation and discrimination against African Americans.

在二十世纪五六十年代，金博士领导了一系列非暴力抗议活动。他斗争的目的是为了终止种族隔离和对非裔美国人的歧视。

His efforts led to passage of the Civil Rights Act of nineteen sixty-four. That year, he won the Nobel Peace Prize.

他的努力促使《民权法案》于 1964 年通过。同年，他获得诺贝尔和平奖。

Forty years ago, Doctor King was in Memphis to organize a strike for workers' rights. The sanitation workers in the city were protesting their low wages and poor working conditions. Doctor King was thirty-nine years old at the time, and had become the nation's chief civil rights leader.

40 年前，金博士在孟菲斯准备组织一场争取工人权益的罢工。城市里的环卫工人正抗议他们的低工资和极差的工作环境。金博士当时 39 岁，却已是美国主要的民权运动领袖。

His murder incited riots in more than one hundred American cities. The race riots lasted for days. Many African American neighborhoods burned. The government ordered about fifty thousand soldiers to help control the violence. An estimated twenty-one thousand people were arrested. Almost fifty people were killed. And millions of dollars in property was damaged or destroyed.

他的被害导致美国超过一百多个城市发生暴乱。种族冲突持续了许多天。很多非裔美国人的社区被焚烧。政府下令派出大概 5 万士兵去帮助制止暴力行动。估计有 21 000 人被捕，近 50 人死亡，价值数百万美元的财产被损毁。

His murder also brought about a divisive and difficult period for race relations in the United States.

他的被害也给美国的种族关系带来一段分裂而艰难的时期。

In the years since his death, Doctor King has often been called one of the most honored Americans in history. But for many, his work for racial equality remains unfinished.

金博士死后多年，仍常被称为历史上最受尊敬的美国人之一。但对于许多人来说，他为种族平等所做的奋斗仍未完成。

In the past forty years, African Americans have become successful in education, business, entertainment and politics. The rise of Democratic Party presidential candidate Barack Obama is a powerful sign of racial progress. If elected in November, Mister Obama would become America's first black president.

40 年来，非裔美国人在教育、商业、娱乐和政治方面都取得很大成就。民主党总统候选人巴拉克·奥巴马的成功就是种族进步的一个有利证明。如果能在 11 月当选，奥巴马先生将成为美国第一位黑人总统。

Yet experts say the black population as a whole has not reached equality with white people socially and economically. Black Americans experience greater rates of poverty and crime than whites.

然而专家称，黑人作为一个整体尚未在社会和经济方面达到与白人平等。美国黑人有着比白人更高的贫穷和犯罪率。

Civil rights leaders say that forty years after his death, many African Americans still seek Doctor King's dream of equality and opportunity.

民权运动领袖说，马丁·路德·金死后 40 年，许多非裔美国人仍在追求金博士所梦想的平等和机会。

Martin Luther King Junior is best remembered for his nineteen sixty-three "I Have a Dream" speech. It brought together millions of people in the United States and around the world to work for racial justice.

马丁·路德·金最让人们怀念的就是他在 1963 年的演讲“我有一个梦想”。它让美国和世界无数人团结在一起为种族平等而奋斗。

(录音：“我有一个梦想”)

(And that's IN THE NEWS in VOA *Special English*, written by Brianna Blake. I'm Steve Ember.)

附　录：

我有一个梦想①

马丁·路德·金

I am happy to join with you today in what will go down in history as the greatest demonstration for freedom in the history of our nation.

今天，我高兴地同大家一起，参加这次将成为我国历史上为了争取自由而举行的最伟大的示威集会。

---

① http://zhidao.baidu.com/question/145277725.html

Five score years ago, a great American, in whose symbolic shadow we stand today, signed the Emancipation Proclamation.

100 年前，一位伟大的美国人签署了《解放宣言》，今天我们就站在他那象征性的身影下。

This momentous decree came as a great beacon light of hope to millions of Negro slaves who had been seared in the flames of withering injustice. It came as a joyous daybreak to end the long night of their captivity.

这项重要法令的颁布，对于千百万灼烤于非正义残焰中的黑奴，犹如带来希望之光的硕大灯塔，恰似结束漫漫长夜禁锢的欢畅黎明。

But one hundred years later, the Negro still is not free.

然而，100 年后，黑人依然没有获得自由。

One hundred years later, the life of the Negro is still sadly crippled by the manacles of segregation and the chains of discrimination.

100 年后，黑人依然悲惨地蹒跚于种族隔离和种族歧视的枷锁之下。

One hundred years later, the Negro lives on a lonely island of poverty in the midst of a vast ocean of material prosperity.

100 年后，黑人依然生活在贫穷的孤岛上，而这孤岛繁荣如翰海般的物资环绕。

One hundred years later, the Negro is still languished in the corners of American society and finds himself an exile in his own land.

100 年后，黑人依然在美国社会中向隅而泣，依然感到自己在国土家园中漂泊流离。

And so we've come here today to dramatize a shameful condition.

所以，我们今天来到这里，要把这骇人听闻的情况公诸于众。

In a sense, we've come to our nation's capital to cash a check.

从某种意义上说，我们来到国家的首都是为了兑现一张支票。

When the architects of our republic wrote the magnificent words of the Constitution and the Declaration of Independence, they were signing a promissory note to which every American was to fall heir.

我们共和国的缔造者在拟写宪法和独立宣言的辉煌篇章时，就签署了一张每一个美国人都能继承的期票。

This note was a promise that all men, yes, black men as well as white men, would be guaranteed the "unalienable Rights" of "Life, Liberty and the pursuit of Happiness".

这张期票向所有人承诺："不论白人还是黑人，都享有不可让渡的生存权、自由权和追求幸福权。"

It is obvious today that America has defaulted on this promissory note, in so far as her citizens of color are concerned. Instead of honoring this sacred obligation, America has given the Negro people a bad check, a check which has come back marked "insufficient funds".

然而，今天美国显然没有承兑这张期票，她的有色公民的期盼遥遥无期，她仅仅给黑人开了一张空头支票，一张盖着"资金不足"的印戳被退回的支票。

But we refuse to believe that the bank of justice is bankrupt.

但是，我们决不相信正义的银行会破产。

We refuse to believe that there are insufficient funds in the great vaults of opportunity of this nation.

我们决不相信这个国家巨大的机会宝库会资金不足。

And so, we've come to cash this check, a check that will give us upon demand the riches of freedom and the security of justice.

因此，我们来的目的是兑现这张支票。让这张支票带给我们宝贵的自由和正义的保障。

We have also come to this hallowed spot to remind America of the fierce urgency of Now.

我们来到这块圣地还为了提醒美国：现在正是万分紧急的时刻。

This is no time to engage in the luxury of cooling off or to take the tranquilizing drug of gradualism.

现在不是从容不迫，悠然行事或服用渐进主义镇静剂的时候。

Now is the time to make real the promises of democracy. Now is the time to rise from the dark and desolate valley of segregation to the sunlit path of racial justice.

现在是真正实现民主诺言的时候。现在是走出幽暗荒凉的种族隔离深谷，踏上种族平等的阳关大道的时候。

Now is the time to lift our nation from the quicksands of racial injustice to the solid rock of brotherhood.

现在是使我们国家走出种族不平等的流沙，踏上充满手足之情的磐石的时候。

Now is the time to make justice a reality for all of God's children.

现在是使上帝所有孩子真正享有公正的时候。

It would be fatal for the nation to overlook the urgency of the moment.

忽视这一时刻的紧迫性，对于国家将会是致命的。

This sweltering summer of the Negro's legitimate discontent will not pass until there is an invigorating autumn of freedom and equality.

自由平等的朗朗秋日不到来，黑人顺情合理哀怨的酷暑就不会过去。

Nineteen sixty-three is not an end, but a beginning.

1963 年不是一个结束，而是一个开端。

And those who hope that the Negro needed to blow off steam and will now be content will have a rude awakening if the nation returns to business as usual.

如果国家依然我行我素，那些希望黑人只需出出气就会心满意足的人将大失所望。

And there will be neither rest nor tranquility in America until the Negro is granted his citizenship rights.

在黑人得到公民权之前，美国既不会安宁，也不会平静。

The whirlwinds of revolt will continue to shake the foundations of our nation until the bright day of justice emerges.

反抗的旋风将继续震撼我们国家的基石，直至光辉灿烂的正义之日来临。

But there is something that I must say to my people, who stand on the warm threshold which leads into the palace of justice.

但是，对于站在通向正义之宫艰险门槛上的人们，有一些话我必须说。

In the process of gaining our rightful place, we must not be guilty of wrongful deeds.

在我们争取合法地位的过程中，切不要错误行事导致犯罪。

Let us not seek to satisfy our thirst for freedom by drinking from the cup of bitterness and hatred.

我们切不要吞饱含仇恨辛酸的苦酒，来解除对于自由的渴望。

We must forever conduct our struggle on the high plane of dignity and discipline.

我们应该永远得体地、纪律严明地进行斗争。

We must not allow our creative protest to degenerate into physical violence.

我们不能容许我们富有创造性的抗议沦为暴力行动。

Again and again, we must rise to the majestic heights of meeting physical force with soul force.

我们应该不断升华到用灵魂力量对付肉体力量的崇高境界。

The marvelous new militancy which has engulfed the Negro community must not lead us to a distrust of all white people, for many of our white brothers, as evidenced by their presence here today, have come to realize that their destiny is tied up with our destiny. And they have come to realize that their freedom is inextricably bound to our freedom.

席卷黑人社会的新的奇迹般的战斗精神，不应导致我们对所有白人的不信任，因为许多白人兄弟已经认识到：他们的命运同我们的命运紧密相连，他们的自由同我们的自由休戚相关。他们今天来到这里参加集会就是证明。

We cannot walk alone.

我们不能单独行动。

And as we walk, we must make the pledge that we shall always march ahead.

当我们行动时，我们必须保证勇往直前。

We cannot turn back.

我们不能后退。

There are those who are asking the devotees of civil rights, "When will you be satisfied?"

有人问热心民权运动的人："你们什么时候会感到满意？"

We can never be satisfied as long as the Negro is the victim of the unspeakable horrors of police brutality.

只要黑人依然是不堪形容的警察恐怖暴行的牺牲品，我们就绝不会满意。

We can never be satisfied as long as our bodies, heavy with the fatigue of travel, cannot gain lodging in the motels of the highways and the hotels of the cities.

只要我们在旅途劳顿后，却被公路旁的汽车游客旅社和城市旅馆拒之门外，我们就绝不会满意。

We cannot be satisfied as long as a Negro in Mississippi cannot vote and a Negro in New York believes he has nothing for which to vote.

只要密西西比州的黑人不能参加选举，纽约州的黑人认为他们与选举毫不相干，我们就绝不会满意。

No, no, we are not satisfied, and we will not be satisfied until "justice rolls down like waters, and righteousness like a mighty stream".

不，不，我们不会满意，直至公正似水奔流，正义如泉喷涌。

I am not unmindful that some of you have come here out of great trials and tribulations.

我并非没有注意到你们有些人历尽艰难困苦来到这里。

Some of you have come fresh from narrow jail cells.

你们有些人刚刚走出狭小的牢房。

And some of you have come from areas where your quest— quest for freedom left you battered by the storms of persecution and staggered by the winds of police brutality.

有些人来自因追求自由而遭受迫害如风暴袭击和警察暴虐如狂飙摧残的地区。

You have been the veterans of creative suffering.

你们饱经风霜，历尽苦难。

Continue to work with the faith that unearned suffering is redemptive.

继续努力吧，要相信：无辜受苦终得拯救。

Go back to Mississippi, go back to Alabama, go back to South Carolina, go back to Georgia, go back to Louisiana, go back to the slums and ghettos of our northern cities, knowing that somehow this situation can and will be changed. Let us not wallow in the valley of despair, I say to you today, my friends. And so even though we face the difficulties of today and tomorrow, I still have a dream.

回到密西西比去吧，回到阿拉巴马去吧，回到南卡罗来纳去吧，回到佐治亚去吧，回到路易斯安那去吧，回到我们北方城市中的贫民窟和黑人居住区去吧。要知道，这种情况能够而且将会改变。我们切不要在绝望的深渊里沉沦。朋友们，今天我要对你们说，尽管眼下困难重重，但我依然怀有一个梦。

It is a dream deeply rooted in the American dream.

这个梦深深植根于美国梦之中。

I have a dream that one day this nation will rise up and live out the true meaning of its creed: "We hold these truths to be self-evident, that all men are created equal."

我梦想有一天，这个国家将会奋起，实现其立国信条的真谛："我们认为这些真理不言而喻，人人生而平等。"

I have a dream that one day on the red hills of Georgia, the sons of former slaves and the sons of former slave owners will be able to sit down together at the table of brotherhood.

我梦想有一天，在佐治亚州的红色山冈上，昔日奴隶的儿子能够同昔日奴隶主的儿子同席而坐，亲如手足。

I have a dream that one day even the state of Mississippi, a state sweltering with the heat of injustice, sweltering with the heat of oppression, will be transformed into an oasis of freedom and justice.

我梦想有一天，甚至连密西西比州——一个非正义和压迫的热浪逼人的荒漠之州，也会改造成为自由和公正的青青绿洲。

I have a dream that my four little children will one day live in a nation where they will not be judged by the color of their skin but by the content of their character.

我梦想有一天，我的四个小儿女将生活在一个不是以皮肤的颜色，而是以品格的优劣作为评判标准的国度里。

I have a dream today!

我今天怀有一个梦。

I have a dream that one day, down in Alabama, with its vicious racists, with its governor having his lips dripping with the words of "interposition" and "nullification" — one day right there in Alabama little black boys and black girls will be able to join hands with little white boys and white girls as sisters and brothers.

我梦想有一天，阿拉巴马州会有所改变——尽管该州州长现在仍滔滔不绝地说什么要对联邦法令提出异议和拒绝执行——在那里，黑人儿童能够和白人儿童兄弟姐妹般地携手并行。

I have a dream today!

我今天怀有一个梦。

I have a dream that one day every valley shall be exalted, and every hill and mountain shall be made low, the rough places will be made plain, and the crooked places will be made straight; "and the glory of the Lord shall be revealed and all flesh shall see it together".

我梦想有一天，深谷弥合，高山夷平，歧路化坦途，曲径成通衢，上帝的光华再现，普天下生灵共谒。

This is our hope, and this is the faith that I go back to the South with.

这是我们的希望。这是我将带回南方去的信念。

With this faith, we will be able to hew out of the mountain of despair a stone of hope.

有了这个信念，我们就能从绝望之山开采出希望之石。

With this faith, we will be able to transform the jangling discords of our nation into a beautiful symphony of brotherhood.

有了这个信念，我们就能把这个国家嘈杂刺耳的争吵声变为充满手足之情的悦耳交响曲。

With this faith, we will be able to work together, to pray together, to struggle together, to go to jail together, to stand up for freedom together, knowing that we will be free one day.

有了这个信念，我们就能一同工作，一同祈祷，一同斗争，一同入狱，一同维护自由，因为我们知道，我们终有一天会获得自由。

And this will be the day—this will be the day when all of God's children will be able to sing with new meaning: My country 'tis of thee, sweet land of liberty, of thee I sing.

到了这一天，上帝的所有孩子都能以新的含义高唱这首歌：我的祖国，可爱的自由之邦，我为您歌唱。

Land where my fathers died, land of the Pilgrim's pride, from every mountainside, let freedom ring!

这是我祖先终老的地方，是早期移民自豪的地方，让自由之声，响彻每一座山岗。

And if America is to be a great nation, this must become true.

如果美国要成为伟大的国家，这一点必须实现。

And so let freedom ring from the prodigious hilltops of New Hampshire.

因此，让自由之声响彻新罕布什尔州的巍峨高峰！

Let freedom ring from the mighty mountains of New York.

让自由之声响彻纽约州的崇山峻岭！

Let freedom ring from the heightening Alleghenies of Pennsylvania.

让自由之声响彻宾夕法尼亚州的阿勒格尼高峰！

Let freedom ring from the snow-capped Rockies of Colorado.

让自由之声响彻科罗拉多州冰雪皑皑的洛基山！

Let freedom ring from the curvaceous slopes of California.

让自由之声响彻加利福尼亚州的婀娜群峰！

But not only that:

不，不仅如此.

Let freedom ring from Stone Mountain of Georgia.

让自由之声响彻佐治亚州的石山！

Let freedom ring from Lookout Mountain of Tennessee.

让自由之声响彻田纳西州的望山！

Let freedom ring from every hill and molehill of Mississippi.

让自由之声响彻密西西比州的一座座山峰，一个个土丘！

From every mountainside, let freedom ring.

让自由之声响彻每一个山冈！

And when this happens, when we allow freedom ring, when we let it ring from every village and every hamlet, from every state and every city, we will be able to speed up that day when all of God's children, black men and white men, Jews and Gentiles, Protestants and Catholics, will be able to join hands and sing in the words of the old Negro spiritual:

当我们让自由之声轰响，当我们让自由之声响彻每一个大村小庄，每一个州府城镇，我们就能加速这一天的到来。那时，上帝的所有孩子，黑人和白人，犹太教徒和非犹太教徒，耶稣教徒和天主教徒，将能携手同唱那首古老的黑人灵歌：

Free at last! Free at last!

终于自由了！终于自由了！

Thank God Almighty, we are free at last!

感谢全能的上帝，我们终于自由了！

Lesson 33　Mars Once Had Moving Plates Like Earth Has Now

By Katherine Gypson, Cynthia Kirk and Karen Legget

November 7, 2005

Part One　Background Information

火星与地球有什么关系

寂寞和好奇的地球人类，总是想在宇宙中寻找自己的伙伴。美国人就数次派火星探测器去火星上“串门”，虽然没有发现什么生命的迹象，却也高兴地宣称火星上曾有过“适宜”生命生存的环境。火星是太阳系九大行星之一，按离太阳由近及远的顺序排在第四。除金星以外，火星离地球最近，距离地球1.9亿公里。火星的质量小于地球质量，它的半径仅为地球半径的1/2左右。但火星在许多方面与地球较为相像：火星的自转周期几乎与地球一样，1个火星日只比1个地球日长41分19秒；火星自转轴的倾角也几乎和地球相同。因而，火星也有四季变化，气温比地球低，生存条件仅次于地球。火星与地球明显不同的是，火星的公转周期几乎是地球公转周期的两倍，所以，火星上每个季节要持续6个月，而不是3个月①。地球人就是根据火星以上情况认为，火星是最适宜人类移民的星球，将来等地球的资源用完了，便把家搬到火星上去。

还有一个很重要的因素坚定了地球人的推测，火星上存在着“极冠”，表面有水的迹象和火山迹象。美国火星勘测轨道飞行器携带的“浅层地下雷达”就是为了证实火星上有过生命这个假设而设置的，它可以指示寻找火星上以前曾经存在水的某个地方的地质环境，比如古代湖床等，从中研究使火星变得干燥和寒冷的气候原因。科学家还可从火星的地质地貌图中了解岩石的年龄和化学组成，以确定火星历史上的一系列事件的顺序。随着前几次火星探测的成功，人们探测火星的兴致也越来越高，21世纪将成为人类探测火星的高潮期，2003年，欧洲空间局和美国先后发射了“火星快车”和两艘“火星探测流浪者”宇宙飞船。当时预计2007年将发射“凤凰”着陆器，2009年将发射“火星科学实验室”。② 看来，在不久的将来，我们很快就会知道火星上是否曾有过生命，什么时候有过生命，有过什么样的生命等问题，那时地球人就可准备向火星进发了。

---

① 佚名. 火星与人类探测火星历程. http://news.xinhuanet.com/ziliao/2003-08/26/content_1044850.htm

② http://www.chinabyte.com/344/2069844.shtml. 2005-08-13

Part Two Exercises

Ⅰ. Listen to the news about the new findings on Mars, and complete the following sentences.

1. American scientists have found evidence that ____.

2. The evidence comes from ______________________________ on Mars. The map was put together from ______________________________, the Mars Global Surveyor.

3. The American space agency sent the Mars Global Surveyor ____.

4. The spacecraft spent nearly four years studying the planet, ____.

5. The spacecraft is now on ____.

Ⅱ. Listen to the second part of the news about the functions of the map, and answer the following questions.

1. What did the space agency say about the new magnetic field map of Mars?

2. What can be found from the map?

1)

2)

3. In what way is the Mars the same as the Earth?

4. How was the plates (地块) formed? (mantle 地幔, hot liquid rock 火熔岩)

5. What happened to the mantle when it reaches the surface?

Ⅲ. Listen to the third part of the news, and translate it into Chinese.

From "The magnetic field (磁场)" to "the Hawaiian Islands (夏威夷群岛)".

Ⅳ. Listen to the last part of the news, and take it down word by word.

The Mars Global Surveyor also...

Part Three Keys to the Exercises

Ⅰ. Listen to the news about the new findings on Mars, and complete the following sentences.

(A possible cause of prostate (前列腺) cancer...

A new campaign to save children from AIDS, and a new kind of vaccine against polio.)

1. American scientists have found evidence that the surface of the planet Mars once moved like that of present-day Earth.

2. The evidence comes from a new map of magnetic forces on Mars.

The map was put together from observations by an American space vehicle, the Mars Global Surveyor.

3. The American space agency sent the Mars Global Surveyor into orbit around Mars in nineteen ninety-seven.

4. The spacecraft spent nearly four years studying the planet, its atmosphere and what lies under its surface.

5. The spacecraft is now on an extended trip to gather more information.

Ⅱ. Listen to the second part of the news about the functions of the map, and answer the following questions.

1. What did the space agency say about the new magnetic field map of Mars?

The space agency says the new magnetic field map of Mars is the first of its kind.

2. What can be found from the map?

1) The map provides images of the full surface of the planet.

2) Scientists say the map shows that the surface of Mars was created in much the same way as Earth's.

3. In what way is the Mars the same as the Earth?

On both planets, the outer surface is broken up into large pieces, or plates.

4. How was the plates (地块) formed? (mantle 地幔, hot liquid rock 火岩石)

These plates are moving over areas of hot liquid rock, called the mantle. As the mantle rises up (隆起) and breaks through the surface of the planet, the plates push apart.

5. What happened to the mantle when it reaches the surface?

The mantle reaches the surface and cools into hard rock.

Ⅲ. Listen to the third part of the news, and translate it into Chinese.

The magnetic field on the planet pulls the rock in one direction. More material pushes from under the planet's surface, building a new rock surface on top of the old. Sometimes different levels of rock will be pulled in different directions. This happens when the magnetic field changes several times every million years.

该行星的磁场将这些岩石推向一个方向。行星表层下面还有更多的物质撞击着，在老的岩石层上面形成了一个新的岩石层。有时，不同层的岩石运动的方向不同。这是因为磁场每几百万年改变几次造成的。

The planet Mars also has a series of mountains called the Tharsis volcanoes. They lie in a straight line. Volcanoes on Mars are ten to a hundred times larger than those on Earth. Scientists have wondered why this is so. With the help of the map, scientists can now see that the mountains were formed in a very hot area between two plates. On Earth, this kind of volcanic activity formed the Hawaiian Islands.

火星上有系列的高山被称为萨丝丝火山。它们坐落在一条直线上。火星上的火山比地球上的大十至一百倍。科学家们对此深感不解，有了此图，他们现在明白了，原来这些高山是在两大地块之间的高温地区形成的。在地球上，类似的火山运动形成了夏威夷群岛。

Ⅳ. Listen to the last part of the news, and take it down word by word.

The Mars Global Surveyor also examined an extremely deep hole. It is called the Valley Marineris. It is six times as long and eight times as deep as the Grand Canyon in the western United States.

The spacecraft also found that the magnetic field on Mars did not cover the planet. Magnetic fields protect planets from some kinds of radiation from space. Scientists think the presence of even a partial magnetic field around Mars may mean that living organisms were able to exist on the planet.

Part Four Translation of the Text

Mars Once Had Moving Plates Like Earth Has Now
火星犹如地球现状，曾经也有移动地块

Voice One:

This is Science IN THE NEWS in VOA *Special English*. I'm Faith Lapidus.

Voice Two:

And I'm Bob Doughty. On our program this week—new findings about Mars...

Voice One:

A possible cause of prostate cancer...

Voice Two:

A new campaign to save children from AIDS, and a new kind of vaccine against polio.

Voice One:

American scientists have found evidence that the surface of the planet Mars once moved like that of present-day Earth. The evidence comes from a new map of magnetic forces on Mars.

美国科学家们找到了证据，证明火星的表面曾经像地球现在的状况一样移动过。其证据来自于一张新的火星磁场引力图。

The map was put together from observations by an American space vehicle, the Mars Global Surveyor. The American space agency sent the Mars Global Surveyor into orbit around Mars in nineteen ninety-seven. The spacecraft spent nearly four years studying the planet, its atmosphere and what lies under its surface. The spacecraft is now on an extended trip to gather more information.

这张图是通过美国太空穿梭机“火星探测器”上的观察拼缀而成。美国太空署于1997年发送了“火星探测器”，此太空船对该行星及其大气层以及地表下层的研究长达4年。目前，该太空船行程已被延长，以便搜集更多的信息。

Voice Two:

The space agency says the new magnetic field map of Mars is the first of its kind. The map provides images of the full surface of the planet.

太空署指出，此图属同类火星磁场图的第一张。此图提供了火星整个地表的形状。

Scientists say the map shows that the surface of Mars was created in much the same way as Earth's. On both planets, the outer surface is broken up into large pieces, or plates. These plates are moving over areas of hot liquid rock, called the mantle. As the mantle rises up and breaks through the surface of the planet, the plates push apart. The mantle reaches the surface and cools into hard rock.

科学家们认为，该图表现了火星诞生的方式与地球非常相似。此两颗行星的外表层都一样爆裂为大块碎片，即地块。这些地块在滚烫的熔岩区上移动，称为地幔。当地幔拱起

来，穿透行星的表层时，地块便被“拉”开了。地幔到达地表，冷却后成为坚硬的岩石。

The magnetic field on the planet pulls the rock in one direction. More material pushes from under the planet's surface, building a new rock surface on top of the old. Sometimes different levels of rock will be pulled in different directions. This happens when the magnetic field changes several times every million years.

该行星的磁场将这些岩石推向一个方向。行星表层下面还有更多的物质撞击着，在老的岩石层上面形成了一个新的岩石层。有时，不同层的岩石运动的方向不同。这是因为磁场每几百万年改变几次造成的。

Voice One:

The planet Mars also has a series of mountains called the Tharsis volcanoes. They lie in a straight line. Volcanoes on Mars are ten to a hundred times larger than those on Earth. Scientists have wondered why this is so. With the help of the map, scientists can now see that the mountains were formed in a very hot area between two plates. On Earth, this kind of volcanic activity formed the Hawaiian Islands.

火星上有系列的高山被称为萨丝丝火山。它们坐落在一条直线上。火星上的火山比地球上的大十至一百倍。科学家们对此深感不解，有了此图，他们现在明白了，原来这些高山是在两大地块之间的高温地区形成的。在地球上，类似的火山运动形成了夏威夷群岛。

The Mars Global Surveyor also examined an extremely deep hole. It is called the Valley Marineris. It is six times as long and eight times as deep as the Grand Canyon in the western United States.

火星探测器还探测了一个极其深奥的、被称为马瑞纳瑞斯谷的深洞。它的长度是美国西部大峡谷的6倍，深度是其8倍。

The spacecraft also found that the magnetic field on Mars did not cover the planet. Magnetic fields protect planets from some kinds of radiation from space. Scientists think the presence of even a partial magnetic field around Mars may mean that living organisms were able to exist on the planet.

太空船还发现，火星上的磁场没有覆盖整个行星。磁场可以保护行星免受太空中的某些辐射。科学家们认为，火星周围即使只有部分磁场，也意味着该行星上的生物有机体能够生存下来。

(You are listening to Science IN THE NEWS in VOA *Special English*, from Washington.)

Lesson 34　Stem Cell Research

By Mario Ritter

August 18，2001

Part One　Background Information

干细胞研究之争

“干细胞技术是近年来飞速发展的一种生物技术。干细胞的干，是‘树干’的‘干’，是‘根源’的意思。干细胞是指尚未发育成熟的细胞，它具有再生为各种组织器官的潜能，医学界称之为‘万用细胞’。科学家认为，绝大多数疾病，从脊髓损伤、帕金森氏综合征、糖尿病到癌症和艾滋病，都有望借助于干细胞技术得到治疗。”①

既然干细胞这么好，为什么对它的研究会引起如此多的争议？其主要原因是胚胎干细胞取自堕胎或流产的胚胎或者胎儿组织。“堕胎或流产胚胎尚未发育完全，未能正常出生，也不能继续存活，并不是社会学意义上的人。”②但要对其进行研究，还得像征集血液和人体器官那样，得到胚胎双亲的同意。由此，则可能导致“经济窘迫的胚胎双亲将面临金钱诱惑，为了金钱而出卖胚胎，这是几乎类同杀人一样的罪恶，是一种灵魂的堕落”③。如果仅仅以捐赠的方式进行，也会引起其他的伦理问题，比如单亲问题。

还有另一种干细胞是成体干细胞，它取自如人体脂肪、胎盘、骨髓中的造血干细胞等成体组织。虽然美国科学家认为，成体干细胞具有惊人的可塑性，和胚胎干细胞一样可以分化为各种各样的组织细胞，但绝大多数科学家还是认为，胚胎干细胞更容易繁殖，在分化为特定的组织细胞时更灵活自如。

除了以上两种方式，科学家还可以克隆人类早期胚胎，从中提取胚胎干细胞进行医疗研究。克隆胚胎也一样存在着伦理问题，首先，不论是胚胎干细胞还是成体干细胞，都要利用细胞嵌合技术嵌合到动物细胞内，以培育出长有人类组织器官的生物。如背上长着人耳的老鼠、产人体血液蛋白的猪、长有人耳的兔子等。这些异形生物的生长不是完全可控制和可预知的，一只猪体内被嵌合了人类细胞后有可能还会长出一颗人心或人脑，这样它就可能具有人类的思维和感情，甚至是痛苦的内心。其次，由克隆胚胎到克隆人，只差一步之遥，它引起了人们的极大恐慌。反对者认为，克隆是单性繁殖，不利于生物进化，克隆人和其母体或父体具有完全相同的遗传基因，在体形和性格上与其母体或父体近乎是一样的，可能会使人类在社会伦理上面临尴尬的处境④。再次，克隆人与人类繁殖的人应该拥有同样的自由意志，如果把他们当作医学试验品，就严重地贬损了他们的尊严和意志。

---

①②③　Mark（成都的乌云）. 干细胞技术的伦理之辩干细胞技术的伦理之辩. http：//bbs. swjtu. edu. cn/bbscon. php board = ethics&id = 1073779649/2002 - 09 - 26

④　佚名. 克隆自体繁殖 再生. http：//tech. enorth. com. cn/system/2001/09/27/000154301. shtml

而赞同克隆人的人认为，“克隆人并不违反生物进化原则。心理学认为，遗传和环境对人的成长的影响是同等重要的。克隆人和其母体或父体首先在年龄，其次在知识、心理经验上是完全不同的，不能认为他是其母本或父本的‘翻版’或‘复活’体。克隆人只是增加了人类的一种繁殖方式而已，他并不能取代人类正常的两性繁殖的主导地位，也不会引起社会伦理的混乱”。

但是，无论科学家们如何怂恿和鼓动，联合国和各国政府都通过了限制干细胞研究或克隆人的协定或法案。早在 1991 年，德国就实行《胚胎保护法》，严格禁止人类胚胎干细胞研究以及克隆胚胎干细胞。2000 年 11 月，德国卫生部又提出一项新的《生殖医学法》草案，再次强调在德国不允许进行胚胎干细胞的培育研究。1998 年 1 月，欧洲 19 个国家在法国巴黎签署了一项有关严格禁止克隆人的协议。美国国会众议院 2001 年 7 月 31 日通过了一项全面禁止克隆人的法案。2001 年 11 月 22 日，英国政府也公布了一项新法案，明确禁止通过克隆技术复制人类个体，即“繁殖性克隆”，成为世界上第一个立法反对生殖性克隆的国家。直至 2005 年 3 月，第 59 届联合国大会以 84 国赞成、34 国反对、37 国弃权的结果，批准了《联合国禁止人的克隆宣言》①。但比利时、中国、英国、新加坡等 34 国投了反对票，因为这些国家不禁止治疗性克隆研究，而这个宣言中“禁止一切形式的人的克隆”等于将生殖性克隆和治疗性克隆都给禁止了。

Part Two　Exercises

Ⅰ. Listen to the first part of news, and complete the following sentences.

1. Last week, President Bush approved limited federal government support of ______________________________.
2. The ______________________________ fertilized（受精的）human eggs called embryos（胚胎）.
3. Many groups ______________________________.
4. Some religious groups believe that ______________________________.
5. Yet, many scientists and some lawmakers believe ______________________________.
6. Private laboratories that ______________________________.
7. Stem cells have qualities ______________________________.
8. The stem cells from embryos are the most useful. They are ______________.
9. Embryonic stem cells are taken from embryos created in laboratories to ______________.
10. During the first days, the cells in the embryo ______________________________.
11. Each of these cells is ______________________________.
12. After about four days of development, ______________________________.

① 高延晶. 危机重重的克隆克隆人根本不可能. http: //news. china. com. cn/chinanet/china. cgi docid = 85052953, 54414424&server = 192. 168. 9. 86&port = 3002

Ⅱ. Listen to the fourth part of the news about adult stem cells, and translate it into Chinese.

Begin from "Adult stem cells. . . ".

Ⅲ. Listen to the last part of the news about the president, scientists and religious groups' attitude toward the research of stem cells, and take it down in the following order.

1. President Bush. . .

These groups of stem cells are now reproducing by themselves in laboratories worldwide.

2. This week, President Bush. . .

3. Yet, some scientists say that it is impossible to know how many groups of stem cells from embryos. . .

4. A number of congressmen. . .

5. The religious groups. . .

6. Other religious groups. . . Parkinson's and diabetes.

7. A national debate. . .

Part Three　Keys to the Exercises

Ⅰ. Listen to the first part of news, and complete the following sentences.

1. Last week, President Bush approved limited federal government support of research on special human cells.

2. The research involves stem cells taken from fertilized (受精的) human eggs called embryos (胚胎).

3. Many groups disagree with the President's decision.

4. Some religious groups believe that all research on stem cells from embryos should be banned.

5. Yet, many scientists and some lawmakers believe no limits should be put on the research.

6. Private laboratories that do not use federal money are not affected by the limits on the stem

cell research.

7. Stem cells have qualities that may make them highly useful in the treatment of many diseases.

8. The stem cells from embryos are the most useful. They are able to develop into all the tissues（组织）of the body.

9. Embryonic stem cells are taken from embryos created in laboratories to help women become pregnant.

10. During the first days, the cells in the embryo divide quickly.

11. Each of these cells is able to become any one of more than two-hundred different kinds of cells in the body.

12. After about four days of development, the embryos are destroyed and the stem cells removed.

Ⅱ. Listen to the fourth part of the news about adult stem cells, and translate it into Chinese.

Adult stem cells are taken from human tissue. These cells have not yet developed to become cells of an organ or a kind of tissue.

成熟的干细胞取自人类肌体组织，但这些细胞还没有发展成器官或者肌体组织细胞。

Removing stem cells does not harm an adult. But adult stem cells are difficult to identify. And, scientists do not know if adult stem cells have the ability to become cells of any kind of organ or tissue. Research suggests that stem cells from embryos can help organs rebuild damaged tissue.

从成年人身上取干细胞不会有任何伤害，但成熟的干细胞很难辨认。况且科学家们不知道成熟的干细胞是否能形成某类器官或组织的细胞。研究表明，胚胎干细胞有助于再生被毁坏的组织。

Currently, adult stem cells, taken from bone tissue, are used to grow several kinds of blood and bone cells. However, researchers believe that embryonic stem cells could treat diseases of the brain, liver, kidneys and heart. Some experts say new tissue could be grown to replace damaged nerve, muscle and even brain cells.

目前，从骨头组织提取的成熟干细胞已被用来培养几种血液和骨头细胞。但研究者们相信，胚胎干细胞可以治疗大脑、肝脏、肾和心脏疾病。有些专家说，可以培养新的组织代替被损坏的神经、肌肉，甚至大脑细胞。

Ⅲ. Listen to the last part of the news about the president, scientists and religious groups' attitude toward the research of stem cells, and take it down in the following order.

1. President Bush limited government financial support to sixty existing groups of cells already taken from embryos.

These groups of stem cells are now reproducing by themselves in laboratories worldwide.

2. This week, President Bush threatened to veto any bill that offers federal support for research on additional stem cells.

3. Yet, some scientists say that it is impossible to know how many groups of stem cells from embryos will be needed to make discoveries that can save lives.

4. A number of congressmen want expanded research to have full federal support.

5. The religious groups that oppose stem cell research consider it the same as taking human life.

6. Other religious groups accept the research because it could lead to cures for diseases such as Parkinson's and diabetes.

7. A national debate continues over the scientific and moral issues involved in research on embryonic stem cells.

Part Four Translation of the Text

Stem Cell Research

干细胞研究

Last week, President Bush approved limited federal government support of research on special human cells. The research involves stem cells taken from fertilized（已受精的）human eggs called embryos. Many groups disagree with the President's decision. Some religious groups believe that all research on stem cells from embryos should be banned. Yet, many scientists and some lawmakers believe no limits should be put on the research. Private laboratories that do not use federal money are not affected by the limits on the stem cell research.

上周，布什总统批准了联邦政府有限度地资助特殊人类细胞的研究。该项目涉及从人类受精卵即胚胎中提取干细胞的研究。许多组织对总统的决定提出了反对。有的宗教组织认为，所有关于从胚胎提取干细胞的研究都应该被禁止。但许多科学家和法律决策者认为，不应该对该项研究进行限制。私营的实验室不使用联邦的资金，因而不受对干细胞研究限制的影响。

Stem cells have qualities that may make them highly useful in the treatment of many diseases. The stem cells from embryos are the most useful. They are able to develop into all the tissues of the body. Embryonic stem cells are taken from embryos created in laboratories to help women become pregnant.

干细胞具有一些特质，对治疗许多疾病具有非常高的使用价值。来自于胚胎的干细胞用处最大，它们可以发展成身体的各种组织。胚胎干细胞是从实验室里产生的胚胎中提取，可以帮助妇女怀孕。

During the first days, the cells in the embryo divide quickly. Each of these cells is able to become any one of more than two-hundred different kinds of cells in the body. After about four days of development, the embryos are destroyed and the stem cells removed. Adult stem cells are taken from human tissue. These cells have not yet developed to become cells of an organ or a kind of tissue.

胚胎中的细胞头几天迅速分裂，每个细胞能成为身体中 200 多个不同的细胞。大约 4 天后，胚胎被毁掉，干细胞离开。成熟的干细胞取自人类肌体组织，但这些细胞还没有发展成器官或者肌体组织细胞。

Removing stem cells does not harm an adult. But adult stem cells are difficult to identify. And, scientists do not know if adult stem cells have the ability to become cells of any kind of organ or tissue. Research suggests that stem cells from embryos can help organs rebuild damaged tissue.

从成年人身上取干细胞不会有任何伤害，但成熟的干细胞很难辨认。况且科学家们不知道成熟的干细胞是否能形成某类器官或组织的细胞。研究表明，胚胎干细胞有助于再生被毁坏的组织。

Currently, adult stem cells, taken from bone tissue, are used to grow several kinds of blood and bone cells. However, researchers believe that embryonic stem cells could treat diseases of the brain, liver, kidneys and heart. Some experts say new tissue could be grown to replace damaged nerve, muscle and even brain cells.

目前，从骨头组织提取的成熟干细胞已被用来培养几种血液和骨头细胞。但研究者们相信，胚胎干细胞可以治疗大脑、肝脏、肾和心脏疾病。有些专家说，可以培养新的组织代替被损坏的神经、肌肉，甚至大脑细胞。

President Bush limited government financial support to sixty existing groups of cells already taken from embryos. These groups of stem cells are now reproducing by themselves in laboratories worldwide. This week, President Bush threatened to veto any bill that offers federal support for research on additional stem cells. Yet, some scientists say that it is impossible to know how many groups of stem cells from embryos will be needed to make discoveries that can save lives.

布什总统将政府的财政资助限制在现存的 60 个已经从胚胎取得干细胞的研究组织。目前，世界各地实验室里的干细胞组织正在繁衍着。本周，布什总统威胁说，将否决任何给额外的干细胞研究提供联邦资助的提案。不过，有的科学家说，人们无法知道需要从胚胎中提取多少组干细胞才能创造拯救生命的新发明。

A number of congressmen want expanded research to have full federal support. The religious groups that oppose stem cell research consider it the same as taking human life. Other religious groups accept the research because it could lead to cures for diseases such as Parkinson's and diabetes（糖尿病）. A national debate continues over the scientific and moral issues involved in research on embryonic stem cells.

好几个国会议员要求联邦政府对扩大研究予以全力资助。反对干细胞研究的宗教组织将之等同于谋取人命。其他宗教组织由于此种研究能够治疗帕金森氏综合征和糖尿病而表示能够接受。关于胚胎干细胞研究的科学与道德问题，全国性讨论正在持续。

(This is Steve Ember with the VOA *Special English* program IN THE NEWS.)

Lesson 35 Climate Conference Opens in Copenhagen

By Sonja Pace

Part One Information Background

关于温室效应的政治争论

温室效应是自然界承受地球表面释放热量的一种现象①。地球目前的平均温度为摄氏14度左右（华氏57度）。如果温室效应不存在，地球表面温度应该在摄氏零下19度（华氏零下2度）。现在人们常提到温室效应中的大气层成分，尤其是二氧化碳含量以及气候变化的后果，主要是因为这些气体的比例在过去250年之内，尤其是过去50年内急速增长。目前二氧化碳在大气层中的占有量为385百万分点，工业化之前为280百万分点。南极空气含量的调查显示，目前二氧化碳的含量大大超过过去56万年间的任何时期。其后果是温室效应增强，地球变暖，至于热到什么程度是争议的焦点。目前最新的数字统计来自联合国政府间气候变化专门委员会2007年的评估报告。报告中指出，1996年至2007年间地球的平均温度提高了0.74度，地面温度较海洋温度上升得更快，地球北部的地面温度比南部高。同时高温天气和强降水现象增加，海洋水位升高，导致地球两极和山脉上的冰雪融化，所有这些现象在大气变暖的过程中是可以预测到的。联合国政府间气候变化专门委员会最新评估报告指出平均温度将会继续上升，但上升速度的快慢和持久程度，以及其造成后果的严重程度，取决于对温室效应控制的速度和效率。

世界各国都要发展经济，而发展经济就避免不了排放废气。欧美国家认为发展中国家对遏制温室效应应负主要责任，因为发展中国家二氧化碳的排放量大于发达国家，所以美国的媒体动辄叫嚣中国人使用汽车越来越多。然而2006年美国每百人汽车拥有量为78.8辆，而中国是2.4辆②。所以总体来说，发展中国家虽然排放量大，但人均排放量少于发达国家。显然，发达国家虽然也感觉到了温室效应将对人类带来的威胁，却不愿意采取实质性的措施减少二氧化碳的排放，而指望其他国家率先减缓发展的步伐。最典型的例子是美国在二氧化碳排放量方面人均世界第一，却两次拒绝签署相应的环保议定书。看来，温室效应集中体现的却是全球化竞争的政治效应。

Part Two Exercises

Ⅰ. Listen to the first part of the news, and fill in the following blanks.

In __________, Denmark, the United Nations ________________ opened this week.

---

① http://www.hjenglish.com/zcyy/page/89423/

② http://www.labour-daily.cn/Web/NewsDetail.aspx IssuanceID = 168060

Around fifteen thousand ____________________ from nearly two hundred countries are there. Some call it "the last best chance" for an agreement to fight __________.

Yvo de Boer is the top climate official at the United Nations.

Yvo de Boer: "The time for formal statements is over. The time for __________ well known __________ is past. The time has come to reach out to each other. I urge you to __________ your __________, take up the work that has already been done and turn it into real action."

But there are questions about how much can be done, and how an agreement would be put into action.

The twelve-day conference ends next Friday. Late next week, leaders from more than one hundred countries are expected at the talks, including President Obama.

Delegates hope to set new ____________ to reduce ____________—the pollution blamed for ____________________ in the ____________. An existing agreement, the Kyoto __________, ends in two thousand twelve. Many countries have offered new proposals for cuts, including the United States and China.

Ⅱ. Listen to the second part of the news, and answer the following questions.

1. What does "China is the leading producer of..." mean?

2. What and why do you think the United States and other industrialized nations should take more responsibilities to do?

3. What is unhealthy to the public according to the Environmental Protection Agency?

4. Under what condition can the US government pass rules on environment protection?

Ⅲ. Listen to the third part of the news, and translate it into Chinese.

Begin from "But developing countries...".

Ⅳ. Listen to and repeat the fourth part of the news, then write it down.

From "Modern..." to "... United States and Canada".

Part Three　Keys to the Exercises

Ⅰ. Listen to the first part of the news, and fill in the following blanks.

In Copenhagen, Denmark, the United Nations Climate Change Conference opened this week. Around fifteen thousand delegates and observers from nearly two hundred countries are there. Some call it "the last best chance" for an agreement to fight climate change.

Yvo de Boer is the top climate official at the United Nations.

Yvo de Boer: "The time for formal statements is over. The time for restating well known positions is past. The time has come to reach out to each other. I urge you to build on your achievements, take up the work that has already been done and turn it into real action."

But there are questions about how much can be done, and how an agreement would be put into action.

The twelve-day conference ends next Friday. Late next week, leaders from more than one hundred countries are expected at the talks, including President Obama.

Delegates hope to set new targets to reduce greenhouse gases—the pollution blamed for trapping extra heat in the atmosphere. An existing agreement, the Kyoto Protocol, ends in two thousand twelve. Many countries have offered new proposals for cuts, including the United States and China.

Ⅱ. Listen to the second part of the news, and answer the following question.

1. What does "China is the leading producer of..." mean?

It means China (is the leading producer) produces most of greenhouse gases.

2. What and why do you think the United States and other industrialized nations should take more responsibilities to do?

Because they were the top polluters for years. So they are under extra pressure to reduce emissions from cars, factories and other sources.

3. What is unhealthy to the public according to the Environmental Protection Agency?

Carbon dioxide and other greenhouse gases a threat to public health.

4. Under what condition can the US government pass rules on environment protection?

First the Environmental protection agency releases a report on the damage of the public health or Congress acts first. (That clears the way for the administration to set limits, unless Congress acts first.)

Ⅲ. Listen to the third part of the news, and translate it into Chinese.

But developing countries are also being urged to do more.

但是发展中国家也被要求有所作为。

And they, in turn, want help.

而他们转而要求援助。

They criticized a proposal for industrialized nations to pay developing countries ten billion dollars a year over three years.

他们对一项工业国家每年支付发展中国家100亿美元，支付时间三年以上的提案提出批评。

The World Bank says dealing with climate change will require hundreds of billions a year in public and private financing.

世界银行称，应付气候变暖问题一年需要公共与私营企业提供几千亿美元。

In New York, the United Nations secretary-general reacted to a dispute over e-mails stolen from the University of East Anglia in England.

在纽约，联合国秘书长对英格兰东安格利亚大学电子邮件被盗的事件作出回应。

Critics say the messages show climate change scientists discussing ways to discredit other theories about global warming.

评论者称，该邮件显示气候变化科学家讨论了如何质疑全球温室效应的其他理论的方法。

But Ban Ki-Moon said Tuesday that the evidence is "quite clear" that humans are the main cause of temperatures rising faster than expected.

但是潘基文周二称，证据“十分明显”，人类是造成气温比预期升高更快的主要因素。

Ⅳ. Listen and repeat the fourth part of the news, then write it down.

The United Nations weather agency says two thousand to two thousand nine was the warmest decade on record. And it said this week that final results will likely show two thousand nine was the fifth-warmest year on record. Current estimates show record warmth this year in large parts of southern Asia and central Africa. The agency reported that the only parts of the world with cooler than average conditions this year were the United States and Canada.

Part Four　Translation of the Text

Climate Conference Opens in Copenhagen
在哥本哈根召开的气候会议

In Copenhagen, Denmark, the United Nations Climate Change Conference opened this week. Around fifteen thousand delegates and observers from nearly two hundred countries are there. Some call it "the last best chance" for an agreement to fight climate change.

在丹麦哥本哈根，联合国气候变化会议于本周召开。大概有近200个国家的15 000名代表和观察员参与会议。一些人称这是达成对抗气候变化协议的"最后的好机会"。

Yvo de Boer is the top climate official at the United Nations.

伊沃·德布尔是联合国气候方面的高官。

Yvo de Boer: "The time for formal statements is over. The time for restating well known positions is past. The time has come to reach out to each other. I urge you to build on your achievements, take up the work that has already been done and turn it into real action."

他说："再也没有时间发表空谈了。重申众所周知观点的时间也已经过去。现在是彼此携手合作的时候。我呼吁大家在已有成果之上继续前期工作，将其变为现实的行动。"

But there are questions about how much can be done, and how an agreement would be put into action.

但是人们怀疑究竟能有何作为，所达成的协议如何能转为行动。

The twelve-day conference ends next Friday. Late next week, leaders from more than one hundred countries are expected at the talks, including President Obama.

12天的会议将在下周五结束。下周末，全世界超过100个国家的领导人将出席会议，包括奥巴马总统。

Delegates hope to set new targets to reduce greenhouse gases—the pollution blamed for trapping extra heat in the atmosphere. An existing agreement, the Kyoto Protocol, ends in two thousand twelve. Many countries have offered new proposals for cuts, including the United States and China.

代表们希望能够就减少温室气体排放制定新的目标，这种污染被认为是将多余的热量困在大气层中的祸首。目前的《京都议定书》将在2012年失效。许多国家都提供了新的减排提议，包括美国和中国。

China is now the leading producer of greenhouse gases. But the United States and other industrialized nations were the top polluters for years. So they are under extra pressure to reduce emissions from cars, factories and other sources.

中国现在是温室气体最大的排放国。但美国和其他的一些工业化国家是多年以来的最大污染国。所以他们在汽车、工厂和其他源头的减排方面承受着额外的压力。

In Washington, the Environmental Protection Agency on Monday declared carbon dioxide and other greenhouse gases a threat to public health. That clears the way for the administration to set limits, unless Congress acts first.

在华盛顿，环境保护机构在周一宣布二氧化碳和其他温室气体对公众健康造成的损害。这为政府限制排放量的管理扫清了道路，以免国会须率先行动。

But developing countries are also being urged to do more. And they, in turn, want help. They criticized a proposal for industrialized nations to pay developing countries ten billion dollars a year over three years. The World Bank says dealing with climate change will require hundreds of billions a year in public and private financing.

但是发展中国家也被要求有所作为。而他们则转而要求援助。他们对一项工业国家每年支付发展中国家 100 亿美元，支付时间在三年以上的提案提出批评。世界银行称，应付气候变暖问题一年需要公共与私人企业提供几千亿美元。

In New York, the United Nations secretary-general reacted to a dispute over e-mails stolen from the University of East Anglia in England. Critics say the messages show climate change scientists discussing ways to discredit other theories about global warming. But Ban Ki-Moon said Tuesday that the evidence is "quite clear" that humans are the main cause of temperatures rising faster than expected.

在纽约，联合国秘书长对英格兰东安哥利亚大学邮件被盗的事件作出回应。批评者称，该邮件显示气候变化科学家讨论了如何质疑全球温室效应的其他理论的方法。但潘基文周二称，证据"十分明显"，人类是造成气温比预期升高更快的主要因素。

Modern climate records date back to eighteen fifty. The United Nations weather agency says two thousand to two thousand nine was the warmest decade on record. And it said this week that final results will likely show two thousand nine was the fifth-warmest year on record.

现代气象记录始于 1850 年。联合国气象局称从 2000 年到 2009 年是有记录以来最暖的十年。同时还称，本周的最终结果将可能显示 2009 年是有记录以来第五热的年份。

Current estimates show record warmth this year in large parts of southern Asia and central Africa. The agency reported that the only parts of the world with cooler than average conditions this year were the United States and Canada.

目前估计今年在南亚和中非大部分地区的变暖情况将破历史纪录。气象局报告称，今年比平均气温低的地方只有美国和加拿大。

(And that's IN THE NEWS in VOA *Special English*, written by Brianna Blake. For the latest news from Copenhagen, go to www. unsv. com. I'm Steve Ember.)

Lesson 36 Shuttle Investigation

By Cynthia Kirk

May 10, 2003

Part One Background Information

布什总统就“哥伦比亚”号失事发表讲话①

我的美国同胞们，今天传来噩耗，巨大的悲痛降临我们的国家。今早9点钟，位于休斯敦的航天地面指挥中心同我们的“哥伦比亚”号航天飞机失去了联系。此后不久，便发现德克萨斯州的上空有残骸飘落。“哥伦比亚”号失事，无一人生还。

机上的7名机组人员是里克·赫斯本德空军上校、迈克尔·安德森空军中校、劳蕾尔·克拉克海军中校、戴维·布朗海军上校和威廉·麦库尔海军中校、卡尔帕娜·乔娜博士和以色列空军上校伊兰·拉蒙。这些男女宇航员为造福全人类承担了巨大的风险。

在一个太空飞行似乎已成为常规作业的时代，人们很容易忽视乘火箭飞行的危险性和在恶劣的地球外层空间遨游的难度。这些宇航员知道这些危险，但他们甘愿面对，因为他们拥有远大而崇高的人生目标。正是因为他们的勇气、胆量和崇高理想，我们会更加缅怀他们。

今天所有美国人都在经受着这种突如其来的打击和牵挂着悲痛的男女宇航员的家人。你们并不孤单，我们全体国民同你们一起哀悼他们。你们所爱的人将永远受到这个国家的尊重和感激。他们为之献身的事业仍将继续。人类正是在探索精神和求知欲望的引导下，超越我们的世界，进入黑暗的外层空间。我们的太空之旅仍将继续。

今天，我们在空中目睹了毁灭和悲剧。然而，在我们看不到的远方，有着慰藉与希望。用预言家弥赛亚的话说：“抬起眼帘，望向天空。是谁创造了这一切？是造物主创造了点点繁星，并将其逐个命名。由于他的伟大才智与神奇力量，才无一遗漏。”

给群星命名的造物主也知道我们今天缅怀的7位亡灵的名字。“哥伦比亚”号航天飞机的机组人员虽未平安返回地球，但我们能祈祷他们安息。

愿上帝保佑这些悲伤的家属，愿上帝继续保佑美国。

---

① http://www.hao360.com/page/details_oral.asp id = 6195

Part Two Exercises

Ⅰ. Listen to the news of a post-catastrophe report, and complete the following sentences.

1. Cause of the accident: Investigators say they now believe ______________ as it re-entered the earth's atmosphere.

2. The investigators: The chairman of the Columbia Accident Investigation Board, Admiral Harold Gehman, ______________ during a news conference Tuesday in Houston, Texas.

3. The accident review:

1) Columbia ______________ as it flew two-hundred-thousand kilometers over the state of Texas.

2) It was ______________ at the Kennedy Space Center in Florida.

3) ______________ when the shuttle came apart.

4. The work now:

1) Since then, ______________ (搁浅) while investigators search for the cause of the accident.

2) Investigators have ______________ of the shuttle. Most of it fell over east Texas and Louisiana.

3) Thousands of people ______________.

5. The findings:

1) After three months of investigating, the board members say they have ______________.

2) Evidence recovered so far supports the belief that ______________ on January sixteenth.

3) Photographs taken during the launch show that a piece of foam (泡沫) insulation (绝缘体) ______________ and struck Columbia's left wing.

4) Investigators believe that the foam ______________ heat-resistant carbon panels on the front edge of the wing, ______________.

5) They noted that an object that came off of the shuttle during its second day in orbit ______________.

6) Investigators believe that shortly after re-entry, ______________ in the wing.

7) A recording device tied to hundreds of sensors (传感器) within the spacecraft helped investigators ______________ inside the wing.

8) The gas ______________ within seconds, causing ______________.

9) Finally, the shuttle ______________, breaking up high above Earth.

10) Within fifteen minutes, ______________.

Ⅱ. Listen to and repeat the third part of the news about the possible problem or future work, then write it doun with the key words given below.

1. possible reasons—weaken, carbon panels

2. manufacturing, the age, poor administration...

3. NASA, planning for...

4. foam insulation, external fuel tanks...

Ⅲ. Listen to and repeat the last paragraph of the news, and try to write it down.

Part Three Keys to the Exercises

Ⅰ. Listen to the news of post-catastrophe report, and complete the following sentences.

1. Cause of the accident: Investigators say they now believe they know what caused the American space shuttle Columbia to break apart as it re-entered the earth's atmosphere.

2. The investigators: The chairman of the Columbia Accident Investigation Board, Admiral Harold Gehman, announced the committee's "working" theory during a news conference Tuesday in Houston, Texas.

3. The accident review:

1) Columbia broke apart February first as it flew two-hundred-thousand kilometers over the state of Texas.

2) It was flying toward a landing at the Kennedy Space Center in Florida.

3) All seven astronauts were killed when the shuttle came apart.

4. The work now:

1) Since then, all space shuttle flights have been grounded (搁浅) while investigators search for the cause of the accident.

2) Investigators have studied evidence from almost fifty-thousand pieces of the shuttle. Most of it fell over east Texas and Louisiana.

3) Thousands of people helped in the recovery effort.

5. The findings:

1) After three months of investigating, the board members say they have a better understanding of the events leading up to the accident.

2) Evidence recovered so far supports the belief that the spacecraft was damaged during lift-off on January sixteenth.

3) Photographs taken during the launch show that a piece of foam (泡沫) insulation (绝缘体) fell off the external fuel tank and struck Columbia's left wing.

4) Investigators believe that the foam struck heat-resistant carbon panels on the front edge of the wing, opening a hole.

5) They noted that an object that came off of the shuttle during its second day in orbit also suggests evidence of a hole.

6) Investigators believe that shortly after re-entry, extremely hot gas entered through the hole in the wing.

7) A recording device tied to hundreds of sensors (传感器) within the spacecraft helped investigators follow the path of the hot gas inside the wing.

8) The gas melted the wing frame within seconds, causing it to bend.

9) Finally, the shuttle rolled and spun out of control, breaking up high above Earth.

10) Within fifteen minutes, all communication with Columbia stopped.

Ⅱ. Listen to and repeat the third part of the news about the possible problem or future work, and write it down with the key words given below.

1. The board is examining many possible reasons for what may have weakened the strong carbon (碳) panels (面板) along the shuttle's wing.

2. They are considering manufacturing problems, the age of the shuttles and poor administration of the shuttle program.

3. NASA (National Aeronautics and Space Administration 国家航空和宇宙航行局) officials have begun planning for the return to shuttle flights, possibly early next year.

4. Board members say repeated incidents of foam insulation breaking away from the external fuel tanks must be fixed before the shuttles can fly again.

Ⅲ. Listen to and repeat the last paragraph of the news, and try to write it down.

Board chairman Harold Gehman says they may never prove the wing was damaged by the foam insulation. He says more tests need to be done before any final conclusions can be made. Investigators will suggest ways to make the shuttle program safer in their final report in a few months.

Part Four Translation of the Text

Shuttle Investigation
太空穿梭机的调查结果

Investigators say they now believe they know what caused the American space shuttle Columbia to break apart as it re-entered the earth's atmosphere. The chairman of the Columbia Accident Investigation Board, Admiral Harold Gehman, announced the committee's "working" theory during a news conference Tuesday in Houston, Texas.

调查人员表示，他们认为已经找到导致美国哥伦比亚号太空穿梭机在重回地球大气层时解体的原因。哥伦比亚号事故调查委员会主席——海军上将哈洛得·格曼于周二在德克萨斯州休斯敦的新闻发布会上宣布委员会所执行的“任务”。

Columbia broke apart February first as it flew two-hundred-thousand kilometers over the state of Texas. It was flying toward a landing at the Kennedy Space Center in Florida. All seven astronauts were killed when the shuttle came apart. Since then, all space shuttle flights have been grounded while investigators search for the cause of the accident.

哥伦比亚号于2月1日在德克萨斯州上空20万公里飞行时解体。当时它正飞往佛罗里达州的降落地——肯尼迪太空中心。穿梭机里的七名宇航员在穿梭机解体时全部罹难。此后，所有太空穿梭机被迫停飞，调查人员也开始调查失事的原因。

Investigators have studied evidence from almost fifty-thousand pieces of the shuttle. Most of it fell over east Texas and Louisiana. Thousands of people helped in the recovery effort.

调查人员对穿梭机遗留的将近五万块的碎片进行了研究，这些碎片大多掉落在德克萨斯州东部以及路易斯安纳州。数千人在这次的碎片寻回过程中提供了协助。

After three months of investigating, the board members say they have a better understanding of the events leading up to the accident. Evidence recovered so far supports the belief that the spacecraft was damaged during lift-off on January sixteenth. Photographs taken during the launch show that a piece of foam insulation fell off the external fuel tank and struck Columbia's left wing. Investigators believe that the foam struck heat-resistant carbon panels on the front edge of the wing, opening a hole. They noted that an object that came off of the shuttle during its second day in orbit also suggests evidence of a hole.

经过三个月的调查，委员会成员表示，他们对导致这起事故的原因有了更好的了解。目前所获得的证据证实了太空舱在1月16日的起飞中已被毁坏的猜测。穿梭机发射时所拍摄的照片显示，一片泡沫绝缘材料从外部的油箱脱落，并击中哥伦比亚号的左翼。检查人员相信，该泡沫绝缘材料击中了机翼前端的隔热碳金属板，并击穿了一个洞。他们指出，穿梭机在轨道运行的第二天，从机上掉落的一个物件也是机身被击穿洞的证明之一。

Investigators believe that shortly after re-entry, extremely hot gas entered through the hole in the wing. A recording device tied to hundreds of sensors within the spacecraft helped investigators follow the path of the hot gas inside the wing. The gas melted the wing frame within seconds, causing it to bend. Finally, the shuttle rolled and spun out of control, breaking up high above Earth. Within fifteen minutes, all communication with Columbia stopped.

调查人员相信，穿梭机重返大气层不久，极热的气体进入了机翼中的洞口。太空穿梭机内一部与上百个探测设备紧密相连的录音器，对帮助调查人员了解热气体进入机翼的路径起了极大的作用。热气体在几秒钟内溶解了机翼的构架，并导致构架弯曲。最后，穿梭机失控地不停旋转，并在地球上空解体。15 分钟内，所有与哥伦比亚号的通讯都中止了。

The board is examining many possible reasons for what may have weakened the strong carbon panels along the shuttle's wing. They are considering manufacturing problems, the age of the shuttles and poor administration of the shuttle program.

委员会正在审查许多可能导致机翼外沿原本坚硬无比的碳金属板变得脆弱的原因。他们将考虑穿梭机的制造问题、穿梭机机龄以及太空穿梭项目的管理不善等问题。

NASA officials have begun planning for the return to shuttle flights, possibly early next year. Board members say repeated incidents of foam insulation breaking away from the external fuel tanks must be fixed before the shuttles can fly again.

美国太空总署的官员已开始计划，大约在明年初重新执行穿梭机飞行计划。委员会成员表示，在穿梭机重新起飞之前，泡沫绝缘材料从穿梭机外部油箱脱落而导致事故不断的问题必须得到解决。

Board chairman Harold Gehman says they may never prove the wing was damaged by the foam insulation. He says more tests need to be done before any final conclusions can be made. Investigators will suggest ways to make the shuttle program safer in their final report in a few months.

委员会主席哈洛得·格曼说，他们可能永远证明不了机翼是由泡沫绝缘材料所损坏的。他表示，在作出任何最终的结论之前，还需通过更多的测试。调查人员会在未来的几个月内，在他们最终的报告里提出有关使太空穿梭计划更安全的方案。

(This VOA *Special English* program, IN THE NEWS, was written by Cynthia Kirk.)

后 记

记得我的博士生导师李良荣教授说，学新闻的学生不能仅仅读新闻的那几本书，否则，知识结构就太狭窄。他认为，学新闻的人得多接触哲学系的老师，并读点经济学的东西，还得去上上社会学的课，最好多跟学法律的同学聊聊。出“门”后，教了二十几年国际新闻听力的我颇有感触，因为发生在整个“国际”上的新闻事件非常复杂，它涉及许多方面的专业知识，尤其是国际政治和经济学方面。在编写这本教材时，我感到最难的部分就是新闻背景知识介绍，一开头几乎是全盘“引用”政治学家和经济学家的大作。为了摆脱“抄袭”的感觉，只好将所有的同类材料再“调”出来，重新学习和“领会”一番，挖掘事件中没有被别人发现的东西，然后将它们加入自己的观点和“调侃”。但终究是学新闻的，在探讨经济学方面的知识时，根本无法超越经济学家们的论述，很多地方还需要“无奈地”采用直接引用的方式（即课文中的注释部分）。借此机会，向本书引用过的资料原创者和大师们表示深深的感谢。尤其感谢中国现代国际关系研究院研究员、全球化研究中心副主任宿景祥博士同意我在本书中引用他的《名词解释：道琼斯指数与纳斯达克》、《国际观察：中美能源合作潜力巨大》和《错综复杂的石油政治》等大作中的内容。

感谢“美国之音”的编辑同意我将其置入“公共领域”内的IN THE NEWS的文字内容和声音材料编入这本非营利性教材。

感谢暨南大学我教过的学生们对本教材成型所作出的贡献！感谢徐钊同学，他负责翻译了如下课文：

Lesson 2　Similarities, but Also Big Differences, between Today's Crisis and 1930s

Lesson 3　World Wealth Report

Lesson 4　Nobel Recognizes Research into Economic Governance

Lesson 15　US States Fight Back to Protect Rights of Property Owners

Lesson 29　Corruption Digs Deepest in Countries in Conflict

Lesson 32　40th Anniversary of Martin Luther King Jr's Death

另外，杨扬同学和我的研究生赵莉城、张莹、朱苏兰、袁娜、宋依吟、李洁玉都为校对该书付出过艰辛的劳动，在此一并表示由衷感谢。

编　者

2010年8月于广州珠江帝景苑